Egypt and the Arabs

Egypt and the Arabs

Foreign Policy and the Search for National Identity

Joseph P. Lorenz

Westview Press

BOULDER, SAN FRANCISCO, & OXFORD

Cover photograph: Egypto-Arab carved wood panel, Fatimid Dynasty, eleventh century. Courtesy of The Metropolitan Museum of Art, Rogers Fund, 1911 (11.205.2).

Published in 1990 in the United States of America by Westview Press, Inc., 5500 Central Avenue, Boulder, Colorado 80301, and in the United Kingdom by Westview Press, Inc., 36 Lonsdale Road, Summertown, Oxford OX2 7EW

Library of Congress Cataloging-in-Publication Data
Lorenz, Joseph P.
  Egypt and the Arabs: foreign policy and the search for national
  identity/Joseph P. Lorenz.
    p. cm.
  Includes bibliographical references.
  ISBN 0-8133-7593-2
1. Arab countries—Foreign relations—Egypt. 2. Egypt—Foreign
relations—Arab countries. I. Title. II. Series.
DS63.2.E3L66 1990
327.62017′4927—dc20   89-49124
                                                                              CIP

Printed and bound in the United States of America

The paper used in this publication meets the requirements
of the American National Standard for Permanence of Paper
for Printed Library Materials Z39.48-1984.

10   9   8   7   6   5   4   3   2   1

*To my beloved wife, Gary, whose zest
for the lands and peoples of the Middle East
turned a career into an adventure*

Contents

Acknowledgments   xi
Introduction   xiii

1 The Geographic and Historical Setting   1

The River and the Sea, 1
Foreign Relations Under the Pharaohs, 3
Egyptian-Israeli Relations in Antiquity, 6
Early Arab Dominion, 7
Egypt Under the Ottomans, 10

**2 Egypt Responds to the West: Pan-Islam,
    Egyptian Nationalism, and Arabism**   13

Reformist Islam in Egypt, 13
The Origins of Modern Egyptian Nationalism, 14
The Arab Awakening in the Fertile Crescent, 16
Egyptian Pan-Arab Policies Before Independence, 17

3 Nasser and the Rise of Arab Nationalism in Egypt   21

Ruling Personalities and the Decisionmaking
    Process, 21
The Making of the Man, 22
The Impact of the Palestine War, 23
Foreign Policy Under Naguib, 25
Nasser and the New Pan-Arabism, 26
Pan-Arabism in Practice, 29
Arab Divisions and the June War, 33
The Retreat from Pan-Arabism, 34

4 Sadat and His Early Foreign Policy   36

The Legacy of Nasser, 36
The Impact of a Peasant Background, 37

Youthful Conspiratorial Activities, 39
Relations with the Muslim Brotherhood, 39
Lessons Learned Under Nasser, 40
Egyptian-Arab Relations Before the October War, 41

5   The October War and Its Aftermath   46

The Problems of a Two-Front War, 46
Arab Unity in Wartime, 47
The Oil Weapon, 48
Arab Objectives and the October War, 49
The Disengagement Agreements Divide the
    Arab World, 50

6   Oil Diplomacy and Arab Reconciliation   55

The Background: Domestic Constraints on
    Egyptian Policy, 55
Egypt and Syria After Sinai II, 58
Quarrels with the Rejectionists, 59
The Lebanese War and Arab Politics, 60
The Egyptian-Saudi Connection, 61
The Trials of an Arab Mediator, 62
The Kaleidoscope Shifts, 65
The Scramble to Make Up, 66

**7   Eight Players in Search of a Peace Conference:
    The Geneva Preparations of 1977**   67

Begin Changes the Picture, 68
The Arabs Prepare for Geneva, 69
Hidden Agendas, 71
The Ba'ath as Vanguard of Arab Nationalism, 72
The Contest for Saudi Support, 73
Arab Rivalries and the PLO, 74
Things Fall Apart, 75

8   The Road to Jerusalem   78

Why Go to Israel? 78
The Jerusalem Initiative and Foreign Policy Theory, 79
The Speech to the Knesset and the Response
    in Egypt, 84
The Arab Response to Jerusalem, 87

9 Camp David and Its Consequences 92

Arab Olive Branches Before Camp David, 92
Sadat and the Issue of Palestinian Autonomy, 93
Jordan and Saudi Arabia Opt Out, 95
The Baghdad Summit and Its Aftermath, 97
Arab Issues at the Blair House Talks, 99
The Collapse of the Autonomy Talks, 100

10 The Making of a New Arab Coalition 102

Changes in the Strategic Landscape, 102
The Impact of Revolutionary Iran, 103
Quiet on the Palestinian Front, 104
The Mixed Legacy of Camp David, 106
Signposts on the Road to Egypt's
  Arab Reintegration, 108
Egypt's Arab Policies Under Mubarak, 108
Dynamics at the Amman Summit, 110
The Algiers Summit and the Palestinian
  Uprising, 112

**11 Foreign Policy and the Search for
National Identity** 115

Sources of Change and Continuity, 115
Recurring Patterns from the Past, 117
The Eclipse of Ideology, 119

12 Arab Politics and the Peace Process 124

New Elements in Inter-Arab Dynamics, 124
Syria and the War in Lebanon, 126
The *Intifadah*, the Arabs, and Israel, 127
Policy Implications for the United States, 128

Appendix A: UN Security Council Resolutions 242 and 338 131
Appendix B: President Sadat's Address to the Knesset 133
Appendix C: The Camp David Accords, September 17, 1978 144
Notes 156
Bibliography 171
Index 179

Acknowledgments

I thank the Department of State for the opportunity to do the initial research for this book as a senior fellow at the Foreign Service Institute's Center for the Study of Foreign Affairs in 1986. Parts of Chapters 10 and 11 were written in early 1988 for the National Defense University and published in 1989 under the title *Egypt and the New Arab Coalition* by the university's Institute for National Strategic Studies. The book was completed after my retirement in the summer of 1988, and the opinions and conclusions in it are mine alone. The royalties have been assigned to Save Lebanon, Inc.

Joseph P. Lorenz

Introduction

Three thousand years after the burned-out kings of the Twenty-first Dynasty yielded to alien rule, Egypt redeemed its independence under the successive leadership of two men whose personalities shaped its destiny as profoundly as did any of its pharaohs. It is hard to imagine a modern Egypt unmoved by Gamal Nasser and Anwar Sadat. Their values and political instincts, their strength of purpose, and the clear vision that each had of Egyptian interests molded the country's internal development and, for close to thirty years, thrust it to the center of regional and international politics. The Arab-Israel conflict, in particular, owes its most important turning points in peace and war to their personal drives and beliefs. With the passing of these two leaders, as Egyptians catch their breath and for the moment turn inward, the time seems fitting to ask what is enduring and what transient in their conflicting legacies to Egypt.

The question has practical importance because the course that Egypt follows will largely determine whether the Middle East remains at peace or turns again to war. Urgent as its economic problems are at home, Egypt remains pivotal to the diplomacy of the region and to its military balance. The country's geographic centrality, its large and relatively skilled population, its disciplined and well-equipped armed forces, and, above all, the sense of national purpose that makes Egyptians expect their government to assert Egypt's leadership in the Arab community—all assure an active and continuing regional involvement. Whether that involvement is driven by the dynamic pan-Arabism of Nasser, the visionary but firmly Egypt-oriented policies of Sadat, or something unlike either clearly affects the possibilities for peace. A main object in the coming pages is to explore the values and interests that animate Egyptian foreign policy—those handed down through the millennia as well as those forged since independence—so that we can make an informed judgment about the direction that Egypt is likely to take in Middle East politics.

Any inquiry into Egypt's place in the Middle East must start, in my opinion, with the things that give Egyptians their sense of national identity and define for them their place in the world. That includes their land and their history, their encounters with Arab nationalism and pan-Islamic thinking, and their development of a purely Egyptian nationalism in practical politics as well as in theory. It covers also their searing experiences since independence with Arab unity and then with Arab rejection.

Because of the richness of Egypt's historic relations with its neighbors, the book's first two chapters are devoted to an overview of the pharaonic, Mediterranean, Arab, Ottoman, and British colonial periods. The aim is to acquaint the nonspecialist reader with the main currents of Egyptian political thought and belief, as they have contributed to present attitudes on Egypt's identity and appropriate role in the region. The diplomatic history of modern Egypt, as seen through the prism of its Arab relations, begins in Chapter Three with a review of Nasser's pan-Arab policies.

The main body of this book is a close study of Egyptian foreign policy under Sadat. There are three reasons for this emphasis. The first is the inherent interest and importance of Sadat's policies, which created the configurations and set the political terms that govern the Arab-Israel dispute today. The second is that Sadat's Jerusalem initiative and the peace treaty that followed led to some persistent myths about the origins and meaning of Egypt's peace with Israel, which I hope to be able to help dispel. Finally, the Sadat years are the period I happen to know best, having been involved with the politics and diplomacy of the Middle East throughout most of Sadat's tenure. (From 1973 to 1976, during and after the October War, I was responsible for Middle East affairs at the U.S. Mission to the UN, during the next two years had similar responsibilities in the State Department, and from 1978 to 1981 was posted to Cairo as counselor for political affairs.) The book's final three chapters examine Egyptian policy toward the Arabs and Israel under President Hosni Mubarak and consider the implications for U.S. policy of the trends and dynamics of Egyptian-Arab relations.

A major hypothesis of the book is that Egyptian history has led to an underlying tension in the Egyptians' views of themselves and of their neighbors. On the one hand is an Egypt that is self-contained and sufficient, the recipient of an unchanging wisdom that need not and probably cannot be exported. On the other is an Egypt that finds its purpose and identity in broader associations, for the last 1,400 years primarily in Arabism and Islam. In the years since independence Egyptians have swung passionately from one extreme to the other. And although the wide swings of the pendulum have subsided with Mubarak's pragmatic approach to foreign policy, the competing visions continue to color Egyptian thinking about the country's regional role and responsibilities.

Egypt's policies in the Middle East do not, of course, flow directly from the values and interests of the Egyptian people or, indeed, from those of their leaders. There are constraints that stem from domestic economic and social imperatives, from great power pressures and the need for continuity of arms supply, from treaty obligations, and from simple inertia. And despite the relative homogeneity of Egyptian society, different groups have different ideas about foreign policy. Sometimes, as in the case of the urban intellectuals, that does not make a great deal of difference. In other cases, that of the army, for example, or the Muslim Brotherhood, or the inflammable masses in Cairo whose main interest is where their breakfast is coming from rather than the state of relations with the Arabs or Israel, it makes considerable difference.

Most of the questions that come to mind about the foreign policy decisionmaking process of any country are relevant to Egypt and its Arab relations. In Egypt's case, however, they are thrown into sharp relief by the country's commitment over a brief period to the contrasting value systems of pan-Arabism and Egyptian nationalism. How much weight, then, should be given to the influence of longstanding strategic interests on policy formulation as against the power of ideology? What kind of interaction takes place between national foreign policy and the dynamics of a regional system? What are the forces that hold together a group of nations like the Arabs, so different and yet so deeply linked, and what interests and attitudes pull them apart? To what extent is foreign policy hostage to domestic political imperatives? Especially in a country like Egypt, where the economic and social problems are serious and difficult to reform, will a leader try to build his legitimacy on the opportunities offered by an active and popular foreign policy?

None of these questions has a definitive answer, and no amount of trying will squeeze the complexity, fluidity, and occasional equivocation of Egyptian foreign policy into the mold of formal theory. I do not, in any case, believe that theories purporting to explain foreign policy behavior are generally helpful. The bias stems in part from my profession. The Foreign Service officer, trying to evaluate the currents that shape a country's policies, cannot help but be struck by a sense of contingency—by the uncertainty and potential inherent in each historical situation. Like Leon Trotsky, the diplomat is inclined to see history as "refracting itself through a natural selection of accidents."

My approach, in short, is to try to understand where Egypt has been and to draw from its experiences with the Arab world the lessons Egyptians themselves draw from their history. One way to do this is to talk to Egyptians who think about such matters. In this I have been fortunate. My Egyptian friends have been generous of their time, not only while I served in Cairo but again in the winter of 1987–1988, when I visited the Middle East to inform myself on recent Egyptian-Arab relations. Whether these friends were part of the regime or opposed to it, whether they were deputies in the parliament, leftist politicians, diplomats, or leaders of the Muslim Brotherhood, they treated me with the warmth and graciousness that distinguish Egyptians of every persuasion and walk of life.

J.P.L.

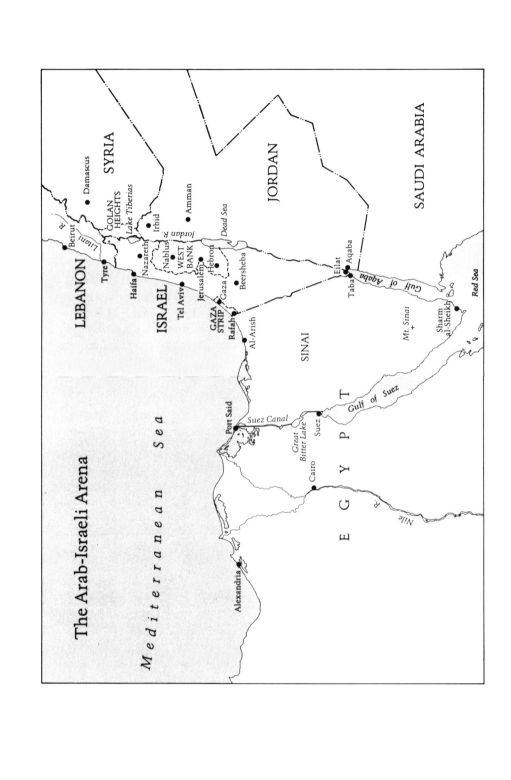

The Arab-Israeli Arena

1

The Geographic and Historical Setting

The River and the Sea

Of all the variables that make up a country's attitudes toward the outside world, the closest thing to a constant is geography. Even that varies in its impact as technology changes: Rapid transportation and instant communications vault the mountains and oceans that once kept nations apart. For nearly 3,000 years Egypt's geographic setting tended to turn its people inward. Pharaonic civilization remained intact and substantially unchanged by foreign contact longer than any other society in history. Even though the ancient world's most vital civilizations shared the Mediterranean Sea with Egypt, they failed to affect its culture in any lasting way.[1]

One key to ancient Egypt's self-sufficiency lies in the combination of a life-sustaining river flowing through an impassable desert. For most of its 900-mile passage through Egypt, the Nile supports a narrow ribbon of cultivation bounded on either side by mountains or desert. The Nile helped keep Egyptians at home by providing a variety of food—birds and game in its marshes as well as abundant fish. Its northern and southern reaches protected against foreign encroachment: The cataracts to the south discouraged raids from Africa; and in the north, mud flats, swamps, and shifting river channels were obstacles to invasion from the sea. Moreover, before the Romans built Alexandria, no major harbor on Egypt's Mediterranean coast could be used as a staging point for invading troops. The Delta, fronting the Mediterranean, had somewhat greater contact with the outside world than Upper Egypt, and it has throughout history tended to be the more cosmopolitan part of the country.

Egypt's other frontiers served, with one exception, to strengthen its natural defenses. The Red Sea discouraged potential African or Asian invaders because of the desert wastes separating its shores from Egyptian population centers. The Libyan desert to the west, though not impenetrable, was another obstacle. What remained was the land route across northern

Sinai, fewer than a hundred miles of coastline separating Egypt from the Fertile Crescent. At its eastern end lay the ancient civilizations of Syria and Palestine, beyond them the Mesopotamian kingdoms of Babylonia and Assyria and, at various times, the restless tribes of Central Asia and Anatolia moving south. In antiquity Egypt had its closest contacts with these peoples, dominating them when united and strong, vulnerable to their invasion when fragmented. As will later become clear, a pattern of relationships developed between Egypt and its eastern neighbors whose chief characteristic was recurring competition between the Nile and Tigris/Euphrates river-valley civilizations for control over Syria and Palestine.

Had ancient Egypt become a maritime power like the other advanced Mediterranean civilizations, the cocoon surrounding pharaonic culture could not have lasted close to 3,000 years. Several reasons in addition to its geography explain why Egypt turned away from the sea: The lack of timber for shipbuilding and the expense of importing it from the Levant were factors,[2] and when Egyptian vessels did sail the high seas, they apparently hugged the shoreline—which explains the minimal contact between Egypt and Crete.[3] Too, the absence of a thriving hinterland of the kind that stimulated the maritime growth of the Phoenicians, and later the Greeks and Romans, isolated the country. Despite these restraints, there were brief periods when Egypt was very much oriented toward the sea. Xerxes, for example, is said to have used 200 Egyptian-built triremes manned by Egyptian sailors when he led the attack on Greece in 480 B.C. During the reign of the Ptolemies—after Greek seafaring had declined—Egypt for a short time became the dominant maritime power of the eastern Mediterranean.

There were other, less direct ways in which Egypt's geography affected its place in the world. The long process of mastering the Nile, draining its marshes, and establishing control over a people stretched out along a thin band of cultivable land has had a lasting impact on the shape of Egyptian government and its methods of making policy. Until the twentieth century, the annual Nile floods dominated Egyptian life. The Nile required extensive drainage and irrigation systems; these in turn called for capital, technical expertise, and coordinated control of labor. The result was the rise of a highly centralized political and economic authority. As the pharaohs came to exercise absolute power over their subjects, habits and expectations formed that help to explain the exceptional latitude that modern Egyptian leaders have had in the formulation of national policy, especially in the area of foreign affairs.

Egypt's river-valley civilization continues to play a dominant part in the way Egyptians look at themselves and the outside world. The Nile remains the embodiment of Egyptian attachment to the land, even among city dwellers. A leader who ignores this does so at peril. In the post–Camp

David period, for example, nothing so irritated Egyptians as President Sadat's proposal to divert Nile water to Israel's Negev Desert in exchange for concessions on Jerusalem. The Nile is Egypt; it is not a bargaining chip in international politics.

Other national traits can be traced to the self-contained nature of Nile villages and to the attunement of rural life to the rhythm of the river's rise and fall. The Egyptian tendency toward complacency and, at times, isolationism combines with a remarkable rootedness to the soil, leading to conservatism and a strong attachment to traditional social values.[4] These attitudes are characteristic not only of the peasantry but of the millions who moved to the cities in the last two generations, among them Nasser and Sadat.

Foreign Relations Under the Pharaohs

Even the casual visitor to Egypt is struck by the dignity and self-assurance of the Egyptian people—by the impression they give of knowing who they are and what their culture represents. Part of this sense of identity stems from the Arab connection, part is the result of Islam, and part derives from the long struggle and eventual victory over colonialism. These influences are, in varying degrees, common to most Middle Eastern nations; in Egypt's case, however, there is the additional consciousness that the nation flourished for more than 2,000 years before Western civilization was born. The educated have an especially keen appreciation of the splendor of pharaonic civilization. Every secondary school graduate has studied pharaonic history for two years and visited the ruins at Luxor. Ancient Egyptian civilization is the backdrop to every Egyptian's view of the world, shaping attitudes toward neighboring countries and affecting the style of Egypt's relations with them. It is also the only period before 1952 in which Egypt conducted its external relations as an independent country.

Until the Roman conquest of 332 B.C., the foreign conflicts that most significantly influenced Egypt's history were with the empires and tribal nations to its east.[5] When Upper and Lower Egypt were united under strong pharaohs, Egypt successfully defended, and frequently enlarged, its frontiers against the Asians. The pharaohs were not, for the most part, interested in acquiring and settling foreign territories, and they certainly had no desire to spread Egyptian culture. Their civilization was centered on the Nile, and their religion and art had the limited objectives of ensuring that they and their high priests were comfortable after death. The country also lacked the compactness and the reserves of population needed for expansion and settlement over the long term. "[T]he truth is that though [Egypt's] agriculture has always exacted unremitting industry, the country's conditions have never been such as to develop great military prowess, and whenever faced by a hardier and more warlike race, Egypt has invariably succumbed."[6]

The earliest recorded contacts outside Egypt proper are skirmishes in the Sinai that took place during the First Dynasty between bedouins and Egyptians working malachite and turquoise mines.[7] It was not until the Sixth Dynasty, when the North and South were integrated under Pepi, that foreign expeditions were launched on a large scale, apparently against tribes of the Fertile Crescent or the Arabian Peninsula. The earliest suggestion of an internal motive for foreign expeditions appears at this time. Pepi's chamberlain states in a report on a campaign that he undertook in Asia that "the warriors brought back with them a great number of living captives, which pleased the King more than all the rest."[8]

In later periods there is clear evidence that the need for mass labor was an impetus to war. Herodotus remarks that "Sesostris" (in reality, Rameses II) "proceeded to make use of the multitudes whom he had brought with him from the conquered countries, partly to drag the huge masses of stone, which were moved in the course of his reign to the Temple Vulcan— partly to dig the numerous canals with which the whole of Egypt is intersected."[9]

The creative energy that marked the last dynasties of the Old Kingdom was followed by a long sleep during which no important monuments were built and no wars were conducted. But Egypt roused itself during the Eleventh Dynasty at Thebes, launching campaigns against all bordering nations. Expeditions were mounted against African tribes to the south, and a naval flotilla was sent through the Red Sea to what is now Somalia. Although no permanent Egyptian settlements in Africa were established, Egyptian trade flourished.

After the prosperity of the Middle Kingdom, another period of decline began early in the eighteenth century B.C. Following a century of internal struggle, the Hyksos, a nomadic people living in Syria, occupied Lower Egypt for about 200 years; however, they left no important mark on society. From the ashes of alien rule, Egypt rose again with its highly distinctive culture intact.[10]

Although the nation that arose from the defeat of the Hyksos closely resembled the Middle Kingdom in culture, art, and religion, it differed in one important respect—it was, for the first time in Egyptian history, a military state. The rulers of the Eighteenth Dynasty inherited the large and effective army that had driven out the Hyksos and campaigned in Asia. Attracted by the wealth of Mesopotamia and the rich cities of Syria, the new rulers extended Egypt's sway east to the Euphrates and south to the third cataract of the Nile in Nubia. The empire that they founded was notable for its tolerance, organization, and effective, decentralized administration.

The dissolution of the Egyptian empire toward the end of the Eighteenth Dynasty is associated with the reign of Akhenaton, the son of Amenophis III, whose interests lay in religion and art rather than foreign ventures. As local princes in Syria and Palestine withdrew their allegiance, the Egyptian rulers used diplomacy to retain what territory they could. In 1278 B.C. Rameses II concluded with the Hittites' King Khatusilis the first treaty in history. Allocating northern Syria to the Hittites and southern Syria to Egypt, the agreement expressed the hope that it would lead to "peace and good brotherhood between the contending parties forever."[11]

As Egypt's power waned, its neighbors exploited its weakness. Ethiopia reciprocated centuries of Egyptian dominance in Nubia by gradually absorbing Upper Egypt and then the Delta. The Ethiopian kings of the Twenty-fifth Dynasty ruled as Egyptian pharaohs, probably considering themselves at least culturally Egyptian. The only remaining archaeological evidence of pharaonic influence in Africa are the ruins of the Ethiopian kingdom of Meroe, which flourished in the sixth century B.C. in what is now northern Sudan.[12]

Unlike the Ethiopians, the Assyrians who supplanted them had no cultural ties with Egypt. On the contrary, they saw Egypt even in its impotence as a rival for imperial dominion. The feuding Egyptian kings tried to stem the Assyrian advance by creating a buffer zone in Israel and the Syro-Palestinian states. In the eighth century B.C., for example, Egypt encouraged King Hosea of Israel to defy the Assyrian invaders from the north.

The Saite rulers of the sixth and seventh centuries B.C. managed to reestablish a measure of Egyptian autonomy in the Delta and to bring order back to Upper Egypt, which had long been ruled by feuding warlords. The Saites consciously looked back to long-passed eras of pharaonic glory, restoring ancient Egyptian religious, governmental, and social practices. Under their rule foreign trade reached new heights of activity both with traditional partners like the Phoenicians and with newcomers like Greece, which was just then setting up mercantile settlements in Egypt and throughout the Mediterranean.

The Greeks found the Egyptians more interesting than the Egyptians found them. "Before the impact of the foreign life which thus flowed in upon Egypt, the Egyptian showed himself entirely unmoved, and held himself aloof, fortified behind his ceremonial purity and his inviolable reserve."[13] The accounts of Greek-Egyptian relations in antiquity that Herodotus and other Greek travelers provide offer fascinating insights into the enduring nature of national character. On the one side were the Greeks, curious, cosmopolitan, and intrigued by the presumed wisdom of pharaonic civilization (hidden from them by hieroglyphics they could not decipher);

on the other were the Egyptians, self-contained, dignified, and disinterested in cultures alien to their own.

The final pharaonic thrust into Asia came in 608 B.C., when Egypt once again invaded Syria and went on to rule over land reaching to the Euphrates. Two years later the Egyptian army was routed by Nebuchadnezzar of Babylon. A few last Egyptian forays against the Babylonians followed, after which the brief moment of resurgent Egyptian empire came to a close. From the Persian conquest in 525 B.C. until Nasser's coup d'état in 1952, Egypt was ruled by foreigners.*)*

Egyptian-Israeli Relations in Antiquity

A special look at Egyptian-Israeli relations in antiquity may be in order, not because history is likely to repeat itself, but because the ancient contacts are part of the historical consciousness of educated Israelis and Egyptians. They give to today's relationship between Egypt and Israel a texture and depth that are absent from the attitudes that Israelis and other Arabs have toward each other.

To Egyptians and Israelis alike, the Exodus is the central event of their relationship in ancient times. The Koran's account of the flight from Egypt is of course drawn from the Old Testament, and in tone as well as factual treatment it differs only slightly from the biblical version.[14] Reflecting Mohammed's regard for the Jews as "People of the Book" whose prophets preceded him and were worthy of veneration, the Koran sides strongly with the Israelites against the pursuing Egyptians. Indeed, the pharaoh is portrayed as the "prototype of the illegitimate ruler . . . [who] oppresses the apostles of God and the faithful."[15] We shall see later that the Koran's insistence that the pharaohs ruled by unlawful power rather than divine law has aggravated the conflicting political loyalties between Islamicists and Egyptian nationalists, who trace the nation's identity to the glories of the pharaonic past.

Like the Bible, the Koran fails to specify which pharaoh led the pursuit of Moses and his followers. Biblical tradition places the Exodus around 1250 B.C., which would put it in the middle of the long reign of Rameses II. Islamic scholars, on the other hand, have argued that this date is almost certainly too late as there are indications that the Israelites were already settled in Canaan by the thirteenth century B.C.[16] They suggest that a more likely candidate is Thutmose I, whose resurgent nationalism in the early sixteenth century B.C. seems compatible with the pharaoh's oppression of the Israelites.

Recent scientific evidence supports the hypothesis of an earlier period. Archaeologists working in Greece have tied the "parting of the waves" and the "deep darkness over the whole land of Egypt" to a volcanic eruption on the Greek island of Santorini in the middle to late fifteenth century

B.C.[17] If their dating is correct, the Exodus would have taken place during the reign of Hatshepshut, the daughter of Thutmose I. The Santorini-Exodus theory was in fact arrived at partly on the basis of an interpretation of inscriptions from Hatshepshut's reign. In the end, however, one cannot help feeling that the Israelites would have been sufficiently impressed at being pursued by one of Egypt's rare female pharaohs to have recorded the fact.

As Egypt began its decline in the Twentieth Dynasty, Solomon and David were leading Judea and Samaria through a period of economic expansion and enhanced international activity. At this junction of rising and falling fortunes, Egypt's influence reached new heights, for it had much to offer that the nascent Hebrew state needed. Jerusalem borrowed from Egypt the administrative skills and techniques the pharaohs had developed during their own periods of expansion. Solomon, for example, divided his labor force into three-monthly shifts as the Egyptians did, and David seems to have adopted many of the functions and titles of the complex Egyptian bureaucracy.[18]

Both the Old and New Testaments contain passages that show Egypt had a reputation for wisdom. Moses, having been brought up by the pharaoh's daughter, is said to have beer. "learned in all the wisdom of the Egyptians" (Acts VII:22). And the most forceful statement that can be made about Solomon's wisdom is that it "excelled . . . all the wisdom of Egypt" (1 Kings 4:30).

The literature of pharaonic Egypt was well known in Israel. Two Egyptian literary styles, in particular, seem to have had a direct influence on the Bible. The pharaonic hymns to Aton influenced certain psalms,[19] and Egyptian didactic treatises, such as the "Wisdom of Amenemope," are reflected in the Book of Proverbs.[20] The Bible is also beholden to Egypt in a technical sense, for the early Old Testament works were almost certainly written on Egyptian papyrus.[21]

In only three periods of ancient history (1000–740, 621–606, and 142–63 B.C.) was Israel able to maintain independence from the river-valley kingdoms to its east and west. The buffeting the Israelites received was typical of the fate that had befallen the fertile strip along the eastern Mediterranean before the Jews arrived and foreshadowed what was in store for the two millennia to come. Through its attractions and its vulnerability the land has imposed a recurring pattern on the foreign policies of the countries of the area throughout recorded history.

Early Arab Dominion

In the twelve centuries that separate the last independent pharaohs from the Arab conquest, Egypt sank ever deeper into subservience until finally, after several rebellions and a brief period of autonomy, it succumbed to poverty, bitterness, and disunity. Four empires exploited the country: Persia taxed Egypt to fund wars with Greece; Alexander and the Ptolemaic Greeks used Egypt's grain; Rome developed Egypt as a military base for the defense of its eastern provinces; and Byzantium, contending with Rome for leadership of the Christian world, persecuted Egypt for its challenges to religious orthodoxy. Each power began its rule with relatively enlightened and efficient administration and ended it in self-indulgence and oppression. In each case, as the interests of ruler and ruled grew apart, there arose a need to justify the occupation, leading to the racial supremacy typical of imperialism in decline.

The bitter hatred that characterized Egypt's relations with Byzantium in the sixth and seventh centuries A.D. had important consequences for early Islam. First, the lack of security that existed in Egypt because of civil disorder and insurrection against the Byzantines resulted in Egypt's becoming the unwitting godfather to Islam. Merchants of the spice trade who for 200 years had used the overland path from the Nile to the Red Sea as their route to the Far East were forced to divert their caravans to the ancient route that led from Palestine along the western coast of Arabia to Yemen.[22] Had this change not taken place, Mecca would have been an out-of-the-way village dominated by a nomadic economy and way of life. There would have been no Jewish and Christian merchants to influence Mohammed's thought, no experienced leaders to administer the caliphate or institutions on which to model it, and no army to expand the frontiers of Islam.

The second, more direct way in which Egyptians speeded the early spread of Islam was by welcoming the Arab forces under Amr Ibn al-As who besieged Alexandria in A.D. 642. The Arabs happened to arrive just when Egyptian-Byzantine relations were at their worst. The Byzantine patriarch of Alexandria had doubly offended the Egyptian Copts: At the same time that he pressed them to compromise their doctrines of monophysite Christianity, he also tightened the collection of imperial taxes. The Egyptian bishop of Alexandria therefore directed the people not to resist the Arabs, and the 50,000-man Egyptian force that had been formed to protect the Byzantine fleet surrendered to an Arab army less than half its size. The Egyptians did not know a great deal about the people they were helping to bring to power nor do they seem to have cared; anything was evidently better than the continued harsh and doctrinaire rule of Byzantium.

In the early years of Islam, the Arabs held themselves apart from the peoples they conquered, whether they were of Persian, Semitic, Berber, or (as in the case of Egypt) Hamitic stock. They set up garrison camps near the chief cities and exacted tribute in much the same way that alien administrations had done in the past and would do in the future. Unlike the Byzantines, they did not try to impose their religion on the peoples they conquered but looked on Islam as an ethnic religion that was an integral part of what it meant to be an Arab.[23]

Aloof though they might have been, the Arabs were very different in their way of life and religion from the Westerners who had ruled Egypt for nearly a thousand years. Their faith was simple and full of the fire of newness, and they lived by the austere, uncorrupted code of the desert. In Egypt they tried to obey the Prophet's charge to "deal gently with the people."[24] They treated the Copts with respect, giving them back their own patriarch and protecting their lives and property. Because Islamic law was considered applicable only to Muslims, non-Muslims remained under the jurisdiction of previously existing civil codes and were governed mainly by notables of their own faith.

It was during the Umayyad period, in the century after Mohammed's death, that the foundations of Arab culture were laid in Egypt. The earliest and most powerful force was Islam. The new faith combined with its powerful spiritual appeal important economic and social advantages, and large numbers of Egyptians converted despite the lack of Arab encouragement. Almost as important in the formation of a sense of common identity was the spread of Arabic as the official language of administration, in Egypt as throughout the empire. Mastery of the language became important not only for the devout who wished to read the Koran but for the ambitious who hoped to get ahead in government or business.

As Islam and Arabic radiated throughout the empire, they became inextricably linked, parting company only at the borders of Persia. Islam, moreover, appropriated to itself the traditions and culture of ancient Arabia. "[The] religious sciences rested on a foundation of Arabic philology, and Arabic philology was based upon the old pre-Islamic poetry . . . so the Muslim scholar steeped himself in the literary and social heritage of the ancient Arabs."[25] The result was "the enduring Arabian impress upon Islamic culture."[26]

As Arabization was taking place throughout the conquered lands, the non-Arab converts to Islam (whom the Arabs referred to as the Mawali) became increasingly offended by the contempt with which they were treated by the Arab aristocracy. In A.D. 750 the Mawali of the eastern empire, rallied by the Abbasid branch of the Prophet's family, conquered and virtually exterminated the Umayyads. With the change in the power base, a new brand of Islam evolved that reflected the cultures of the empire's many races rather than that of the founding Arabs alone. A process had begun in which people of different ethnic backgrounds and faiths would consider themselves Arab by virtue of their contributions to Arabic civilization. It was a conception that was articulated more than a thousand years later by a group of twentieth-century Arab leaders: "Whosoever lives in our country, speaks our language, is brought up in our culture and takes pride in our glory is one of us."[27]

Beginning in the early ninth century A.D., the Abbasid caliphs took to recruiting Turkish mercenaries from the northeastern part of the empire to staff their palace guards and serve as provincial commanders. The practice was to dilute further the earlier identification of Islam with Arab culture. In A.D. 868 the first of a long succession of Turkish and Central Asian-dominated regimes was established in Egypt and Syria by a local Turkish commander named Ibn Tulun. With few interruptions, for the next 650 years Syria was ruled from Cairo rather than from Damascus or Baghdad, first by Tulunids, then by Fatimids, Ayyoubids, and Mamlukes.

The Fatimid caliphate made Egypt for the first time the center of gravity of the entire Muslim world. Shortly after conquering Cairo in A.D. 969 the Fatimids defeated the Abbasid armies and extended Egyptian dominion over Syria, Palestine, and the coasts of the Red Sea. Once again, as in pharaonic times, the Fertile Crescent was the prize over which the Middle East river-valley civilizations fought. This time the conflict was cloaked in ideology, the Sunni orthodoxy of the Abbasids being pitted against the extreme Shi'ism of the Fatimids.

The Fatimids are not especially admired by Egyptians today. The real Egyptian heros of the Arab empire are a Kurd and a Turk who appeared on the scene in the twelfth and thirteenth centuries. Saladin, the Kurd who founded the short-lived Ayyoubid Dynasty, and Beybars, the first of the Mamlukes, are revered for driving the Crusaders out of Palestine. Saladin has a special place in Egyptian hearts for returning Egypt to the fold of Sunni orthodoxy. That they were not Arab is immaterial. They brought dignity to Egypt by expelling Western invaders from Islamic soil and by guiding Egypt to the leadership of mainstream Islam.

Egypt Under the Ottomans

The Ottomans who in 1517 defeated the Mamluke army outside Cairo paid as little attention to Egyptian interests as was consistent with maximum short-term profits. For more than three centuries Turkish was the language of administration and commerce, and Turks alone were assumed to be fitted to govern. The Ottomans nevertheless shared the religion of the people, and as "Defender of the Faith," the Emperor had a legitimacy that commanded the allegiance of his subjects. Through their support of Islam, the Ottomans also encouraged the emergence of a group of religious leaders who spoke for the Egyptian people on secular as well as religious matters. Through these sheikhs and imams the voice of the Egyptian people could be heard at the end of the eighteenth century.

Napoleon's invasion of Egypt in 1798 was the country's first encounter with modern Europe, and the confrontation followed a script that continued with little change for the next 150 years. Napoleon understood that Egypt suffered from misrule and oppression, and he expected the kind of welcome that had been given previous invaders in such circumstances. In fact, he was opposed from the start. The people of Alexandria initially tried to prevent his army from landing; then, as French troops marched on Cairo, the *fellahin* (peasants), at the urging of the imams, retreated with their animals into the desert, falling upon the forage parties that followed them. Napoleon had not reckoned on the power of militant Islam nor on Egypt's long and bitter memory of the West.

Seven years after the French invasion, the Egyptian people, again working with local Islamic leaders, replaced the Ottoman pasha with Mohammed Ali, the commander of the Albanian contingent sent by the Ottomans to fight Napoleon. Mohammed Ali's foreign policy followed a familiar pattern. Like the dynamic and restless rulers who preceded and followed him, he sought to expand his authority eastward. With French help he built an effective modern army. By 1818 he had subdued the whole of the Arabian Peninsula, and in 1833 his son, Ibrahim Pasha, conquered Syria and Palestine.

Over the next seven years, Ibrahim tried to create the foundations of an Arab empire for Egypt by forging among Syrian intellectuals a sense of Arab identity and community of interest with Egypt.[28] These were the first, tentative steps toward an Egypt-oriented pan-Arabism. To the age-old pattern of Egyptian efforts to gain control over Syria was added the ideological rationale of pursuing goals common to the Arabs as one people.

When the Middle East was reintroduced to the West by way of Napoleon's ineffectual campaigns in Egypt and Palestine, Islamic civilization had sunk into seemingly endless apathy and decay. Egypt, once the granary of the Roman Empire, had barely enough food to support itself, even though its estimated population of 2.5 million was about a quarter of what it had been during the Roman occupation. In the Levant as well agriculture languished under regimes that taxed ruthlessly and provided no protection from the raids of the Bedouin. Pestilence and famine were endemic, government was capricious, and the young were taught that human suffering was the will of God. Higher education was limited to Islamic jurisprudence and theology, and few read deeply beyond these subjects.

Into this bleak situation came Napoleon and his company of French scholars, fired by the Enlightenment's faith in the potential for social and economic progress through rational human endeavor. The interplay between these scholars and educated Muslims had far-reaching consequences. In Egypt it brought "to the attention of a few men . . . a keen sense of the advantage of an orderly government, and a warm appreciation of the advance that science and learning had made in Europe."[29]

By the late nineteenth century, largely as the result of Mohammed Ali's efforts, thousands of Egyptians had received educations grounded in Western rationalistic values. The stage was set for a debate on the conflicting demands of nationalism, Islam, and pan-Arabism that could not have occurred earlier in the century. But if Western nationalism, with its emphasis on territorial bonds, added a new dimension to the old questions of political allegiance, it by no means resolved them. Four centuries of Ottoman rule had reinforced the idea that the body of Islamic believers was the natural source of political community. For Arabs who regarded the mission of Mohammed as the central fact of history, that conception was a powerful foundation for political allegiance.

2

Egypt Responds to the West: Pan-Islam, Egyptian Nationalism, and Arabism

Between the decade before the British occupation in 1882 and the outbreak of World War I, three strains of thought emerged in Egypt that are important to understanding contemporary relationships in the Middle East. Two of them, pan-Islam and Egyptian nationalism, were direct Egyptian responses to the political and military challenges of the West. The third, Arab nationalism, was mainly a product of Westernized Syrian and Lebanese intellectuals—although Cairo was to become one of its most active centers.

The period was a kind of way-station in Egyptian political thought, which stood between the sometimes inchoate attitudes of the past toward political community and the mass ideologies of the future. By coming to grips with the implications for Egypt of the modern nation-state, the scholars and politicians of the era built the theoretical framework for much of the debate since independence about the competing loyalties of nation, religion, and the communal ties forged by language and culture. The ideas that emerged also served to explain and legitimize Egyptian foreign policy and, occasionally, to help shape it.

Reformist Islam in Egypt

Even before the British occupation, Egyptians had begun to ask questions about the relevance of Islamic revelation in the face of Western technical and military superiority.[1] The radically new techniques that Mohammed Ali had borrowed from the West presupposed a human ability to control events that was at variance with traditional Islamic thinking. People felt a need to adapt Islam to modern philosophic and scientific principles—a process that had taken Christianity several hundred years. But most urgently they sought ways to protect Islam against the threat from non-Muslim power.

One man, Jamal ed-Din al-Afghani, put the stamp of his personality on these concerns and turned them into a movement. Coming to Cairo in 1871 from Constantinople, where he had watched Europe pick apart the corrupt and ineffectual Ottoman Empire, Afghani was convinced that the only practical defense against Western encroachment was a union of all Muslim countries. His concerns were broader than the problems of Egypt: He sought, above all, to generate a sense of community with which Muslims could confront the challenges from the West. Although he supported the efforts of Western-educated Egyptians to limit the power of the khedive, he did so not because he questioned the khedive's legitimacy under the Ottoman caliphate, but because he hoped through economic and political reforms to forestall foreign intervention.

Most Egyptian thinkers writing before the British occupation shared with Afghani the traditional Islamic premise that the *umma*, the community of believers, was the body to which ultimate political allegiance was due. At the same time they recognized that the *watan* (country or nation, depending on the context)[2] existed within the universal *umma* and not only demanded, but was owed, the loyalty of its subjects. It thus became the concern of Islamic scholars like Rifa'a al-Tahtawi and Mohammed Abduh to explain and justify the concept of an Egyptian nation in terms of Islamic thought.[3] Both Tahtawi and Abduh explored the bonds that lead men to form a civilized society. For Tahtawi there was no conflict between love of one's fatherland and fidelity to a larger spiritual community. The Egyptian nation, in his view, drew its unique character and cohesiveness from pharaonic civilization, and the patriotism that the land evoked reinforced the bonds of spiritual community. Abduh, more deeply involved in national politics than Tahtawi, spent much of his life locked in combat with the conservative *ulama* (spiritual leaders), who "busy themselves with what might have been suitable for a time that is long gone by."[4] Yet Abduh accepted the tenet that the community of believers was the basic political unit, an indivisible whole whose separation into national or regional units was unnatural. A belief that came to be strongly contested by Egyptian and Arab nationalists, it nevertheless remains central to the beliefs of fundamentalist groups like the Muslim Brotherhood.

The Origins of Modern Egyptian Nationalism

As Afghani and Abduh were arguing for religious reform, Egyptians with a more secular perspective were also making their voices heard. Led by Sherif Pasha and organized into a party known as the Constitutional Nationalists, these advocates of political liberalization consisted mainly of wealthy landowners of Turkish and Circassian background who had come to identify with Egypt. What united them chiefly was concern over the growing British and French restrictions on Egyptian sovereignty that followed Khedive Ismail's profligacy and the near bankruptcy of the country in the 1870s.

Between the Islamic reformers and the Constitutionalists—and used by both groups—was the army. The native Egyptian officers were stirred by Afghani's rhetoric, but they were also motivated by grievances of their own, the most fundamental of which was that all higher-rank billets were held by Circassians. More broadly, the army reflected the growing discontent of the masses, who had suffered the most from the levies imposed to pay the country's foreign debts.

At the point where these various forces converged stood the son of a village sheikh, Colonel Ahmad Bey Urabi. Urabi began his rise to power in 1879, playing a minor part in an officers' riot and cooperating with the Constitutionalists in their efforts to regain control of the national budget. In 1881, as the mood of the country hardened and popular support moved from the Constitutionalists to the Islamic elements, Urabi moved with it. By the time the British invaded Egypt in July 1882, the Sheikh al-Islam was calling for holy war and the Constitutionalist leaders had taken refuge with the khedive in Alexandria under British protection.

For the next seven decades the story of Egyptian nationalism is the story of efforts to dislodge the British. Every element of society took part— Westernized intellectuals, imams in the villages and sheikhs at al-Azhar University, the army, the urban masses of Cairo and Alexandria, and even from time to time the king. The almost exclusive focus on one goal had important consequences. By submerging differences among disparate groups, it forged a sense of political community where none had existed for hundreds of years. Moreover, the clear-cut character of the struggle and final victory made it clear to Egyptians that they were in control of their own destiny. Unlike peoples who experienced a more ambiguous and less direct colonial control, as was the case, for example, in Iran, Egyptians were not haunted by the sense that their affairs continued to be directed by foreign powers after they won their independence.

Between the British occupation and World War I, the secular and religious branches of Egyptian nationalism went their separate ways, cooperating only occasionally when it served their interests. The leading oppositionist figure of the period was Mustapha Kamil, radically anti-British but conservative enough to find common ground at times with the *ulama*. Kamil saw the Egyptian nation as the center of three larger associations— Islamic, Ottoman, and Eastern—and he advocated strengthening Egyptian bonds with all of them. Yet, like most educated Egyptians of the time, he did not consider the Arab community itself as an object of political allegiance for Egyptians. He was in fact strongly opposed to Arab separatist tendencies, and in 1898, in *The Eastern Question*, he attacked the notion of an Arab caliphate as a British device for speeding up the dissolution of the Ottoman Empire.[5]

Kamil's main competition came from the People's party (al-Hizb al-Umma), whose principal theoretician was Ahmad Lutfi al-Sayyid, a close friend of Abduh and a key figure in the development of Egyptian political thought. Lutfi al-Sayyid unambiguously rejected the idea that Egyptians owed allegiance to the Ottoman Empire. The nationalism that he espoused was secular and territorial, and there was no room in it for political allegiance to any entity beyond the nation. Islam might properly claim the loyalty of Muslims, in Egypt as elsewhere, but that was a matter of religious conscience that had no bearing on the nature of the political community.

The Arab Awakening in the Fertile Crescent

In Syria and Lebanon during the early twentieth century, a rebirth of Arab consciousness was taking place that was to have a delayed impact on Egyptian political thought. It developed partly as a result of the publication by Christian missionaries of the great works of Arab literature, partly as a response to the oppression and Turkish-centered policies of the Ottomans. The movement was largely literary and philosophical, and its content varied from country to country. In Lebanon, where Christians dominated the movement, the emphasis was on protecting the autonomy that had already been won. The Lebanese wanted close association with western Christendom and had no more desire to be ruled by Damascus than by Constantinople.[6] The Syrians, on the other hand, alternated between advocating an independent "greater" Syria and a true pan-Arab union encompassing the entire Arab world.

For Syrians and Lebanese alike the revival of Arab consciousness was at bottom an effort to come to grips with the nature and boundaries of their nation.[7] Egyptians, constituting a nation by any criterion and absorbed in their struggle for independence, had little interest at the time in such existential issues. Moreover, as Arab nationalism turned to political activism, the differences in immediate goals drove Egypt and the Arabs further apart. During the first World War, for example, Egyptians had scant enthusiasm for Sherif Huseyn's British-backed revolt in the desert, in part because of their anti-British sentiment but also because of their lingering pro-Ottoman loyalties.

For all their differences, the Arab and Egyptian national movements had considerable contact. Cairo was a haven for Syrian and Lebanese activists, who had more freedom to publish and meet under Lord Cromer, the British high commissioner, than under Sultan Abdel Hamid. Through a number of periodicals devoted to science and philosophy, the Syrians who moved to Cairo introduced Egyptians to the main currents of French and

British thought.[8] One of the more prolific émigrés was a native of Aleppo named Abdel Rahman al-Kawekebi, who argued that Islam could be purified and strengthened only by transferring the caliphate from Turkey to Arabia. The idea had its Egyptian supporters—so long as the caliph's new seat was to be Cairo rather than Mecca.

In Egypt as well as in the eastern Arab world, Christians constituted a large, active, and well-educated segment of society. Yet their roles in the independence movements of the two areas were very different. In Syria and Lebanon the Christians worked closely with Muslim nationalists, despite their uneasiness about long-term Islamic goals. In Egypt, on the other hand, the strong Islamic coloration of much nationalist thinking frightened the Copts, who as a small minority felt more vulnerable than their coreligionists in the eastern Arab world. They came to believe that their interests lay in cooperation with the British, and in the emotional atmosphere that prevailed before independence that collaboration was often viewed by Egyptian Muslims as treasonous. Since independence Coptic intellectuals have often been staunch supporters of an activist pan-Arab Egyptian policy. It may be that the more secular Arabism of the Levant has seemed less threatening than the alternatives at home, at least during periods of Islamic resurgence.

Indeed, Islam is for many Egyptians today almost as inextricably a part of the concept of nation as it was for Afghani, Abduh, and Tahtawi. Now, as in the past, the deepest attachments are to religion and to the land. However powerful a force Arab nationalism was to become, it remained an import lacking the roots of these native products.

Egyptian Pan-Arab Policies Before Independence

The pan-Arabism that emerged in Egypt in the late 1930s and 1940s took a form different from what it had been and from what it was to become. Left behind was the literary/philosophical phase; still to come were the mobilization of the masses, the appeal to the disenfranchised outside of and within Egypt, and the efforts to legitimize power through ideology and propaganda. Not the least of the differences between the new and the old pan-Arabism was that whereas in the first act of the drama Egypt had played a role that swung between understudy and audience, in the second and third acts it directed the production.

Egypt's active involvement in Arab politics before its independence was closely connected to a renewed awareness of the importance to Egyptian security of the support of other Arab states, especially Syria and Palestine. Mohammed Ali and Ibrahim Pasha had reached that conclusion before, and it was to become the foundation of Nasser's Arab policy.

The Response to Domestic Pressures

By World War I the nationalist movement in Egypt had come to be expressed in the language of Western politics. Political parties, parliamentary groups, and trade unions were instruments in the struggle for independence. The great nationalist figure of the period, Saad Zaghloul, shared with other Egyptian politicians the Western, territorial view of the nation. He had little interest in the Arab struggle that was taking place against the Ottomans, and indeed was later to be criticized by the Nasser regime for taking too narrow a view of nationalism.[9]

In 1919 Zaghloul founded the Wafd party, which for close to twenty years was the authentic voice of Egyptian nationalism. Both the inspiration for the Wafd and most of its founding members (largely urban intellectuals and middle landowners) came from Lutfi al-Sayyid's Umma party.[10] After the 1936 treaty with Great Britain, the Wafd became increasingly concerned with the pursuit of power for its own sake. By 1952 Nasser and his contemporaries viewed the Wafd as a reactionary force catering to the landed aristocracy.

After Zaghloul's death, alienated by the corruption of the Wafd and Western-style institutions in general, Egyptians turned increasingly to more traditional forms of political expression. In the 1940s opposition movements sprang up in the conservative Islamic community, in the army, among neofascist "socialists," and among groups of students and workers on the left. Although it was Nasser's tight little group of junior officers that was to change Egyptian history, it was the Muslim Brotherhood, founded in 1928 by Hassan al-Banna, that most troubled the authorities.

Like Afghani before him, Banna argued that Islam contained in its law and tradition everything necessary to reform a society corrupted by the West. What distinguished Banna from other Egyptian sheikhs was his exceptional organizational ability, which he used to develop a large, responsive, and highly motivated organization. Assembled into a covert paramilitary army known as the Battalions of the Supporters of God, Brotherhood volunteers fought with the Palestinians in the Arab rebellion against the British from 1936 to 1939. (Later, during the 1948 War, units of the Brotherhood from Gaza were to fight alongside the Egyptian army in Palestine.) Meanwhile, within Egypt, the Brotherhood upstaged the Wafd by proposing that a pan-Arab coalition be formed as a forerunner to a full-fledged Islamic union.[11]

The resurgence of Islamic fervor and pro-Palestinian sentiment among Egyptians had a noticeable impact on the Wafd's foreign policy. Both in office and out of it, the party courted the Palestinians, raising funds for Palestinian causes and holding receptions for visiting Palestinian leaders.[12] The Wafd's activist Arab policy was the more striking in light of its traditionally Egypt-centered conception of nationalism.

Another internal political factor that led to greater Arab involvement was the desire of Prime Minister Mustapha al-Nahas to strengthen the Wafd's position at the expense of the palace. One of King Farouk's recurrent proposals after the breakup of the Ottoman Empire was to relocate the caliphate to Egypt, where the mantle of leadership would fall to him. The creation of the secular League of Arab States deprived Farouk of the ostensible reason for his project—the need for a forum for pan-Arab cooperation. It also put the conduct of Egyptian relations with the Arabs just where al-Nahas believed it belonged, in the hands of the Wafd.

Intellectual sentiment in Egypt, though less a factor than domestic pressures in the government's pan-Arab policies, had also come to favor a more active Arab policy. This was due partly to the views of Sati al-Husri, a Turkish-educated Syrian living in Egypt. Husri argued that the most important determinant of national identity was commonality of language.[13] Regarding Egypt as the center of gravity in the Arab world, he believed that Cairo had a duty to lead the struggle for unity among all Arabic-speaking peoples. One Egyptian whom he influenced with his blend of pan-Arabism and Egypt-centrism was the Arab League's first president, Abd al-Rahman Azzam. Like Mustapha Kamil before him and Gamal Abdel Nasser to come, Azzam had his own trinity of allegiances. "We are Egyptians first, Arabs second, and Muslims third," he declared.[14]

Arab Rivalries and the Formation of the Arab League

The new pan-Arabism was closely tied to the struggle for Palestine, in which Egypt became increasingly involved in the late 1930s. The first clear sign of a more activist Arab policy was Egypt's attitude toward the Palestinian general strike of 1936. Cairo refused to endorse the Arab Higher Committee's appeal to Palestinian workers to return to work, arguing that Britain's undertaking to consider suspending Jewish emigration could not be trusted. In 1937, at a pan-Arab conference in Syria, the Egyptian delegates took the position that a Jewish state in Palestine would be as great a threat to Egypt as to its immediate neighbors.[15] The following year 2,500 people from a dozen countries came to Cairo for the World Inter-Parliamentary Congress of Arab and Muslim Countries for the Defense of Palestine. Egypt's primacy in Arab multilateral councils had been established.

In the early 1940s, as the eastern Arabs were achieving independence, the old struggle for regional dominance surfaced again and led directly to the formation of the Arab League. The breakup of Syria into four mandated territories—Syria, Transjordan, Palestine, and Lebanon—after World War I had set the stage for a recurrence of Egyptian-Iraqi competition. Once Syria became independent, Damascus worked to create a broad federation of Arab nations, a more feasible goal in its view than an independent

Greater Syria. In an effort to exploit Syrian ambitions, Iraqi Prime Minister Nuri al-Said in 1943 advanced a two-stage plan envisaging the immediate federation of Syria, Lebanon, Palestine, and Jordan, to be followed by the establishment of an Arab League made up initially of Iraq and the four federated states.

Egypt viewed Nuri's plan as no more than window-dressing for the extension of Hashimite authority throughout the Fertile Crescent. With Saudi cooperation and British encouragement,[16] Nahas persuaded other Arabs to join Egypt in a League of Sovereign States. From its inception the league was dominated by Egypt: Its covenant was drafted in 1944 in Alexandria, its first meeting was held in March 1945 in Cairo, its first secretaries-general were Egyptian, and its headquarters remained in Egypt until March 1979, when they were moved to Tunis after Egypt's expulsion from the league for concluding the peace treaty with Israel.

From the late 1930s to the late 1980s there have been few periods when Egypt has not devoted its talents and resources to efforts to settle the Palestinian problem. The policy clearly has rested on a national consensus that it is right. But another major reason for spending so much time on the world's most intractable problem is that, for more than fifty years, leadership on behalf of the Palestinians has translated into leadership in the Arab world.

3

Nasser and the Rise of
Arab Nationalism in Egypt

Ruling Personalities and the Decisionmaking Process

Any study of Egyptian foreign relations since independence soon establishes that Egyptian rulers have played an unusually dominant role in the foreign policy decisionmaking process, particularly during the nearly thirty years that Nasser and Sadat held power. It is a pattern and a theme that began with the activism of the pharoahs of the Middle Kingdom and the Ramesside dynasties, persisted in the outward-looking policies of Islamic leaders like Saladin and Mohammed Ali, and culminated in Sadat's trip to Jerusalem and the Egyptian peace with Israel. Nasser himself understood the country's need for a strong leader in times of crisis: "It seems to me that within the Arab circle there is a role wandering aimlessly in search of a hero. . . . This role, exhausted by its wanderings has at last settled down, tired and weary, near the borders of our country and is beckoning us to move . . . since no one else is qualified to play it."[1]

We will explore the reasons Egyptian leaders have enjoyed exceptional latitude in the formation of foreign policy (compared to the rulers of developing countries generally and other Arab countries in particular) when we examine the Jerusalem initiative. For the moment, as we begin our survey of Nasser's Arab policies, it may be useful simply to note some of the implications for the decisionmaking process of the overriding importance in Egypt of ruling personalities.

The first consequence is the relatively small part played in the making of foreign policy by formal institutions like the parliament, political parties, and even the foreign affairs bureaucracy. Yet this holds only for those issues that the leader deems important and worth his personal involvement; hence the need in any analysis to determine just what those issues are. This in turn requires an understanding of the leader's values, personal drives, and objectives for his country. The other side of the coin is that the more removed formal institutions are from the decisionmaking process, the greater is the input of informal mechanisms. On key issues both Nasser and Sadat consulted with trusted friends, who were sometimes in the army or government but more often worked outside the administration in journalism, business, and other fields.

Although domestic economic and political forces are unquestionably important, they do not drive Egyptian foreign policy in quite the same way that they do in many developing countries. Since independence—and through the Mubarak regime—some of the boldest diplomatic strokes have been made not because of economic and political pressures but despite them. Egypt's leaders have more latitude than most to put off responding to internal pressures (a very different thing from ignoring them entirely), and this gives rise to the increased flexibility and potential for drama and surprise that have been so characteristic of Egyptian foreign policy.

One final result of the leader's maneuverability in foreign affairs, I believe, is to justify the analyst's telling the story with Egypt as the central character—discussing foreign policy in terms of Egyptian initiatives and actions rather than viewing the country's policies simply as a response to the external forces that act upon it.

The Making of the Man

The stark, dusty little hamlet of Beni Morr, which Nasser always referred to as "my village," has more than doubled in size since the early 1920s when Nasser lived there as a child but has not changed much otherwise. Today about a third of the villagers are Coptic, a higher proportion than early in the century. Like all Saidis of Upper Egypt, the people of the area are considered by Egyptians from Cairo and the Delta to be hot-blooded, easily offended, and quick to avenge any slight to honor or dignity. It is a stereotype that corresponds to some fundamental characteristics of Nasser, though the passion and the intensity were usually kept under tight rein.

If Beni Morr came to evoke for Nasser the solidarity of family, the bond to the land, and the warmth of shared work, Alexandria, where he was born and for a time attended secondary school, represented the opposite end of the scale of social values. In post–World War I Alexandria, one inhabitant in three did not speak Arabic. The economic, cultural, and political life of the city was in the hands of Greeks, Italians, Armenians, and British, who communicated little with each other and hardly at all with Egyptians. The orientation was to the western shores of the Mediterranean rather than to the land within. It was a city that "seemed moored to the African earth like a vessel straining to stand out to sea."[2]

For the people of Beni Morr, on the other hand, the view was inward, toward the river. As in similar villages, there was a strong sense of social cohesiveness, partly because of the need for cooperation during the irrigation and harvest, partly because the community was made up of extended family groups and clans who had worked the same land for generations. Indeed, the village seems to have gotten its name from the Beni Morr tribe of the Hejaz in Arabia who, according to tradition, settled the area 1,300 years ago during the Arab conquest of Egypt. The Nasser family, one of the larger, more prosperous clans in the village, came to Beni Morr in the late seventeenth century. A former foreign minister who worked for Nasser believes that the sentimental side of Nasser's Arabism—as distinct from the hard, strategic interests that drove his Arab policy—may have stemmed in part from his family's Arab tribal origin.[3]

From 1924 to 1936 Nasser was moved about to different schools in Cairo and Alexandria. He lived first with his uncle, then with his grandparents, and finally with his father and stepmother, never really having a home that he could call his own. The lack of family stability (intensified by the death of his adored mother when he was eight) may have helped to shape characteristics that were to become apparent later: a sense of insecurity and restlessness, a leaning toward suspicion, and a tendency to repress his true feelings.

As a boy Nasser found an important emotional outlet in street politics. From the age of eleven through his last year of high school (when he spent a total of forty-five days in the classroom) he was involved in countless demonstrations and clashes with the police. The object was always the same—faster movement toward total British withdrawal. The means varied, from the Wafd, to the National party, to Ahmad Hussein's mix of fascism and Islam known as "Young Egypt." By the time he entered the military academy in March 1937 Nasser had become a thorough political animal. He developed a keen sense of timing, a sense that formed the basis of much of the style, and some of the substance, of his foreign policy when he came to power.

The Impact of the Palestine War

For Nasser, as for many of his contemporaries, the first war with Israel, in 1948, was the crucible in which a new conception of Egypt's Arab relationships was formed. The fighting sensitized him to the kinship of Arabs in their common subjection to imperialism. In *The Philosophy of the Revolution* he recalled that the war caused him to think hard about the Palestine question and brought him his "first notions of Arab consciousness." His empathy for the Palestinian Arabs and their cause was to infuse his Arab and anticolonial policies when he became president and to communicate itself to Arabs everywhere.

In terms of later foreign policy, however, the war's most important consequence was the extent to which it shaped Nasser's strategic conception of Egypt's role in the Middle East, for it taught Nasser the critical importance to Egyptian security of the area of the Fertile Crescent.[4] "Palestine," he often said, "is not only an Arab but an Egyptian problem."[5] The strategic importance of the eastern Arab countries was a principle widely accepted by previous Egyptian governments and especially by the Egyptian military. Lord Allenby (victor of the Palestine campaign in World War I and later high commissioner) was fond of pointing out to officers of Nasser's generation that Egypt had never been seriously threatened except from the east and that "the security of the country begins at Beersheba."[6] Yet the principle seems to have been even more fundamental to Nasser's thinking than it was to that of other members of the Revolutionary Command Council. Discussing the sources of Nasser's Arab policies, a former Free Officer expressed the view that it was Nasser's belief in the strategic centrality of Greater Syria, rather than any deep-seated affinity with the Arabs, that was at the heart of his Arab nationalism.[7] The ideology of modern pan-Arabism, the officer continued, was largely the work of Nasser confidant Mohamed Hasaneyn Heikal, starting with the latter's preparation of the final draft of The Philosophy of the Revolution.

That Nasser should have given sustained thought to military strategy and geopolitical theory is hardly surprising. For an officer of his probing intelligence that would have been natural whatever his position; but as an instructor at the military academy in Cairo in the early 1940s he was compelled to examine Egypt's strategic interests and to develop his thinking about their implications. He seems to have started from two basic geographic and historic facts. First, Egypt and Greater Syria formed the bridge and barrier between the Mediterranean and the Indian Ocean, together constituting the region's natural center of economic and political gravity; and second, Egypt's seasons of past greatness coincided with periods of maximum control in the area.[8] To conclude that Egypt's Arab policy should be based on the exercise of Egyptian influence in Syria and Palestine was not a great leap of the imagination. And while Egyptians have understandably not offered this rationale publicly to explain their foreign policy, there is no other interpretation that explains so much about Egyptian actions in the Middle East—especially in Nasser's time, but also before and after him.

There is no invective against Israel in The Philosophy of the Revolution. Nasser regarded Israel as the product of British efforts to preserve its imperial position in the Middle East. He blamed Western colonialism rather than Israel for displacing the Palestinians. In armistice talks with an Israeli officer (as recalled by both participants) Nasser showed a keen interest in the techniques used by the Jews to organize an underground resistance movement against the British and mobilize international support. His relatively unimpassioned attitude toward Israel was to change in 1955 and

1956; until then, however, it seems clear that Israel and its actions played but a small part in this thinking.

The war in Palestine shaped Nasser's future in other ways as well. By holding out against encircling Israeli forces at Faluga, he captured the attention and approval of his military colleagues in a war that left little for Egyptians to admire. More broadly, the conflict exposed the moral bankruptcy of the regime and led to a climate of dissatisfaction that paved the way for revolution. For not only did postwar trials implicate the palace in graft involving the supply of defective weapons to the front, but the military was happy to blame its political leaders for defeat in a conflict in which the Arabs greatly outnumbered the enemy. In short, the war ruptured the bond between the army and the king and provided Nasser fertile ground for the development of a clandestine movement.[9]

Three years after the end of the Palestine war in 1949, as Egyptian attitudes toward established authority moved along a scale ranging from cynicism, to repugnance, to opposition by terror, Nasser carried out a coup d'état that met virtually no resistance. For the next eighteen years, the destinies of Egypt and its ruler were linked to a degree not seen since pharaonic times. At the time of the revolution, Nasser's overriding goals were to rid Egypt of its foreign occupiers and to destroy the power of those who served them. He had the soldier's faith in action and contempt for theories. "If the army does not act," he wrote, "who else will?"[10]

When he took power on July 22, 1952, Nasser shared with his compatriots a sense of outrage, not only over the defeat in Palestine but over what Egyptians perceived as British contempt for their sovereignty.[11] In a deeper sense the humiliation—and the search for national dignity that it inspired—grew out of 2,500 years of foreign rule, some of it good, most of it bad, but all of it marked by the occupiers' feelings of superiority toward the Egyptian people. It is hardly surprising that after their independence Egyptians took satisfaction in foreign policies that highlighted their place in the sun. What is surprising is that it took Nasser nearly three years to embark on such a course.

Foreign Policy Under Naguib

The first years of the Egyptian republic under General Mohammed Naguib's presidency shed light on the directions that Nasser was to take, through both the contrasts and the similarities between the two men and their policies. Naguib's personality was the antithesis of Nasser's. He was a warm and comfortable father-figure, with the self-assurance born of a secure middle-class background. His dearest wish was to turn over authority to a constitutionally elected civilian government as soon as possible. He did not have the talent Nasser was to develop of holding an audience spellbound, nor did he inspire in ordinary Egyptians any special sense of identification. In short, he lacked Nasser's personal magic.

Naguib was nevertheless extraordinarily popular. He challenged the Wafd in the area of its greatest strength, the Delta, and was greeted with rapturous enthusiasm in every village and town. The people were "delighting in a new order—any new order so long as it were not the old order."[12] Naguib's popularity during his short tenure is a reminder that there was more to Nasser's sway over the Egyptian people than charisma or, put another way, that charisma is a two-way street, requiring readiness and a spirit of acceptance on the part of the people governed as well as special qualities on the part of the leader.

The foreign policies of Naguib in 1952 and 1953 and of Nasser in 1954 were very similar. Both men believed that a tranquil period in Egypt's foreign relations was needed in order to consolidate political control and resolve the serious financial problems facing the country. Their emphasis was therefore on a fast and peaceful settlement of the big problems, primarily the evacuation of British troops from Egypt and the independence of Sudan. One of the military regime's early moves was to abandon Egypt's claim to possession of Sudan on the assumption that the Sudanese would voluntarily associate themselves with Egypt after independence. Despite Egypt's best efforts to make this happen (and to some extent because of them), Sudan opted for full independence from Egypt and from Britain alike.

Egyptians accepted the decision with the best grace possible. They took some comfort in the belief that abandonment of their claim to sovereignty in Sudan would at least remove the main obstacle to agreement with Britain on the status of its forces in Egypt. In fact it took nearly two years of hard bargaining after the Sudan settlement before the Anglo-Egyptian treaty, providing for the total withdrawal of British troops in twenty months, was signed on December 19, 1954.

Nasser and the New Pan-Arabism

Within a few months of Nasser's agreement with the British on troop withdrawal, Egyptian foreign policy took a dramatic turn toward pan-Arabism. The two events are close enough in time to raise the question whether they were related—whether, that is, the agreement with the British opened the door to a more assertive Egyptian regional posture by removing the constraints that had existed while Cairo was negotiating its independence. That a clear and conscious decision was taken to change course and identify Egypt publicly with Arab-wide interests is certain. The new emphasis was immediately apparent to Egyptians, to other Arabs, and to everyone else concerned with the Middle East. During the first months of 1955 Arab nationalist themes in Radio Cairo newscasts ("Arab solidarity," "Arab Egypt,"

"Arab people of Egypt," and so on) jumped from approximate parity with Egyptian nationalist themes ("Egyptian people," "sons of the Nile Valley," "glory and dignity of Egypt," and so on) to about five to one in favor of the pan-Arab themes. By midyear the ratio was about twelve to one, where it remained through 1959.[13]

Many Arabs had concluded by late 1954 that Nasser cared only about matters of direct concern to Egypt. It is certainly true that, from the problems of land reform to the threat from the Muslim Brotherhood, Nasser had his hands full with domestic problems. A contemporary cartoon portrays Egypt after independence as a shrouded mummy rising from the grave.[14] Nasser had in any case little use at the time for Arab nationalist slogans. "Power," he wrote, "is not merely shouting. . . . [It is] acting with all the components of power."[15]

In fact, however, Nasser did not neglect Egypt's Arab relations before 1955. On the contrary, he gave them the priority he believed they deserved, though treating them as matters for private diplomacy rather than public rhetoric. His principal emissary to the Arab world was Major Salah Salem, who visited most of the important Arab capitals between 1952 and early 1955. In August 1954 Salem met quietly with Nuri al-Said at Sarsank in northern Iraq to discuss Nuri's proposal for a U.S.- and British-backed defense system that would link Egypt with Iraq and Turkey and protect against Soviet penetration into the Middle East. Although the talks ended in misunderstanding and failure, Nasser made no attempt to exploit publicly Nuri's efforts to continue the Iraqi partnership with Britain.

In October 1952 Nasser gave an interview that illustrates the interest-driven, nonideological view of Arab power and nationalism he held during his first years in power. He began by identifying the bases of Arab power as its oil and strategic location as well as its spiritual bonds to and relationships with neighboring states.[16] Two years later, after Nasser had replaced Naguib as president, the interview was reprinted without this passage.

Four events led Nasser to move in 1955 and 1956 toward a foreign policy that found its main justification in the ideologies of Arab nationalism and nonalignment: the Baghdad Pact, Egyptian-Israeli military clashes in Gaza and the subsequent Czech arms deal, the nonaligned summit in Bandung, and the Suez crisis. The result was not only a shift in the style of Egyptian foreign policy but a change, ultimately, in the way that Egyptians saw themselves in the Arab world.

The Challenge of the Baghdad Pact

Nasser's intense opposition to the signing of the Baghdad Pact in April 1955 was in part the natural wariness of a revolutionary leader toward a conservative monarchy still tied to its colonial master. But more fundamental was Nasser's conviction that Britian hoped to achieve through an alliance with Iraq the concessions it had not been able to obtain from him—most importantly, British base rights in the event of a Soviet attack on Iran. And in the background was the longstanding competition of the two river-valley civilizations for regional autonomy. As usual, the prize was Syria, which was wavering between association with Iraq and Egypt.

For the first time Nasser became deeply involved in inter-Arab relations and rivalries,[17] using mass propaganda in saturation doses to achieve his diplomatic goals. The end result was Iraq's virtual isolation in the Middle East. Saudi Arabia and Syria joined Egypt in bilateral defense agreements, and other Arab governments either lent diplomatic support or remained neutral. But more important in the long run was the widespread resonance of the anti-Western propaganda in the towns and cities of the Arab world.[18] A chord had been struck, somewhat by chance, and Nasser was quick to hear its significance.

Clashes with Israel and the Czech Arms Deal

The border clashes between Egypt and Israel that took place in Gaza in February 1955 are interesting for what they suggest about the Egyptian military's role in the making of foreign policy. Before 1955 the Free Officers do not seem to have planned much in the way of foreign involvement. The government had limited resources and grave problems at home, and the army realized that it was in any case unprepared for a second round with Israel.[19] Nasser himself continued to view Israel with ambivalence, publicly commenting that at the time Zionism and Israel were "progressive elements in contrast to the rotten Arab regimes in the Middle East."[20]

Each step in the escalating violence in Gaza was marked by Egyptian miscalculation of the impact of its public statements on Israel. To begin with, Nasser had no conception of the seriousness with which Israel treated Radio Cairo propaganda targeted at other Arabs. One listener was David Ben-Gurion, who viewed the shrill Egyptian propaganda as evidence that Nasser intended to attack Israel as soon as he had the means.[21] On February 28 Ben-Gurion sent a powerful Israeli column against Egyptian army headquarters in the town of Gaza and then destroyed a truckload of Egyptian soldiers sent as reinforcement. Nasser's predicament was that of any military leader challenged by superior force. He knew that to acquiesce to his officers' insistence that he strike back was to invite destruction of his forces, but he could not ask the army to stand by while their units were attacked. In the end, he responded by training increased numbers of Palestinian guerrillas. Then in September 1955, after the West had pro-crastinated in meeting his arms requests, he turned to the Soviet bloc for arms.

Bandung and the Suez Crisis

To the elemental appeal of anti-Westernism, Nasser grafted the ideologies of nonalignment and Arab nationalism. At the Afro-Asian Conference at Bandung in April 1955, Nasser was treated by India's Jawaharlal Nehru, China's Chou En-Lai, and other notables as the foremost figure of the Arab world. He of course recognized the importance to his internal position of being accepted by Third World leaders as a key player in international politics. But he also seems to have concluded that nonalignment made sense for Egypt in the growing confrontation with the West. The large number of newly independent African and Asian states that identified with nonalignment virtually assured Egypt of widespread support in any actions it might take against the West.

During the abortive 1963 talks on Arab unity held by Egypt, Syria, and Iraq, Nasser remarked that it was not until the Suez crisis of 1956 that Egyptians began to take Arabism seriously.[22] Clearly the magnitude of the crisis following nationalization of the canal made the events of 1956 critical to Arab nationalism. The events put Nasser at the center of the world stage, seizing the imagination of the Egyptian people and of Arabs and Muslims everywhere. Many Arabs who had not paid much attention to Nasser's warnings about the neoimperialist threat were persuaded by the Franco-British-Israeli invasion of Egypt that he was right. Certainly in Nasser's own mind the invasion confirmed the need for Arab support. "Other Arab nations," he was later to write U.S. president John F. Kennedy, "cannot isolate themselves from the aggression launched on one of them, for it . . . threatens the other Arab states with the same danger and the same fate."[23]

After the Suez crisis the full force of the media was turned to propagating Arab nationalism. Even the Free Officers had taken to saying that the revolution never had any purpose except to lead the Arabs to strength and solidarity.[24] There is no doubt that the propaganda had an important effect on Egyptian attitudes, reinforcing the growing view that Egypt had a unifying mission in the Arab world. How deep and how enduring these feelings were is a question to be considered in later chapters.

Pan-Arabism in Practice

The Egyptian-Syrian Merger

In February 1958, about a year after Nasser's popularity in the Arab world had reached its height, Egypt and Syria agreed to merge their countries into the United Arab Republic. The new republic was not to be a loose federation but a total, organic integration of the two states. The Arab dream that had for so long been frustrated seemed on its way to becoming reality: Ideals were to be put into practice and rhetoric was to be tested in institutions. For three years the national interests of Egypt and Syria competed with the imperatives of pan-Arab ideology.

The merger took place during unusual turbulence in the Middle East. Syria was at the center of the storm and was propelled by the violence around it to seek safety in unity with a stronger partner. On one side Iraq bombarded Syria with propaganda, while on the other Lebanon, through its Muslim community, drew Syria ever more deeply into its own tragic drift toward civil war. The United States and USSR added their weights to the tug of war. The Eisenhower Doctrine of January 1957, pledging financial aid to Middle Eastern governments threatened by "overt armed aggression from any nation controlled by international communism," increased Syrian nervousness by strengthening the positions of the surrounding conservative governments. Partly in response, Syria concluded a major agreement with the USSR in mid-1957 for military and economic aid.

Within Syria power had gradually become concentrated in two parties, the Ba'ath party and the Communist party. Ardent advocates of pan-Arab unity, the Ba'athists had strongly supported Nasser and his policies since 1955. In addition to being drawn ideologically toward unity with Egypt, the Ba'athists were concerned that Syria was likely to drift further toward communism unless it obtained outside help. Egypt had the advantage of being both anticommunist and anti-Western.

By 1958, when Syria proposed integration, Nasser had become a victim of his own propaganda. He could hardly turn Syria down when the call to unity had become central to his influence in the Arab world and increasingly important to his legitimacy within Egypt. Yet he foresaw many of the difficulties that lay ahead and initially suggested putting off the union until the Syrians had straightened out their internal problems. The Ba'athists were somewhat taken aback by the cool response to their proposal. After the merger, Michel Aflaq, one of the party's founders and its main theoretician, was to say that Nasser was "in need of a philosophy."[25]

The Trials of Union

One of the many problems the new republic faced was in trying to unite the divergent approaches to Arab unity: Syria was rigid and doctrinaire, Egypt pragmatic and cautious. Even though the two peoples shared language, religion, and a sense of pride in Arab culture, their governmental systems could hardly have been more different. Politics in Syria was a national game nearly everyone played. In addition to the Ba'ath (at first mainly the party of the intellectuals), the landed oligarchy, the left, and the capitalists were also represented in government. The army intervened frequently and without consistency of purpose. Within the parliament, alignments shifted and coalitions formed as politicians sought to further their interests or their convictions. All this activity reflected a number of national charac-teristics, among them individualism, disdain for authority, and acceptance of diversity as a fact of social and political life. The Egyptians, by contrast, were accustomed to strong, centralized rule and believed the proper role of government was to ensure order and class harmony.

The decision to proceed with total integration had the effect of lodging effective power in the hands of Egypt, as the dominant partner. The Ba'ath had agreed to dissolve all parties except the unified National Union on the assumption that, as the best organized political group in Syria, it would dominate the union and become the main force in the eastern province of the United Arab Republic (UAR). In the event, the Ba'athists were outmaneuvered in the negotiations setting up the National Union, and when local committee elections were held in July 1959 they won only about 5 percent of the seats.

Cut off from power except for a few largely ceremonial cabinet posts, the Ba'ath ended its association with the UAR in late 1959. Its bitterness at finding itself unnecessary even to the running of the Syrian province was matched by Nasser's sense of betrayal at the inconstancy of those who had urged union in the first place. The UAR limped along for two more years, but with little enthusiasm on either side. In mid-1960 Nasser made an effort to address Syrian grievances, convoking a national assembly that included well-known Syrian political figures. The problems, however, were not to be solved. The end came on September 28, 1961, when Syrian army officers carried out a coup against those who had, in their words, "humiliated Syria and degraded her Army."[26]

Unity of Purpose Versus Unity of Ranks

During the three years of union with Syria, Egypt's relations with other Arab states went through rapid and often unpredictable change. The very fact of the UAR's existence upset old power alignments and led to new coalitions. Within a month of the merger, Iraq and Jordan joined forces to resist what they saw as a rising tide of revolutionary Arab nationalism. In May 1958 Lebanon complained to the Security Council that the UAR was interfering in its affairs by training antigovernment forces and providing them with arms. Then, at the height of the turmoil, the Iraqi army overthrew the monarchy, and for a few days the momentum of pan-Arabism seemed unstoppable.

Once he had consolidated power, however, Brigadier Abdel Karim Kassem adopted a violently anti-Egyptian posture, moving against Nasserist and pan-Arab elements in Iraq. The antagonism of revolutionary Iraq raised problems of principle for Egypt. If the radical, antimonarchical populists of Iraq opposed unity with like-minded Egypt, who was left to unite with? Nasser dealt with the question by ignoring it. The Egyptian propaganda machine simply reverted to the name-calling techniques used against the old regime—except that Iraq became a stooge of international communism instead of Western imperialism.

The challenge to Egypt's power in the region was not so easily handled. Nasser had to take his allies where he found them, and once again he patched up relations with Saudi Arabia and Jordan. The reconciliation with the Arab monarchies lasted only until Syria's secession from the UAR. After the secession Nasser concluded that he had been wrong to try to work with the conservative elements in Syria; the better course was to encourage revolution in the Arab states that leaned too far to the right (or, in the case of Iraq, too far to the left).

At this point the regime developed a formula for pan-Arabism that permitted Egypt the theoretical flexibility it needed to accommodate its state interests. On the one hand, Egypt reaffirmed its dedication to pro-pagating Arab unity; on the other, it acknowledged that Arab unity was, at the time, impractical. Henceforth Cairo would try to achieve "unity of purpose" rather than work for a specious "unity of ranks" among Arab states that had different political systems and were at different stages of economic development. In this way Nasser managed to retain the rhetoric of Arab nationalism, which had given him so much leverage, at the same time that he postponed indefinitely the effort to unite dissimilar countries, which had caused him so much trouble.

Within two years of Syria's secession, military coups in Iraq and Syria had returned to power the still pro-union Ba'ath Party. If the Ba'athists were willing to forgive and forget, that was not entirely so of Nasser. His revolutionary posture was paying dividends, even in Yemen, where in 1963 Egyptian support of rebel forces served to remind the Saudis and others not to take Egypt lightly. The price for unity had by this time become clear and unmistakable: Cairo insisted on controlling the political leadership of any union that might be created.

In tripartite negotiations in April 1963, Egypt, Syria, and Iraq agreed on a constitutional framework that included a president with strong powers, a bicameral legislature, and three regional vice-presidents. There was no consensus, however, on the nature of the "political fronts" that were to be created in each region or the functions of the "unified political leadership" that was to operate on the federal level.[27] With the negotiations for unity at an impasse, the best that could be done was to proclaim a two-year transition period, after which, if all went well, the constitution would be implemented. Even this agreement to agree in the future was greeted with euphoria in much of the Arab world. But before four months had passed, Nasserists had been purged from the Syrian armed forces, Iraq was in a state of renewed internal crisis, and the propaganda machines of all three countries were again operating at full throttle.

Arab Divisions and the June War

The collapse of the Egyptian-Syrian-Iraqi endeavor marked the end of serious attempts to achieve even partial unity during Nasser's lifetime. In Egypt the reaction was a sense of wounded pride and a feeling that other Arabs probably lacked the ballast to make a success of union. Outside Egypt the reactions differed. Conservative governments rejoiced at the divisions among their radical neighbors, Ba'athists and other pan-Arab ideologues resolved to try again when they had increased their bargaining power, and many others "felt that Arab unity was a harmless fiction."[28]

Even by earlier standards, the intensity of Egypt's swings between 1963 and 1967 from confrontation with other Arabs to cooperation and back again was remarkable. In October 1963, a few months after the collapse of the unity talks, Egypt was engaged in quarrels with Saudi Arabia over Yemen, with Morocco over the dispatch of Egyptian arms to Algeria, with Jordan as a matter of ideological principle, and with Syria and Iraq over the purges of pro-Nasser elements in their countries. Then in late December Nasser called for an Arab summit. Ostensibly convened to confront Israel over its plan to divert the headwaters of the Jordan, the conference had in reality the twofold objective of undercutting Syria's call for war against Israel and persuading Saudi Arabia to cooperate with Egypt in ending the war in Yemen. The conference managed to clear the air, and for the next two years inter-Arab relations were at their most cordial.

The era of civility ended in mid-1966. It was in part the victim of the diehard positions of the warring factions in Yemen, who no longer responded fully to their Saudi and Egyptian patrons. Adding to the friction was Syria's renewed encouragement of Palestinian guerrilla operations through Jordan; for when King Hussein turned to Saudia Arabia for help in maintaining the integrity of his country, Egypt backed Syria, and the usual split between radicals and conservatives again spread through the Arab world. A process had been set in motion that led directly to the 1967 War. The Palestinian raids resulted in Israeli reprisals against Jordan, Saudi Arabia then reproached Egypt for not coming to Jordan's aid, and Nasser finally felt obliged to prove his Arab credentials by taking a bellicose stand toward Israel. "[To] put an end to the Arab maneuverings," wrote Sadat, Nasser gave orders "for the Tiran Strait to be closed and the United Nations Emergency Force to be withdrawn," knowing that "war [was] a one hundred percent certainty."[29]

The Retreat from Pan-Arabism

During the last three years of his life, Nasser had neither the means nor the desire to pursue an active Arab policy. With his army nearly destroyed by Israel and the economy close to collapse, outside help was essential. Saudi Arabia, Kuwait, and Libya together contributed $280 million a year as compensation for wartime damage, which included the loss of revenues from the Suez Canal and the Sinai oil fields. The Soviets undertook to rebuild the Egyptian armed forces, establishing themselves throughout the country as military and economic advisers and as custodians of the military facilities granted them. Defeat thus brought with it military and economic dependence and the abandonment, at least temporarily, of the two pillars of Egyptian foreign policy, nonalignment and leadership of the Arab world.

The most fundamental change in Egypt's priorities resulted from the loss of the Sinai: The return of occupied territory became the cornerstone of Egyptian foreign policy, every other action being judged according to its impact on that goal. Egypt and the other Arab states were not, however, allowed to forget the Palestinian problem. The PLO, set up in 1964 by Arab leaders meeting in Alexandria and supported by Egypt mainly as a means of restraining large-scale Palestinian incursions into Israel, became a political force in its own right after 1967. The PLO's prestige among Arabs grew rapidly after the June war, partly because of a number of high-profile guerrilla operations against Israel, partly because of a growing recognition that Arab state support for the Palestinian cause was necessarily tempered by the pursuit of national interests. The last straw for the Palestinians was UN Security Council Resolution 242—accepted by Egypt, Jordan, and later Syria, as well as Israel—which called for Israel's return of territory occupied in 1967 in exchange for secure boundaries, relegating the Palestinian problem to a question of refugee status.

The PLO's challenge to Arab state interests came to a head in September 1970, as the PLO created a virtual state-within-a-state inside Jordan from which to launch its operations against Israel. Infuriated by Egyptian and Jordanian acceptance of the Rogers Plan calling for Arab-Israeli talks to implement Resolution 242, the PLO carried out a multiple hijacking in Jordan and engaged in increasingly fierce clashes with the Jordanian army. By mid-September Jordan was in a state of civil war. Nasser called for an emergency summit meeting to end the fighting: He could neither sit by as the Palestinians were massacred nor accept a Jordan so radicalized as to isolate Egypt in its effort to recover its territory.

The summit exhausted an already ill Nasser, but not before he had persuaded the PLO's Yasser Arafat to make the concessions required for peace with Jordan's King Hussein. To those who opposed the compromise he said: "You issue statements but we have to fight. If you want to liberate, then get in line in front of us."[30] On September 28, the day after the agreement was reached, he died of a heart attack.

The eighteen turbulent years that Nasser ruled Egypt set the inner and outer limits of Arab nationalism. To all but the most romantic, the inability of Egypt, Syria, and Iraq to merge their governments brought home the impracticality of the kind of union that earlier pan-Arab theorists and politicians had urged. At the same time, Nasser's success in mobilizing mass Arab opinion in the pursuit of common objectives underlined the potential power of Arab solidarity. Even if the ideal was rarely achieved, Egyptians, no less than other Arabs, came to look upon unity of Arab action as a central objective of their countries' foreign policies.

4

Sadat and His Early Foreign Policy

The Legacy of Nasser

Anwar Sadat's first three years as president were heavily influenced by Nasser's policies and personality. The immediate foreign policy legacy was unambiguous: The Sinai had to be recovered by force or diplomacy, and every move had to serve that end. Had Sadat been inclined to avoid this commitment, which he was not, he would almost certainly have lost the support of the military.

Foreign policy aside, Sadat's ability to hold on to the presidency and establish his authority was affected in different ways by Nasser's character and political style. On one side was the heroic dimension of Nasser's personality, the hold he continued to have on Egyptian emotions even after his death. For any successor the problem of developing the legitimacy and support needed to govern effectively would have been grave. For Sadat it was especially so. He had been outside the mainstream of power until Nasser named him vice-president in 1969, and most Egyptians did not take him seriously. At the same time, his being Nasser's choice—even though he was the last of the original members of the Revolutionary Command Council to hold the vice-presidency—gave his claim a sanction that appealed to the Egyptian taste for order and continuity. This held true of the military and internal security forces in particular, whose support was to be critical in the coming struggle for power.

Once president, Sadat had at his disposal the prerogatives of an office that had become enormously powerful during the previous eighteen years of centralized rule. Even though widespread discontent over abuses of power existed in the late 1960s, Nasser's style of governing seems on balance to have reinforced Egyptian acquiescence in the tight control of decision-making at the top. There were, in short, few constraints on the personal management of foreign policy once Sadat consolidated power. It was a great advantage to a leader who believed, as he did, that it was possible to control events—or at least that it was useful to appear to do so.

Sadat used his power to guide Egypt in a direction that was in many respects a complete turnabout from Nasser's. "As he steered Egypt, he always had a range of options and consistently he chose a 'rightist' course, conservative, stabilizing, adaptive, pro-Western, while imparting to the Presidency a strongly traditionalist character all in almost exact contrast to Nasir."[1]

The contrast to Nasser is the more striking as both men were born into the same social class in the same year, attended similar schools and read the same books, supported the same political movements and demonstrated against the same British actions, and entered the military academy together in the same year—the first in which candidates outside the aristocracy and upper-middle class were accepted. The similarities of background make the reasons behind their radically different political behavior seem inexplicable. Yet we must attempt an explanation, even if we can only reach W. S. Gilbert's conclusion that

Every little boy and girl
That's born into this world alive
Is either a little liberal
Or else a little conservative.[2]

The Impact of a Peasant Background

Throughout his life Sadat conveyed the impression that his peasant childhood was the formative period of his life. He often returned to the village of Mit Abul Kom where he spent his early childhood, praying there on religious holidays and donating to the village community the profits from his autobiography. There is a ring of authenticity to the opening scene of *In Search of Identity*, which recalls the simple pleasures of childhood in the "quiet village in the depths of the Nile Delta." The harmony of village life was for Sadat a metaphor for the nation as it ought to be, its individuals bound to one another by ties to the land. "That kind of collective work—with and for other men—with no profit or any kind of individual reward or prospect—made me feel that I belonged not merely to my immediate family at home, or even to the big family of the village, but to something vaster and more significant: the land."[3]

The stories told to Sadat by his grandmother were neither ancient pharaonic fables nor Islamic legends, but political tales dealing with the exploits of modern Egyptians struggling against the British. Indeed, because very little remains in Egyptian folk literature of the traditional myths and fables,[4] Sadat was treated early in life to heavy doses of Egyptian patriotism and anticolonialism.

Some of the apparent contradictions in Sadat's character reflect the dichotomies typical of Egyptian village culture. The same peasant, for example, can be at once "wonderfully cheerful and contented, with a ready wit, dearly loving a joke, lighthearted, kindly and hospitable" and yet "very emotional, inflammable . . . and nearly always conspicuously lacking in self-control."[5] Village culture, in particular the customs governing intravillage disputes, may also have played a part in shaping Sadat's distinctive approach to the use of force. Peasants from rival villages are frequently at odds, in part because honor dictates that every affront to communal honor or dignity requires a counterstroke. Yet an integral part of the code governing village disputes is that special honor attaches to the peacemaker, who is usually the head of the village.[6] Sadat himself saw force and diplomacy as closely interrelated; they were, he believed, mutually reinforcing means to the same political ends.

The more well-to-do peasant families like Sadat's, who own a bit of land and have a stake in the existing order, tend to be among the most conservative Egyptians. At the family and village level the social organization is patriarchal and the approach to authority respectful and submissive. The just society is seen as an organic unit. The state is a body directed by a brain, the head of state; its members work together in harmony.[7] This approach to political organization does not leave much room for the competitiveness of liberal democracy or the class conflict of Marxism. And indeed Sadat had little use for pluralistic politics. He believed that differences of opinion and conflicting group interests would disappear (as he felt they had in India under Gandhi and Nehru) when a nation "live[d] together as one family,"[8] like the villagers of Mit Abul Kom in his nostalgic memories of childhood. In short, Sadat saw his relationship to the people as one of a father to his children, and he expected them to recognize his good will and to respond with obedience.

Sadat's youth had its share of unhappiness, especially after his family moved to Cairo, and it can be argued that his personality was permanently scarred by blows to his self-esteem that occurred in late childhood and early adolescence. In Cairo Sadat's father took a third and then a fourth wife, after which Sadat's Sudanese mother (the second wife) was scorned and reduced to a household drudge. Heikal, in a book notable for its unbalanced hostility toward Sadat, concludes that Sadat's fear of his father and ambivalent feelings toward his mother compelled him to escape into a world of fantasy, finally turning him into an actor in search of a role in life.[9] Heikal's theory has a certain plausibility, although it is built on such meager evidence as Sadat's acknowledged attraction to the theater. Its most serious weakness lies in its disregard of certain accepted premises in psychology: Since Freud, psychologists have recognized the overwhelming dominance in personality formation of infancy and early childhood (which in Sadat's case Heikal concedes to have been unusually happy) rather than of late childhood and adolescence. Modern analytic psychology also generally acknowledges Jung's concept of the "persona," or social façade, as an element in the makeup of every normal personality. Indeed, the phenomenon of "acting" is most apparent in the narcissistic drives that typically motivate politicians.

Youthful Conspiratorial Activities

If Sadat's peasant origins and family relationships were fundamental to his view of the world and Egypt's place in it, the conspiratorial activities of his early manhood explain much about his methods for managing Egyptian foreign policy. Between 1938 and 1952, Sadat spent about six years in the army helping to create the organization that made the revolution, another three in jail, and a good part of the rest planning political assassinations. Of all the Free Officers, he was the most audacious, impulsive, and violent.

Convinced that the military held the only key to dislodging the British, Sadat started to prepare the way for revolt as soon as he entered the army. In 1938, at the garrison village of Manqabad in Upper Egypt, he met with Nasser and a small group of contemporaries to discuss the political problems of the country. The following year in Cairo, members of the group organized themselves into a secret society that, somewhat enlarged, was to become the Council of the Revolution.

During World War II Sadat became involved in a number of quixotic escapades designed to help Germany defeat the British. It is clear that he was acting not only on the principle that his enemy's enemy was his friend, but also out of admiration for Adolf Hitler. Like Napoleon and Ataturk, two of Sadat's other heroes, Hitler's main appeal seems to have been that he used shock tactics to take charge of history and alter its direction. "[We] might have struck a quick blow at the British, joined forces with the Axis and changed the course of events," Sadat said somewhat over-optimistically about an effort to spirit a pro-German general out of Egypt in order to coordinate Egyptian resistance activities with the German high command.[10] Sadat's efforts to change history landed him in jail in 1942, and from then until his reinstatement as an officer in 1950 his battles were fought as a civilian.

Relations with the Muslim Brotherhood

Sadat's relationship with the Muslim Brotherhood was intense, ambivalent, and ultimately fatal. Sadat's first meeting with Hassan al-Banna took place in 1940 at the request of his military colleagues. Sadat was impressed by

Banna's intelligence and by his determination to bring about the moral regeneration of Egypt. At the same time, he recognized that Banna would accept nothing less than total control of the revolutionary movement. He and Nasser agreed that their close-knit society should be kept independent of the Brotherhood—and indeed of all opposition groups—except in terms of the broadest kind of mutually supportive cooperation.

Before the 1952 revolution the Brotherhood had exerted, as we have seen, a powerful impact on Egypt's Palestinian policy. Through its terrorist wing, it held the threat of assassination over Egyptian leaders who might be inclined to abandon the Palestinians or accommodate Israel. And through sermons and the media it was able to keep the Palestinian question constantly before the Egyptian people. Even the great majority of Egyptians—then as now—who have no use for religious fanaticism and see the Brotherhood's attacks on Israel as anti-Semitic bigotry, are moved by the call to defend the interests of fellow Arabs driven from their homeland. Nasser, who was shot at by the Brotherhood, and Sadat, who was killed by a fundamentalist, had to reckon with the organization's appeal to Arab and Muslim solidarity as an important part of the domestic and foreign policy environment.

As well as opposing the Brotherhood's mixture of the secular and the spiritual—or, more precisely, its claim to be sole arbiter of what was right for both church and state—Sadat was never at ease with Muslim funda-mentalism. His religious beliefs were in the mainstream of Islam, as interpreted by the Egyptian *ulama*. Such an outlook is conservative, tolerant up to a point, and generally disposed to follow the central course of Islamic thinking. What Rome is to Catholicism, the clerics of al-Azhar consider themselves to be to Islam. While Sadat's general approach to religion was similar to that of the religious establishment, he was not deterred from manipulating the *ulama* for his own needs whenever it suited him.

Another side to Sadat's religion, which seems from his autobiography to have developed while he was in jail, was a mystical sense of the immanence of divine love, somewhat akin to Sufism. This side of Sadat is hard to reconcile with the side that ordered the near random bombings and assassinations of pro-British Egyptians in the mid-1940s. It is one more apparent contradiction in a complex personality.

Lessons Learned Under Nasser

During his years with Nasser, Sadat held several positions that influenced his later approach to Egyptian-Arab relations. For much of the period he had overall responsibility for Egyptian affairs in the Arabian Peninsula and the Gulf. As a natural corollary, he became the regime's point man in its efforts to court the Islamic world and in this role was appointed secretary-general of the Islamic Congress. He also played a leading part in Egypt's intervention in Yemen.[11] The net effect of these experiences (including the Yemen war, which was a cautionary lesson to the entire leadership) was to strengthen Sadat's conservatism and belief in the importance to Egypt of the Arab monarchies.

In early 1955, when the Islamic Congress was founded under Sadat's chairmanship, the regime had not yet settled into an active pan-Arab posture but was still trying to burnish its image as the leader of Islamic nationalism. At this time, and later when representing Egypt at Islamic conferences in the 1960s, Sadat established close relations with a number of younger Arab leaders who had come to power by the time he became president. Among them were Crown Prince (later King) Feisal of Saudi Arabia, Jabir al-Ahmad of Kuwait, and Hassan II of Morocco. These personal relationships smoothed the way for the later rapprochement with the Arab monarchies. "They [the conservative Arab leaders] all welcomed me as President and showed that they were willing to help. My clear and declared policy was that Egypt could not distinguish one Arab country from another on the basis of so-called progressive and reactionary or republican and monarchical systems."[12]

Sadat's unwillingness to base Egypt's Arab relations on ideological distinctions was a function not only of his conservatism but of an innate pragmatism that became increasingly apparent during the late Nasser years. With the Arabs he was willing to try whatever worked for Egypt. The only countries to give Egypt financial aid after the 1967 defeat, he observed, were the Arab monarchies that Nasser had branded reactionary. "I have always mistrusted theories and purely rational systems," he wrote in *Revolt on the Nile.* "I believe in the power of concrete facts and the realities of history and experience. My political ideas grew out of my personal experience of oppression, not out of abstract notions."[13]

Nondoctrinaire though he was, by the time he took office in 1970 Sadat had a reputation as the most conservative of the Free Officers. Egyptians saw the battle for succession between Sadat and the Ali Sabri group in May 1971 as an ideological struggle between left and right. Yet Sadat's victory over those who regarded themselves as Nasser's rightful heirs had much more to do with practical politics than with ideology. His "corrective revolution" showed that in the long climb to the top he had mastered the techniques of consolidating support and dividing the opposition, the qualities of shrewdness and calculation, the art of waiting for the right moment, and the tactics of shock and surprise—all as applicable to the conduct of foreign affairs as they are to domestic politics.

Egyptian-Arab Relations Before the October War

Egypt's Arab relations before the October War of 1973 had two objectives: to help Sadat consolidate internal power and to develop the Arab solidarity needed for the return of Egyptian territory—through diplomacy if possible, through force if necessary. Until his position was secure, Sadat felt obliged to move cautiously in abandoning Nasser's brand of Arab nationalism, even though Nasser had himself been compelled in his last years to change course. The same changes that Nasser could explain away as temporary expedients were branded heresy by Sadat's opponents when Sadat proposed them.

Military planning for an offensive to recover the Sinai was fairly well advanced by the time Sadat came to power. With non-Arab states the aims were to obtain arms and to develop broad diplomatic support for the return of Egyptian territory. With the Arabs, the goals were military or economic or both. Egypt courted Libya and the Sudan in order to achieve strategic depth and to open the way for the acquisition of advanced Soviet weaponry from Libya, established coordination with Syria because of the need for a second front, and nurtured relations with Saudi Arabia and the other Gulf Arabs for the time when it would need massive financial aid and the political leverage of oil.

The Federation of Arab Republics

Less than two months after Nasser's death, Sadat picked up the thread of Egypt's Arab relations where Nasser had left it during the last of his zigzags between association with the "progressive" and "reactionary" Arab states. In December 1969 Nasser had explored the possibility of federation with Libya and the Sudan. The move may have been meant partly as a warning to Saudi Arabia (which had refused Egypt additional financial aid) not to take Cairo for granted. Such a federation would also have decreased the vulnerability of Egyptian airfields, as Libyan and Sudanese air bases were outside the range of Israeli bombers. Nasser, Muammar Qadhafi of Libya, and Ja'afar Numeiry of the Sudan did in fact sign a pact in Tripoli that "envisaged a complete union of their countries,"[14] but the agreement did not come into force during the remaining months of Nasser's life.

For Sadat the federation must have seemed useful politically as well as militarily, conveying as it did the impression of continuity in Nasser's foreign policy. Once in power he tried to breathe new life into it. Resurrecting the pact involved some reconciliation, however, for Libya and the Sudan had fallen out over Qadhafi's objections to communist participation in the Sudanese government.[15] Although that obstacle was overcome in early November 1970, Numeiry in the end declined to join because the Sudanese had not yet established the constitutional bodies needed to ratify the federation.

The Sudan was replaced in the unity discussions by Syria, which, ever since President Hafiz al-Assad's recent accession, had been eager to federate with Egypt. On April 17, 1971, in Benghazi, the presidents of Egypt, Libya, and Syria agreed to a federation that was considerably watered down from the Tripoli Pact. The Federation of Arab Republics, as it was called, was to be headed by a council of the three presidents, who were responsible for coordinating policy and drawing up a plan leading to ultimate unity.

An important provision required that fresh elections be held in the member countries. This would have led to new political institutions in Egypt, giving Sadat the opportunity to replace his rivals in the developing struggle for power. Sadat's opponents, who controlled the Supreme Executive Committee of the Arab Socialist Union, were determined that this should not happen. They forced a showdown over the federation proposal, arguing that Sadat had failed to learn the lessons of the Arab unity disasters of 1958 and 1963. In the end Sadat succeeded in moving the debate to the full Central Committee, where, after lengthy discussion, he received the support he sought.

The main issue at stake in these moves was of course political power, not foreign policy. Yet it does not seem from the Central Committee debate that there was much enthusiasm for the federation on its merits—or indeed for any Arab unity scheme. The provision that most bothered the Egyptian representatives was one that permitted Libya and Syria to outvote Egypt on the Presidential Council, each member of the council having one vote and decisions to be taken by the majority. Before approving the federation, the Central Committee insisted that Egypt retain the right of veto.

In early 1971 Sadat's proposal for a cease-fire and an interim withdrawal agreement with Israel gave rise to more serious foreign policy differences between Sadat and the leftist opposition led by Ali Sabri. Sadat's initiative, with its emphasis on a partial rather than comprehensive settlement, was a genuine departure from Nasser's policy. It was also the opening move in Sadat's practice of using the drama of unexpected initiatives to achieve his objectives.[16]

Although Sadat won the struggle for power—and with it a free hand to federate with Libya and the Sudan—little was done to give shape to the association for over a year. This seems to have been partly because of Sadat's diminished interest in the merger once he had consolidated his internal position, and partly because of Qadhafi's hesitation in associating Libya with an Egypt that seemed increasingly dependent on the USSR. Then, in July 1972, Sadat dismissed some 15,000 Soviet military advisers from Egypt, and in less than two weeks Qadhafi presented Sadat with a concrete proposal for union. A variety of joint committees were set up the following month to consider how best to coordinate and integrate the two systems of government.

As the committees struggled with the problems of union, Sadat seems to have realized that Qadhafi's concept of war with Israel was completely at odds with his. For Qadhafi, the conflict could only be a holy war, with no quarter given or taken; for Sadat, war was to be limited to the achievement of defined political ends. Qadhafi's view was all the more troublesome because the Egyptian high command was itself divided on the nature and scope of the war. Finally, in the summer of 1973, Libya was dropped as an active participant in military planning and the plans for unity were shelved. Nevertheless, in keeping with his search for Arab allies wherever he could find them, Sadat avoided a complete break with Libya before the war.

High on the list of those whose help would be needed during the war were Jordan and the Palestinians. If either or both joined the battle, Israeli troops that would otherwise be used against Egypt and Syria would be tied down. Relations between Egypt and Jordan remained strained during Sadat's first year in office, evidently in part because Sadat wished to avoid seeming to bless the king's rumored contacts with Israeli leaders. Arafat, in contrast, was warmly welcomed in Cairo, and as early as March 1971 discussions between the PLO and the Egyptian military were in train to coordinate Palestinian-Egyptian military operations in wartime.

In the summer of 1971, secure in his own position, Sadat worked with King Feisal in trying to mend relations between Hussein and Arafat. While the mediation was unsuccessful, the effort underlined the importance Egypt attached to Arab solidarity. By 1973, largely owing to Sadat's efforts, Jordan was brought back into the fold, and the united Arab front that had been a principal object in Egyptian foreign policy was nearly complete.

The Damascus-Cairo-Riyadh Axis

At the heart of Arab solidarity in 1973 were the close relations among Egypt, Saudi Arabia, and Syria. Assad saw a two-front war as the only means of regaining Syrian territory and seems to have had little faith in Sadat's alternative diplomatic efforts. He had compelling domestic reasons as well for pursuing a close association with Egypt. Somewhat like the Ba'ath party in 1958, Assad and his Alawite supporters had come to power in November 1970 as a minority regime and needed the cachet of Egyptian approval to neutralize opposition from the Sunni majority.

By the summer of 1973 cooperation between the Egyptian and Syrian military commands was close and generally harmonious. Three days before the war, differences over the precise day and hour of the attack having been settled, the Syrian chief of staff said to his Egyptian counterpart: "If Damascus falls it can be recaptured; if Cairo falls the whole Arab nation falls."[17] Allowing for the flourishes of Arab discourse, the comment acknowledges Egyptian centrality in the Arab world and marks the brief high point of cooperation between Egypt and the Syrian heartland of pan-Arabism.

If Egypt's alliance with Syria was militarily the most important part of the three-power axis that confronted Israel in 1973, the Saudi connection was the crux of Sadat's economic and political strategy. The association was closely tied to the state of Egyptian relations with the United States and the USSR. Certainly Sadat's decision to expel the Soviet advisers from Egypt, while the result of a number of factors, was designed in part to clear the way for better collaboration with the Saudis. And the close relationship between Saudi Arabia and the United States assured Sadat of a friendly interpretation of his actions in Washington.

At the heart of the Egyptian-Saudi rapprochement was the longstanding friendship between Feisal and Sadat, who seem not only to have liked one another but to have known instinctively how best to influence one another. For example, in early 1972, just before Sadat was to leave for the USSR on a mission to replace outdated Soviet bombers, Feisal offered to provide Egypt with twenty fighter-bombers Saudi Arabia had bought from Britain. Feisal announced the offer as a way to strengthen Sadat's hand in the Moscow talks. To show his gratitude, Sadat informed the Saudi minister of defense that the Egyptian command had been instructed to take orders from Feisal if an emergency should arise while he was in Moscow. Sadat's gesture made a strong impression on the Saudi leadership; indeed, it appears that on both sides the incident helped to break down some of the psychological barriers that had grown up during twenty years of strained relations.

By the time of the October War, Egypt's Arab relations had reached a new level of solidarity, mainly because of the compelling need for Arab cooperation in wartime, among the conservative monarchies and the revolutionary republics alike. But another factor was Sadat's long-term diplomatic strategy, which required a new basis for Egyptian-Arab relations. Sadat was convinced that the full recovery of Egyptian territory was linked to U.S. diplomatic influence with Israel, which in turn depended on Egypt's moving toward the middle ground in Arab as well as great power relations. Together these factors transformed Egyptian policy toward the Arabs in the early and mid-1970s, ultimately affecting Egypt's role in the Middle East as profoundly as had Nasser's radical changes in Arab policy two decades before.

5

The October War and Its Aftermath

The October War of 1973 lasted less than three weeks, but it was long enough for a spirit of solidarity unprecedented in modern history to develop among the Arabs. The important decisions of the war were governed by a willingness to accommodate conflicting interests, a factor long absent from Arab affairs. Yet if the success in policy coordination and the respectable performance in battle created a new atmosphere of self-confidence, the war also inevitably revealed differing objectives. There were disagreements among the combatants, among the oil producers, and between the states fighting to recapture their territory and the rejectionists who wanted the war fought to the last Egyptian and Syrian soldier.

The Problems of a Two-Front War

Egypt and Syria agreed on the basic concept of a limited war to break the stalemate and generate pressure on Israel to return occupied territory. They found it harder to achieve the close military coordination needed to carry out a two-front war. In the absence of joint headquarters and a supreme commander with the power to issue operational orders to both armies, coordination took the form of personal appeals from one president or minister of war to the other. Because both Sadat and Assad preferred to communicate by telegram, even though a direct telephone line had been set up for their use, a full day sometimes passed between message and response. After the first four days of Arab success on both fronts, Israel was able to exploit the problems in Egyptian-Syrian coordination by concentrating its power on one front at a time.

Both at the beginning of the war and at its end, Egypt and Syria differed over the desirability of introducing a UN cease-fire resolution. More important in terms of the war's outcome was their disagreement over whether Egypt should press forward to the Sinai passes after consolidating its position on the east bank of the canal. Sadat and Minister of War Ismail Ali were reluctant to push on for fear of jeopardizing the political gains they had achieved. (Later Sadat was to admit that he had become so obsessed with the war's political purpose that he had failed to exploit the military situation on the ground.) Syria meanwhile was taking the full brunt of the Israeli counterattack and badly needed a renewed Egyptian offensive to relieve the pressure.

Late in the second week of battle, mainly in response to Syrian appeals,[1] Egypt launched a tank attack against Israeli forces defending the Mitla and Gidi passes. To do so it transferred the Twenty-first Armored Division to the front from its position in strategic reserve on the west bank of the canal. The move had far-reaching consequences. Not only did the Egyptian attack fail to dislodge the Israelis, who had the time to build up their forces guarding the passes, but the way was open for the Israeli counterattack that changed the course of the war. General Ariel Sharon's armor reached the west bank of the canal and cut off the Egyptian Third Army from food, water, and other supplies. The most important political effect of the encirclement was that it led to U.S. negotiation of an Israeli pull-back; that success, in turn, was the final element in persuading Sadat to rely on U.S. diplomacy after the war.

Arab Unity in Wartime

Military contributions from the other Arab states were significant but of a different magnitude from those of Egypt and Syria. Their impact was undercut, moreover, by command and control problems that dwarfed even those between Egypt and Syria. Military planning before the war had of course been strictly limited by the need to maintain secrecy. The result was that on the eastern front heavy losses occurred because of poor communications, especially among Syrian, Iraqi, and Jordanian armored units.

Because of its border with Israel, its well-trained if small army, and the Palestinian troops on its soil, Jordan was regarded by Egypt and Syria as militarily the most important of the other Arab states. In the spring of 1973, Sadat brought Hussein into the general military picture. The king was not convinced, however, that even a limited war could succeed. In mid-May he wrote to his generals: "It is clear today that the Arab nations are preparing for a new war. . . . The battle would be premature."[2] Nevertheless, to break out of the Arab isolation that had followed Jordan's suppression of the Palestinians in September 1970, Hussein sent envoys to Egypt and Syria in the summer of 1973 to negotiate a rapprochement. On September 12, Hussein, Sadat, and Assad signed a tripartite pact restoring Jordan's diplomatic relations with Egypt and Syria.

Jordan entered the war on October 13, 1973. In the first week of the conflict Hussein had been subjected to Arab pressure to open a third front and to U.S. pressure not to do so. Perhaps as a result of U.S. urging, perhaps because of his country's vulnerability to air attack, Hussein did not in the end engage Israel along the Jordanian-Israeli frontier, although he did send two armored brigades to the Syrian front. The possibility of a third front nevertheless seemed real enough at the time and must have been a factor in Israeli strategy.[3]

The PLO made an effort to open its own third front from Jordan with Palestinian troops. On October 11 Arafat wired Sadat that the Jordanian army was blocking Palestinian *fedayin* units that were trying to move across the border into southern Israel and asked him to intervene with Hussein. Sadat at first declined. Later, changing his mind, he asked Hussein to allow the Palestinians to cross the frontier in order to disrupt Israeli communications. The king responded that he could not, as his frontier was unprotected in the absence of the armored brigades fighting in Syria. This decision to rein in the PLO was later to become a bitter issue, the Arabs complaining that Jordan's contribution to the war had been inadequate. For the Palestinians, the virtual exclusion of their troops from combat was one of the more galling aspects of a war that had little to do with them.

Among the Arab nations sending troops and material to the front, Iraq's contribution was the most significant. Although Egypt and Syria had not hoped for much from Iraq, four squadrons of Iraqi aircraft and a large contingent of armor joined the battle. Iraq was able to move troops from its eastern border by the simple expedient of calling a halt to its war with Iran. (The intermediary between Iraq and Iran was Soviet President Nikolai Podgorny, who prevailed upon the shah to suspend border operations for the duration of the war with Israel.)

Other Arabs contributed to the war in different ways, some with troops, some with weapons, some with money, and some by way of their oil leverage. On the eastern front a Moroccan expeditionary force had been in place since before the war. The Saudis fought there as well, although their entire army consisted of four infantry brigades totaling 36,000 soldiers, of whom 4,000 were deployed in Jordan. West of the Suez Canal, a Kuwaiti brigade and the only Palestinian troops to serve in the war helped to defend Cairo. Algeria and Libya each sent a tank brigade and, with the other oil producers, provided substantial financial help.

The Oil Weapon

The use of oil for political purposes was one of the war's most tangled issues. There were differences over what would and would not work, over tactics and strategy, and, as might be expected in a forum comprising conservative monarchies and radical republics, over exactly what was to be achieved. That the oil producers were able in these circumstances to bury their differences and forge a common policy was one reason for Arab optimism after the war.

Egypt's influence on the oil producers was in the direction of pragmatism and flexibility.[4] The Egyptians argued that oil was a political lever, not a weapon, whose effect on the industrial nations varied according to each country's degree of dependence on it. The Egyptian strategy boiled down to putting pressure on the vulnerable states of Western Europe and Japan so they in turn would press the United States to limit its support to Israel. While Europe and Japan played their part in the scenario, the United States did not. Hence the main practical consequence of the embargo and the production cutbacks was to deny Israel a relatively small amount of European military equipment. The Egyptians may not have expected much more.

Sadat had talked to Feisal about Egyptian objectives before the war but had made no specific request. His approach was characteristic: Having established a warm relationship with the leader of a country important to Egypt, he relied on enlightened self-interest and the claims of friendship to bring about the desired action. "His negotiating tactic," said U.S. Secretary of State Henry Kissinger, "was never to haggle over detail but to create an atmosphere that made disagreement psychologically difficult."[5]

Arab Objectives and the October War

On October 15, Assad gave a speech celebrating the Arab unity brought about by the war, "the pan-Arabism of battle," as he described it. The implication that unity was easier to achieve in war than peace became clear enough a week later when Egypt accepted the UN cease-fire mandated by Security Council Resolution 338. Assad was annoyed on two counts: First, he had not been consulted by Egypt, and, second, he believed that Israel had been able to launch a successful counterattack against his forces just before the cease-fire because it knew Egypt would soon be out of the war. After two days Assad grudgingly agreed to the cease-fire on the understanding (which he knew was not Israel's) that Resolution 338 required the complete withdrawal of Israel from all the Arab territories occupied in 1967.

Iraq and Libya rejected the armistice entirely, Iraq in anger withdrawing its forces from Syria. Jordan immediately accepted it. As the war wound down, it became apparent to the Arabs who rejected any limited peace with Israel that the countries doing most of the fighting had objectives different from theirs. It took some time for the full implications of these opposing views to become clear; until then, the pride in wartime solidarity and a creditable military performance outweighed the recriminations that marked the war's end. But the stage was set for the most divisive confrontation that the Arab nations had yet faced.

The war had important implications for Sadat's attitude toward the use of force in the achievement of Arab objectives. One of the main lessons he learned was that total victory over Israel—the only kind that could lead to the satisfaction of all Arab state and Palestinian demands—was ruled out by great power politics. The U.S. nuclear alert at the time of the Third Army's encirclement made this starkly clear. Earlier the United States had matched Soviet weapon resupply to the Arabs almost ton for ton to show that the war could not be won by indirect Soviet intervention. When the Soviets appeared to be considering the dispatch of troops, the United States sent an unambiguous message that direct Soviet intervention would risk a nuclear war. In the end, it was not détente that assured a limited war but the fundamental interest of both superpowers in avoiding nuclear confrontation.

The Disengagement Agreements
Divide the Arab World

In the three years following the October War, many of the issues that came to divide the Arabs after Camp David first crystallized. As Sadat moved along the path of limited agreements that he believed to be the only feasible approach to settlement, the other Arabs became increasingly concerned that Arab-wide objectives would be sacrificed for the return of Egyptian territory. For the time being these problems were still on the horizon. Assad needed his own disengagement agreement after the war to move back the Israeli salient from the plains of Damascus and to show that he, as well as Sadat, could win back territory from the fighting.

As the UN cease-fire took hold in late October, Egypt and Syria were both faced with situations on the ground that they would almost certainly have tried to change by force if diplomacy had failed. And indeed they knew that their best card in obtaining a negotiated settlement was the implicit threat of renewed hostilities on both fronts. Sadat was no more anxious than Assad to give up the possibility of joint action before U.S. diplomatic efforts had been put to the test. Yet with his Third Army virtually encircled, he could not wait for Syria to complete its own disengagement agreement.

The First Two Agreements

After the war Sadat tried to help Syria achieve a satisfactory disengagement agreement. He recognized that Syria alone could generate the kind of Arab pressure that could be troublesome to Egypt, and he meant to make it worth Syria's while to stay with the step-by-step negotiating process. Right after the first Egyptian disengagement agreement he warned Kissinger that he was bound by honor to help Syria recover the territory it lost in the war: "If Israel returned less than the newly conquered territories and Syria went to war, [Sadat] would support his ally even though it would wreck the design of his entire policy."[6] Kissinger, for his part, did not have to be persuaded of the importance of Syrian involvement. He regarded it as the key to preventing Sadat's isolation and the precondition to later movement toward a settlement with Jordan and the Palestinians.[7]

Sadat visited the key conservative Arab states after the first disengagement to make sure that Egyptian postwar objectives were understood. He cared little about the reaction of the rejectionists. As Kissinger told Foreign Minister Abba Eban at the time, Sadat was "ready to alienate the Arab extremists all the way from Baghdad to Tripoli."[8] Sadat's efforts with the mainstream Arabs were rewarded at an Arab summit in November 1973, where the actions that Egypt had already taken were approved.

None of this made much impression on Assad, who could not forgive Sadat for refusing to hold up the first Egyptian agreement until Syria had concluded its own accord. The intensity of Syrian anger is worth trying to understand, for it is the passion behind the Cairo-Damascus rivalry that was later to be largely responsible for the disruption of the Arab world. Much of the fire was plainly fed by wounded pride—a sense of being taken too lightly by the complacent Egyptians, convinced of their centrality in Islam and the Arab world. For historical reasons the Syrians were unusually sensitive to Sadat's ill-concealed view that after the war Damascus had no choice but to follow Egypt's lead.

If the Syrians were prickly about their junior-partner relationship, they also saw their national interests as different from Egypt's. Assad knew that a separate Egyptian peace with Israel would entail serious constraints on Syria's wide-ranging ambitions in the Middle East. Syria wanted its territory back, it was deeply involved in Palestinian politics for reasons of national security and principle, it was engaged in a struggle for influence in Iraq, and it had aspirations and commitments in Lebanon that were to entangle it in ways that could not have been foreseen at the time. In most of these areas, Syrian interests clashed with those of Israel. As the option of joint Arab action diminished, Assad could expect to find his scope for action in the Middle East increasingly constricted.

The friction caused by differing national interests and the stresses of history were aggravated by the very different power positions of the two leaders. Sadat had behind him an army whose honor had been vindicated, a people who yearned for peace, and a tradition of one-man rule that enabled him to rise above the hate and prejudice fanned through thirty-five years of conflict. Assad's situation was not so simple. Although firmly in control, he could not be sure how far the Ba'ath and the military would follow him on a path of accommodation with Israel. And beyond the ideologues at home were the Iraqi Ba'athists, always on the lookout for an opportunity to accuse their Syrian counterparts of selling out.

Probing for a West Bank Agreement

In December 1974 Secretary of State Kissinger visited a number of Arab capitals, ostensibly to prepare the ground for the end-of-year Geneva Conference, but more fundamentally to create a favorable atmosphere for U.S. negotiation of the next-stage agreements—first among Israel, Egypt, and Syria, and then, if all went well, between Israel and Jordan. The first stop was Houari Boumedienne's Algeria. Whether Boumedienne was persuaded of Kissinger's sincerity, flattered by the attention paid him, or convinced that the situation called for U.S. mediation, he gave his implicit approval to U.S. efforts. The blessing of revolutionary Algeria cleared the way for the Arab consensus that was essential at this stage for both Sadat and Assad.

After the difficult negotiations over the Golan Heights ended in agreement in late May 1974, hopes soared throughout the region that a beginning might have been made toward an irreversible peace. The feeling was that if Syria could sign an agreement with Israel, there should in principle be no barrier to negotiations between Israel and any other Arab nation. But the mood was fragile; its durability depended on further progress. The place to start, it seemed clear, was the West Bank, especially since Israel and Jordan already had a history of practical accommodation. (The PLO had done much to undermine its own claim to represent the Palestinians by launching a murderous attack on school children in the Israeli village of Ma'alot during the Syrian shuttle; far from disrupting the negotiations, the incident served to concentrate the minds of Syrians and Israelis alike on the importance of what they were doing.)

Sadat had reservations about Jordan's effectiveness as a negotiator for the Palestinians, and he said as much to U.S. President Richard Nixon during the latter's visit to Egypt in June 1974. Nixon assured him that in any negotiations on the West Bank the United States would work to bring in the Palestinians at an early stage.[9] A month later, after talks with Hussein in Alexandria, Sadat announced that he would support the king as the spokesman for the Palestinians living in Jordan. Despite Egyptian efforts, the question of Palestinian representation was resolved in the PLO's favor on October 28, 1974, at an Arab summit in Rabat.

Sinai II and Its Consequences

In the period leading up to the Rabat decision, as it became obvious that Israel was not prepared to enter negotiations with Jordan any more than with the PLO,[10] Kissinger weighed the possibility of a second disengagement involving further Israeli withdrawal on the Syrian and Egyptian fronts. The key to Arab acceptance was, as before, a Syrian agreement as a companion piece to Egyptian disengagement. But Assad was not to be persuaded. "War is not our hobby," he told Kissinger. "But I warn you, if there is not equal progress on all fronts—and for the Palestinians—then we shall not endorse what you do in Egypt."[11]

To protect himself from the drumbeat of Syrian and Palestinian criticism, Sadat insisted that only the military issues associated with Israeli withdrawal behind the Sinai passes were a proper subject for discussion. In Israel, meanwhile, the Labor government was doing its best to widen the gap between Egypt and Syria. In an interview with the Hebrew-language daily *Haaretz* on December 3, 1974, Foreign Minister Yitzhak Rabin declared that Israel's chief aim in the negotiations was to separate Egypt from Syria. This was not news to Sadat or Assad, but it made it easier for the rejectionist Arabs to argue that Egypt could not negotiate with Israel without sacrificing Arab interests.

After the conclusion of Sinai II, Assad complained to Kissinger that the new agreement "removed Egypt from the Arab-Israeli conflict and left Syria an orphan."[12] The terms of Sinai II do not in themselves bear out the assertion. Egypt had resisted Israel's demand for a formal declaration of nonbelligerency and had agreed only that for the three-year duration of the agreement the conflict should not be resolved by military force. It is true, however, that as a practical matter Sinai II took an important step toward ending the state of war between Egypt and Israel by locating a U.S.-manned early-warning station between their opposing armies. In private assurances Sadat reportedly pledged that Egypt would abstain from battle should Syria attack Israel, and at the same time secured from Israel an assurance that it would not attack Syria. The other two secret assurances relevant to the settlement process were made by the United States to Sadat: first, that the United States "would honestly endeavor to ensure Palestinian involvement in a peace treaty" and, second, that it "would make a serious effort to help bring about negotiations between Syria and Israel."[13]

On August 22, 1975, on the eve of Kissinger's arrival in the Middle East for his final shuttle, Syria and Jordan jointly announced the formation of a supreme command to direct political and military action against Israel. Hussein had plainly concluded that he had more to gain by protecting his flank from radical Arab attacks than by identifying himself with Egypt, the United States, and a settlement process that seemed to have run its course. For Assad, however strange his new bedfellow, the association strengthened Syria's claims to Arab preeminence and broadened its resources for a concerted campaign to isolate Sadat. Damascus had succeeded in consolidating a northern Arab front in opposition to Egypt.

During and after the Sinai II negotiations, the Egyptians worked hard to obtain Arab backing for their actions. In the first half of 1975 Vice-President Hosni Mubarak made two swings through the Gulf, Presidential Adviser Ashraf Marwan stopped in several Arab capitals before the agreement was signed, and in mid-May Sadat spent a week in Iraq, Kuwait, Jordan, and Syria. For Iraq and Jordan, Sadat's was the first by an Egyptian head of state.

By mid-1975, after Sinai II had been concluded, all discussion of the negotiating process centered on the possibility of an international conference. Egypt and Israel, each for its own reasons, agreed that the end of the road to partial agreements had been reached. Sadat may have had his doubts about the viability of a conference to which the Syrians and Palestinians came armed with proposals that were at the same time nonnegotiable and unacceptable to Israel. But he needed a breathing space, and the best way to neutralize Arab criticism was to seize the initiative by calling for a peace conference with the participation of the PLO. It was in this context that Sadat, with Arafat standing by his side, announced that he had received a mandate from the confrontation states to speak for them in a forthcoming meeting with U.S. President Gerald Ford to discuss next steps of the peace process.

6

Oil Diplomacy
and Arab Reconciliation

The Background:
Domestic Constraints on Egyptian Policy

The Intellectual Climate

Even before Sadat came to power—and increasingly in the early 1970s—there were renewed stirrings of a traditional, Egypt-centered nationalism ✗ throughout the country. The impact on foreign policy was in the direction of alliances that demonstrably furthered hard Egyptian interests (the return of territory above all) and away from relationships that were based on such abstractions as pan-Arabism or even regional prestige and influence. This new emphasis on self-reliance and pragmatism in foreign affairs is evident in an April 1972 memorandum to Sadat written by ten well-known Egyptian political figures, including two former Free Officers. The memorandum makes the following points, among others:

- "Israeli occupation of a part of Egypt has gone on for five years and it seems that this is going to be permanent. . . .
- The Arab countries are in disagreement and have not realized the danger that threatens [Egypt] and them. . . .
- Egypt has made her past by herself and she must make her future in this way. . . . [T]he policy of national liberation must be based on Egypt's resources alone—spiritual as well as material. This ought to be the only pillar of our policy since it is our honor and dignity that has been wounded, our land that has been occupied and no one can restore them to us except ourselves.
- The birth of the liberation will be dependent on our capabilities alone.
- Egypt is once again fighting for her independence against the occupation by Israel and the objectives of the Great Powers. . . .

• We would not object to an alliance with the devil if it leads to our advantage and not to his, but unless the alliance is between two equal parties it is bound to lead to our disadvantage, because our ally is not our equal. . . ."[1]

After the October War, the Egypt-first tendencies became more pronounced. Most Egyptians were clearly ready for a respite from rhetoric and the opportunity to confront Egypt's problems. If there was one sentiment that cut across all classes, it was that Egypt had shed more blood for the Palestinians and exhausted more resources for their cause than was reasonable or warranted. Flowing from this was indignation at those Arabs, especially the champions of all-out war who had never fired a shot in anger, who presumed to instruct Egypt in its duty to the Arab World.

Experiments in Democracy

The rigid state control of political expression and organization that marked the 1960s had led to a situation in which most authentic political life took place beneath the surface. Sadat set out to relax the atmosphere, partly because he knew it would be popular, partly because he must have sensed that he would have better control of the situation if the opposition were revealed. In 1975 the two-steps-forward-one-step-backward process of allowing the return of political parties began. The result was a glimpse into the country's changing political forces.

The formation of the New Wafd party in the mid-1970s suggested the emergence of a class of middle-income professionals and people in business with an interest in a free economy and political liberalism. The left was represented by the National Progressive Unionist Grouping (NPUG), headed by the respected former Free Officer, Khaled Mohieddin. Consisting mainly of intellectuals whose politics had formed under Nasser, the NPUG was not a serious force in the middle and late 1970s. Yet precisely because of its weakness, Sadat often singled it out for criticism when his policies misfired and were opposed by a range of opinion that extended well beyond the left. Viewing itself as the guardian of Nasserism, the NPUG often criticized Sadat for disregarding Arab opinion as he moved toward peace with Israel.

The most consequential of Sadat's liberalization measures were the release of Muslim Brotherhood leaders who had been imprisoned by Nasser and the loosening of restrictions on their activities. The Brotherhood quickly recaptured considerable public support through the organization of secondary school and university students, the provision of vital services to the urban poor, and the publication of a widely read periodical, *al-Dawa*. The Brotherhood remained as steadfastly pro-Palestinian and anti-Israel as it had been in 1948; in the mid-1970s it vigorously opposed the disengagement agreements, arguing that they separated Egypt from the Arab and Islamic communities.

Economic Constraints

Sadat's moves toward a more liberal political system were paralleled by actions to open the tightly controlled socialist economy to Arab and Western investment. This economic opening was developed in response to the requirements of foreign policy as well as to internal economic needs. The encouragement of foreign investment through legal incentives and safeguards clearly was meant to reassure those who in Sadat's view held the keys to a Middle East settlement—notably the United States, the Arab oil producers, and, to a lesser extent, Western Europe. The message was that Egypt's more conservative political orientation had economic roots and would endure.

By 1975 the country was virtually bankrupt, the economy having reached a state of stagnation that demanded more private and foreign investment. Egyptian economists, including Abdel Aziz Higazi and Abdel Munim Kaissuni, pleaded for an economic opening to the noncommunist world in order to increase exports and tap into Arab oil revenues. Describing the country's economic plight, Sadat did not mince words: "We had reached the 'zero stage' economically [before the October War]. . . . What this meant in concrete terms was that I could not have paid a penny towards our debt installments falling due on January 1 [1974]; nor could I have bought a grain of wheat in 1974. . . . [B]ut we are now in the same situation we were in a year ago, perhaps worse."[2]

In turning to the oil-rich Arabs to help meet Egypt's foreign exhange needs, Sadat was following Nasser's path after the war of 1967. The difference was that Sadat took pride in his ability to extract aid from the Gulf Arabs whereas Nasser submitted to the necessity with reluctance. The real deluge of Arab aid money came after the October War. It rose from about $350 million annually in the years right after the 1967 War to about $3 billion annually from October 1973 to November 1977.[3] Sadat's critics maintain that he accepted a degree of economic and political dependence on his benefactors that Nasser would not have countenanced. Yet there is no evidence that he in fact adopted any policy advocated by Egypt's creditors against his better judgment. On the contrary, as we shall see, he went to Jerusalem knowing that Saudi Arabia would be unhappy and signed a peace treaty with Israel realizing that it would jeopardize Arab economic assistance.

The Impact of Urban Riots

Egypt's economic difficulties led to eruptions in the streets of Cairo. In 1974 and 1975, riots, strikes, and demonstrations protested the desperate living conditions of the fixed-income wage earners. On January 1, 1975, iron and steel workers from Helwan marched through downtown Cairo chanting, "*Ya batal al-Ubur, feen al-futur?*" ("O hero of the crossing, where is our breakfast?")[4]

Sadat's response to mass protest was ambivalent. Publicly, he accused the particular demons of the day—communists, religious fanatics, or Nasserist ideologues—of trying to bring him down, dismissed them as powerless, and pledged to continue on course. Privately, he recognized that the poor, and especially the urban poor, posed the greatest threat to his policies and to his hold on power. He knew that his political adversaries could not normally ignite and maintain mass protests by themselves, but there was no question of their ability to fan the flames of urban unrest.

The urban demonstrations had their greatest impact on economic policy. In the wake of the serious riots protesting price rises in food and fuel in January 1977, Sadat firmly opposed the demands of the International Monetary Fund (IMF) and the gulf donors for a reduction of government subsidies on bread, butane gas, and other staples of the poor. The 1977 riots were doubtless a factor in slowing down plans for a return to domestic party politics, but (as we will see in our discussion of Camp David) they did not significantly affect the foreign policies on which Sadat had embarked. The peace initiative was a high-risk policy that broke radically with past patterns and conventions; yet Sadat pressed forward as if the economy were booming and the people contented with their living conditions.

Egypt and Syria After Sinai II

During the three years leading up to Camp David, inter-Arab politics were largely driven by Syria's efforts to block further Egyptian accommodation with Israel. Syria's basic concern, shared by Jordan, was that Egypt would agree to a separate peace with Israel, after which Israel would have no further incentive to negotiate the return of Arab territory. Egypt's worry, the mirror opposite, was that Syria, backed by the USSR, would prevent it from recovering its land by insisting on unrealistic and non-negotiable conditions at an international conference. The Egyptians were also deeply suspicious of joint Syrian and Jordanian plans for a confederation. Their fear was that Syria would use its influence to prevent Jordan from entering negotiations on the West Bank, leaving Egypt the only Arab nation to negotiate with Israel.

Within a month after the conclusion of Sinai II, the propaganda war between Egypt and Syria was back in full swing. On October 10, Cairo's *al-Akhbar* (one of several daily newspapers) carried Lebanese government charges that the Syrian Ba'ath was sabotaging Lebanon. The second main story reported Assad's sudden departure for Moscow, implying that he was running to the Soviets for instructions on what to do next in Lebanon. Four days later the Syrian press gleefully quoted Israeli officials as saying that Syria had taken a "hard line concerning any eventual political negotiation on the Golan." And in Damascus *al-Thawra* (a paper that tends to reflect Assad's views) claimed that the atmosphere of Sinai II had "immobilized the Egyptian front." The propaganda is unlikely to have had much influence on public attitudes in either country: The educated had through long exposure become inured to Arab propaganda, and the masses had a long history of skepticism toward established authority and its pronouncements.

The Cairo-Damascus rivalry was aggravated in 1975 by Egyptian fears that the United States believed Syria held the key to reactivating the peace process. The U.S. media, with greater access than before to Assad, gave Syria the kind of attention previously reserved for Egypt and Sadat. Sadat's primary goal was to get the negotiating process started again, but he was not prepared to do so at the expense of relinquishing to Syria Egypt's Arab leadership.

Quarrels with the Rejectionists

Egypt was on bad terms at this time not only with Syria and Jordan but also with Libya, Iraq, Algeria, and the radical Palestinian factions. The Libyan connection seemed something like a comic opera, and Sadat generally had the sense to treat it as such. Normally he dismissed Qadhafi's periodic calls for the Egyptian people to rise up and overthrow him with the suggestion that Qadhafi return to the mental hospital outside Cairo for further treatment. Twice, however, in 1976 and 1977, Sadat lost his composure and used force or the threat of force to retaliate against alleged Libyan terrorist activities.

The first confrontation began in July 1976 with an unsuccessful coup attempt against President Numeiry, which Sadat and Numeiry accused Qadhafi of instigating. Egypt and the Sudan promptly concluded a military cooperation agreement and discussed with Saudi Arabia the possibility of joint action against Libya. This was followed on July 17 by a series of meetings in Saudi Arabia among the Egyptian, Sudanese, and Saudi heads of state and their ministers of war.[5] The following month three terrorist acts against Egyptians occurred in quick succession, Egypt blaming them on Libya. After Sadat ordered troops to the frontier, Qadhafi lodged a complaint with the Arab League and tried unsuccessfully to convene the Federation of Arab Republics, which had ceased to exist except on paper. By this time Egypt had deployed two divisions along the border, including two armored brigades and three squadrons of MIG 23s.[6] Suddenly, in late September, the danger of war passed as quickly as it had appeared. Perhaps

Sadat had been bluffing, simply showing Qadhafi what he would face if he continued to goad Egypt.

In July 1977 the Egyptian air force did in fact bomb Libyan targets along the frontier, the ostensible reason being that Libya had received so many weapons from the USSR that it could only have been planning to attack Egypt. Later Sadat maintained that he had ordered the miniwar in response to an Israeli intelligence report that Qadhafi was planning to assassinate him. The purpose, he said, was "to teach Qadhafi a lesson."[7]

Iraq, like Libya, opposed not only the particular agreements that Egypt had just concluded, but any form of negotiation with Israel. The total rejectionism of Libya and Iraq may not have been unwelcome in Cairo, for it placed both countries outside the pale of rational discussion of a Middle East settlement and, in doing so, prevented the formation of a solid Arab bloc against Egypt. Nor could Libya and Iraq expect support from their Soviet ally, as the USSR was pressing hard for an international conference as its own re-entry tricket to the negotiating process.

The divisions within the PLO in some ways mirrored the split between Syria and the rejectionist states. The Palestinian factions were for the most part bound to individual Arab states by proprietary ties, adding an unusual dimension to inter-Arab political dynamics.[8] On the one hand, Arafat and most members of his dominant group, al-Fatah, accepted the objective of a Palestinian state coexisting with an Israel defined by pre-1967 borders. (A special relationship of sorts continued to exist between Egypt and Fatah after Sinai II, presumably because Arafat believed that Egypt had a better chance than any other country of bringing the PLO into serious negotiations.) On the other hand, George Habash's Popular Front for the Liberation of Palestine (PFLP) and the other still more radical groups within the PLO continued to demand an end to the Jewish state of Israel.

With Sadat's opponents divided among themselves, the Arab line-up was not at the time heavily weighted against Egypt. Most of the conservative Gulf states, along with the Sudan and Morocco, were sympathetic toward Sadat's efforts to move in stages toward the return of Arab territory and the achievement of Palestinian rights. The result of the differing Arab positions was to give Saudi Arabia and Kuwait the maneuverability they needed to mediate between Egypt and Syria.

The Lebanese War and Arab Politics

By late 1975 the spreading conflict in Lebanon began to have a serious impact on Middle Eastern politics. One effect was to intensify the rivalry between Egypt and Syria, for as Syria began to exploit the opportunities for increasing its influence in a divided Lebanon, Egypt inevitably looked for ways to block Syria's ambitions. The conflict also widened the breach between Syria and the PLO: The more tenuous the authority of the Lebanese government, the more concerned Syria became that a PLO-dominated regime might emerge in Beirut and launch guerrilla operations against Israel, leading to a confrontation that Syria could not control. As the PLO and Syria drifted farther apart, the PLO became increasingly dependent on Egyptian support.

The Arab monarchs had their own reasons for trying to prevent a civil war from breaking apart the Lebanese nation. They feared that the rising violence would lead the Maronite Christian community to seek partition, further polarizing the Arab world and leading to the kind of radical agitation that had threatened their regimes not long before. They no doubt also realized that further movement toward a Middle East settlement was hopeless in a divided Arab community. In this context Saudi Arabia and Kuwait launched their initiative to reconcile Egypt and Syria.

The Egyptian-Saudi Connection

The mediators had a formidable task ahead of them. With neither Sadat nor Assad in any hurry to mend fences, their leverage and powers of persuasion were crucial. One might suppose that the financial dependence of the quarrelers on the peacekeepers was leverage enough, but the Gulf leaders knew from experience that it had to be used with considerable finesse if it was to be effective with either country.

Egypt's relationship with Saudi Arabia was especially delicate. Saudi Arabia and the other Gulf sheikhdoms—awash in petrodollars, as Egyptians saw it, because of Egypt's sacrifices for the Arab cause—held the key to Egyptian financial and economic health. Moreover, the Gulf donors had begun to fix conditions to their loans, patterning their demands on the stabilization packages drawn up by the IMF. Egyptian feelings about this practice were expressed by Ibrahim Nafi'a, *al-Ahram's* economics editor, in an article of July 24, 1976: "It is inconceivable that any Arab state—because they too are developing countries, whatever their level of wealth—should impose the same conditions as the great wealthy nations upon the poorer countries."[9]

In February 1976, Sadat and his principal advisers flew to Saudi Arabia, Kuwait, the United Arab Emirates (UAE), Bahrein, and Qatar in search of $10 to $12 billion to support Egypt's five-year plan. They received only a pledge from the Gulf Organization for the Development of Egypt (GODE) of up to $2 billion, with conditions attached that were aimed at reducing Egypt's swollen consumer subsidies. Sadat stated publicly that this commitment was inadequate.

The special sensitivity of the Egyptian-Saudi relationship goes deeper than the awkwardness between the giver and the beholden. At its root is each people's view of itself as heir to the leadership of Islam and Arab culture. The Saudis see themselves as the source of Arabism in its purest form, that of the desert Arab, and take pride in their status as the land of the Prophet and protector of the holiest Muslim shrines. The Egyptians, far from admiring the Bedouin, regard them as backward and uncouth, fated to live in an infertile land and denied the blessings of a great river. They equate culture with urbanity and national preeminence with accomplishment in science, history, and the arts. Al-Azhar's centuries of ascendancy in Islamic theology and Arab scholarship are for Egyptians as strong a claim to spiritual leadership as the chance birthplace of Mohammed and his first followers.

An important element in the Egyptian-Saudi relationship has been the Palestinian issue. The Saudis have been relatively consistent in their support of the Palestinians. No doubt they see a Palestinian settlement as the key to a Middle East solution, but they must also view the Palestinian movement as a useful counterweight to expanded Syrian influence in the region. Although they have been comfortable with the Jordanian-Lebanese buffer between themselves and Syria, they would probably be happier still if the buffer were reinforced with a Palestinian state that was dependent for its viability on Saudi largesse. For these reasons the Saudis are accustomed to lecturing the Egyptians about the need for a Palestinian solution, and whenever Egypt has seemed less than wholehearted in that pursuit, the Egyptian-Saudi relationship has suffered.

During the Lebanese war the positions were reversed. For a time, at least, the Saudis found themselves in an unfamiliar position beside Egypt, defending Syria's use of force against the Palestinians. They evidently believed that the immediate need was to end the civil war and prevent partition, goals it seemed could be achieved only through Syrian intervention.

The Trials of an Arab Mediator

In October 1975, soon after the conclusion of Sinai II, the mediation efforts of Saudi Arabia and Kuwait began with preliminary feelers sent out by the Saudis to Egypt and Syria; they ended ten months later with a minisummit in Riyadh, where Sadat and Assad agreed to cooperate in Lebanon and work together toward a comprehensive Middle East settlement. The mediation and the Arab reactions to it are a case study in modern inter-Arab politics. It was the first time that the new political power of the Arab oil producers was brought to bear on inter-Arab relations. And for the last time before Egypt's isolation following Camp David, the national interests, personalities, and competing values of the principal actors in the Arab Middle East were actively engaged.

Direct contact between the Egyptian and Saudi leaders was infrequent. They generally communicated through their emissaries, Ashraf Marwan for Sadat, and Saudi Chief of Intelligence Kemal Adham for Fahd. (The embassies and foreign offices seem to have been rarely used for important exchanges.) While the dialogue was apparently fairly open and candid, it would have been surprising if the emissaries had handled in any but the most gingerly way those matters on which their principals had not yet agreed.

When the Saudis began their mediation, it was under the new leadership of King Khalid, who succeeded Feisal after Feisal's assassination in March 1975, and Crown Prince Fahd, the strongest voice in Saudi foreign policy. In December Fahd and Sadat met in Cairo, where they seem to have agreed generally on the direction of their Middle East policies. Sadat evidently gave his blessing to the proposed mediation, with the caution that Egypt would neither withdraw from nor apologize for the agreements that it had concluded with Israel.

Early in 1976, Saudi Arabia and Kuwait began the search for enough common ground to call a meeting between Syrian and Egyptian representatives. It was not until May that the mediation first surfaced publicly, with the arrival in Damascus of Prince Saud and Kuwaiti Foreign Minister Sheikh Sabah al-Jaber. The day after the Damascus meeting the Syrian and Egyptian governments announced that the prime ministers of Egypt, Syria, and Kuwait would meet in Saudi Arabia the following week. It seemed that the feud between Cairo and Damascus was about to end.

Nevertheless, on the day scheduled for the meeting between prime ministers, the talks were postponed without explanation. The Egyptians soon let it be known that they had refused to meet unless given an ironclad guarantee that the provisions of Sinai II would not be discussed. This, they said, the Saudis had not been able to provide despite earlier assurances that the agreements with Israel would not be an item on the agenda. The mediators were plainly annoyed and offended by the abrupt cancellation. On May 20, Kuwait's *Time* complained that "mediation diplomacy has severe limitations in inter-Arab disputes." The worst of it, the article continued, was that Arab aid donors were given no substantive role in Middle East diplomacy but were regarded by the confrontation states as good for nothing but giving money.

Sadat clearly saw no compelling reason to accommodate the Gulf kingdoms despite Egypt's acute dependence on Gulf financial aid. He also no doubt regarded the Syrian demand to discuss Sinai II, with its implication that Egypt should back away from the agreement, as a serious misreading of the relative power positions of the two countries. He had evidently concluded that Syria was in deep trouble in Lebanon and that he had only to wait for Assad to come pleading for reconciliation.

The Syrians' trouble in Lebanon was, as might be expected, partly Egypt's fault. Egypt had sent the Ain Jalut Brigade (made up largely of Palestinians who had moved to Egypt from the Gaza Strip) to augment the Palestinian forces in Beirut. Alexandria became a staging point for Iraqi troops, who were flown to Egypt and then ferried to Sidon and Tyre to fight alongside the Palestinians and Lebanese Muslims who controlled those ports. Finally, Egyptian shortwave broadcasts beamed at Damascus made the most of the spectacle of Syrian troops attacking Palestinians.

None of this allayed Cairo's frustration at being forced to sit on the sidelines, powerless to change the outcome of the Lebanese war. Egypt had few resources in Lebanon: It was still wary of the PLO and had little contact with the Sunni and Shi'ite communities. In the early stages of the conflict, when Syria's military victories were matched by its apparent success in consolidating political influence in Beirut, it seemed that leadership of the Arab world was passing from Egypt to Syria. Damascus was, moreover, the center of international attention and praise for its perceived efforts to bring peace to the region.

In early summer 1976 the tide began to turn. Iraq built up its troops along the Syrian border[10] and seemed prepared to act on its calls for the overthrow of the Assad regime. Assad had to take Baghdad's action seriously: Iraq, because of its common border with Syria, was a far more direct threat to the Ba'athist leadership than Egypt could ever be.

Despite the rising tension, the Saudi and Kuwaiti mediators carried on their efforts to arrange a high-level Egyptian-Syrian meeting. The Saudi and Kuwaiti foreign ministers arrived in Damascus on June 5, about half an hour after Syrian demonstrators had finished sacking the Egyptian embassy. Later in the month the four prime ministers finally met in Riyadh. After two days of discussion, they issued a communiqué announcing the end of hostile propaganda and the resumption of full diplomatic relations between Cairo and Damascus. The Egyptians called the Riyadh meetings a success, emphasizing that no discussion of Sinai II had taken place. The Syrians, for their part, were pleased at having achieved their main objectives— Saudi and Kuwaiti agreement to the full resumption of financial aid and acquiescence in Syria's continuing military presence in eastern Lebanon while it was withdrawing its troops from Beirut.

Although Egypt and Syria were not ready for the full rapprochement that was being urged upon them, they were careful to avoid a direct confrontation. Egypt even helped to launch the Arab peacekeeping force that ultimately legitimized the Syrian presence in Lebanon. The force had the advantage in Egyptian eyes of serving as a partial brake on Syria's efforts to establish its hegemony and at the same time of preserving the military presence that seemed needed to restore stability. Cairo no doubt also hoped to ease Syrian pressure on the Palestinians through "Arabization" of the conflict. Although the idea for the peacekeeping force was ostensibly the Arab League's, Egypt initiated the plan and the Arab League's Egyptian secretary-general, Mahmoud Riad, conducted the negotiations with Syria on the operation's size and composition.

The Saudi-Kuwaiti mediation initiative languished during the summer of 1976 as Egypt worked to increase its leverage in Lebanon by building bridges to the parties to the conflict. At Sadat's invitation, high PLO officials visited Cairo in early September. At about the same time Lebanese Christian and Muslim leaders came to Egypt for discussions on ways to end the war. As Egypt tried to carve out a role for itself in Lebanon and the months passed, the mediators' patience began to wear thin. They became increasingly supportive of Syrian policies and disturbed at Egyptian resistance to their efforts at reconciliation.

The Kaleidoscope Shifts

Saudi Arabia and Kuwait were rewarded for their persistence when, in late October, their efforts of nearly a year culminated in a meeting in Riyadh of the leaders of Egypt, Syria, Kuwait, Lebanon, and the PLO. The summit seemed to herald a new era of Arab cooperation. Overnight, old enmities were dropped and new alliances formed. A contemporary observer wrote that "Lebanon and the Middle East scene this week were like a kaleidoscope that had been given a sudden jolt. Abruptly, all the shapes and colors have changed. . . . Clearly the Riyadh conference of Arab leaders has brought a new alignment of forces in the area."[11]

To convene the summit the mediators had capitalized on a military confrontation between Palestinians and Syrians. A week before the meeting, the Palestinians, their forces concentrated in the mountains east of Beirut, had been on the brink of disaster as Syria mounted a major attack aimed at ending the war. The Saudis stepped in, called for an immediate cease-fire and a meeting of leaders concerned with the Lebanese dispute, and rescued Arafat from a desperate military situation. The Saudis wanted to freeze what for them was a good balance in Lebanon: The PLO had been brought under a measure of Syrian influence, enough to prevent it from establishing a militant Palestinian state in Lebanon and perhaps enough to bring it to the negotiating table; Syria had been unable to gain the hegemony that might have led to a combination of radical states on Saudi Arabia's border; the Maronites had resisted the domination that could have driven them to partition; and Egypt, through its support of the Arab peacekeeping force, was playing the kind of constructive role that would end if Syria were to threaten Egyptian interests by establishing control over Lebanon.

Saudi diplomacy had made it possible for the main Arab actors to move beyond Lebanon to preparations for a Middle East peace conference, which it was assumed would be held in 1977 after new administrations in the United States and Israel had settled in. Over the longer term, however, the main significance of the successful mediation was its clear message that Saudi Arabia could no longer be ignored in decisions affecting the common Arab interest. Saudi power, a mixture of oil wealth and ambition, exercised with prudence and Bedouin courtliness, had become a pivotal factor in Arab politics. With Saudi support, a Middle East policy that broke with conventional Arab doctrine might succeed; without it, it had no chance.

The Scramble to Make Up

For several months after the Riyadh summit, Egypt and Syria worked at developing a common political front, both between themselves and with the other Arabs concerned with the peace process. The immediate aftermath of the summit was a meeting between Sadat and Assad on October 25 in Cairo. There the presidents began the task of mapping out a joint strategy for Geneva, and Assad began to smooth the way for a reconciliation between Sadat and his two nemeses, Qadhafi and Hussein. At about the same time reports that Egypt, Syria, and Libya might revive the moribund Federation of Arab Republics also circulated.

A month later, Mubarak and Foreign Minister Ismail Fahmy visited Baghdad and Damascus, using Egyptian good offices to bring about a mutual withdrawal of Iraqi and Syrian troops. Syria and the PLO, lately in armed conflict with each other, worked to devise a formula to permit Palestinian participation at a peace conference. In mid-November Hussein made a surprise visit to Syria; Arafat joined the action by offering to mediate between Libya and Egypt. Then on December 9 Assad and Hussein issued a statement announcing the creation of a committee to develop a plan for the union of their countries. (This turned out later to be a body for policy coordination, and a rather ineffective one at that.) Some weeks later, in an effort to patch up one of the few remaining quarrels in the suddenly amicable Arab world, Hussein made plans to visit Sadat in Aswan.

The biggest turnabout came as the year drew to a close, when Sadat and Assad, meeting again in Cairo, announced that they had decided to form "a united political leadership" and would soon set up committees to study the possibility of union. Both sides said the unhappy experience of the UAR had not been forgotten; they intended to work seriously for unity, but carefully and without haste. The mood in the Arab world was jubilant. The Cairo press glowed with reports of Arab governments' praise for the Egyptian-Syrian "unionist" movement, and on December 23 al-Ahram predicted that Egypt and Syria would work together to convene a peace conference in Geneva early in the coming year.

7

Eight Players in Search of a Peace Conference: The Geneva Preparations of 1977

The search for a Middle East settlement is like the child's game that requires several small balls on a card to be maneuvered into the same number of holes: One can usually get most of the balls into most of the holes, but hardly ever all of them at the same time. At the beginning of 1977 the main actors in Middle East diplomacy seemed as close to fitting into all the holes as at any time since 1948. The Labor government in Israel was committed to negotiations toward an overall settlement that could include substantial withdrawal from the West Bank so long as Israel's security requirements were met. The United States was in a good position to be helpful: A new administration included a president bent on becoming actively engaged and experienced advisers who had concluded that the time was ripe for a high-priority effort. The USSR, since December 1973 co-chair (with the United States) of the Middle East Peace Conference, seemed prepared to work for the reconvening of the conference without undue posturing. Within the PLO, the elements that accepted Israel's existence and sought a practical solution to the conflict were in no worse a position than usual relative to the rejectionists—somewhat better, in fact, as they were actively backed by Egypt and Saudi Arabia. But the biggest change was the emergence of a relatively moderate coalition of key Arab states. Egypt, Syria, Jordan, and Saudi Arabia had undertaken to work together toward a settlement based on the pre–June 1967 lines and the creation of a national homeland for the Palestinians in the occupied territories.

The ten months leading up to Sadat's decision to go to Jerusalem were a period of intense diplomatic activity and, ultimately, of sharp disappointment as the hopes for an overall settlement were frustrated.[1] It was the one time since Israel's establishment when all of the parties grappled with the complex problems of launching a peace conference. In the Arab camp timeworn positions were reexamined and national interests scrutinized. In the end, however, the emergence of an Israeli government committed to retaining the West Bank and the resurfacing of the old divisions between Egypt and Syria combined to frustrate the consensus needed to convene a conference.

Begin Changes the Picture

Before we look at the part played by Arab divisions in barring the way to Geneva, we might consider whether Menachem Begin's accession as prime minister in June 1977 doomed from the start efforts to convene a conference on terms minimally acceptable to the Arabs. Begin had, after all, made plain his total opposition to the relinquishment of any part of the West Bank—even to Jordan, had Hussein been interested in a partial return, which he was not. During the summer of 1977, Begin continued to expand and "thicken" Israeli settlements on the West Bank. To anyone who was listening, he left no doubt about the nonnegotiability of the land of biblical Israel while he was in office.

The administration of U.S. President Jimmy Carter refused to believe that Begin's policies were more than an early negotiating tactic. "It would take Carter more than a year to understand that Begin was as adamant in refusing to negotiate Judea and Samaria as Sadat was in refusing to give up any of Sinai."[2] The result was that Israel's inflexible positions on the Palestinian issue, the Golan Heights, and Jerusalem were less damaging to the prospects for a conference than they would have been had they been taken at face value.

The Arabs were at first no more inclined than was the United States to write off the Begin government. Sadat, Assad, and an emissary of Hussein met with the Saudi leadership in Riyadh after Begin's election and, in Fahd's words, agreed that "it was a time for steady nerves on everyone's part."[3] There seems to have been a feeling, especially on Sadat's part, that Begin, because of his hard-line credentials, might be able to deliver an agreement that more moderate Israeli leaders could not.

Indeed, Begin acceded without much argument to the U.S. strategy of holding a peace conference that would launch negotiations on all aspects of a comprehensive settlement. Why he did so if he was unwilling to accept meaningful changes in the status of the West Bank, the Golan Heights, or Jerusalem is a fair question. One answer must lie in a natural reluctance to provoke a confrontation with the United States at the outset of his administration. But probably equally important was his belief (which Moshe Dayan strongly shared)[4] that an opportunity to reach a separate peace with Egypt might exist and that an international conference could provide the cover for such an agreement. Indeed, in September 1977 Dayan proposed to Egyptian Deputy Prime Minister Hassan Tuhamy that direct negotiations take place between the Egyptian and Israeli leaders. He was turned down: Sadat demanded as the price for such talks a prior Israeli commitment to withdraw from all occupied Arab territory. Sadat also made it clear that he had no interest in signing a peace treaty with Israel in the absence of parallel agreements with Syria and Jordan, which "included solving the Palestinian problem."[5]

Whatever Begin's private reasons for agreeing to go to Geneva, the responsibility for the collapse of efforts to convene the conference was not entirely Israel's. Yet it is hard not to conclude that the Geneva conference, and any bilateral talks that followed it, would have foundered on Begin's unwillingness to consider meaningful withdrawal from the West Bank and the Golan Heights, especially when confronted with the equally unbending demands of Syria and the PLO for total Israeli withdrawal. Certainly that is how Sadat came to see it by the fall of 1977.

The Arabs Prepare for Geneva

Two procedural questions were at the center of the preparations for a peace conference. In different ways each went to the heart of the ambitions and fears of the Arabs involved. The first issue, how to arrange for representative participation of the Palestinians, raised the question of what kind of Palestinian entity the Arab parties wanted as their neighbor and who they wanted to run it. The second issue, whether to negotiate with Israel as a single, unified delegation or as separate national delegations, was even more closely tied to Arab rivalries. Although the Geneva preparations involved other considerations as well, these two did the most to bring to the surface the Arab interests and objectives that lay hidden beneath the rhetoric.

The issue of Palestinian representation came up in various ways as the consultations progressed. At first the focus was on the possibility of PLO participation as part of a Jordanian delegation. During his first, exploratory trip to the Middle East in February 1977, U.S. Secretary of State Cyrus Vance discussed this possibility with Prime Minister Rabin and Foreign Minister Yigal Allon and was told that although Israel would not negotiate with the PLO under any circumstances, "a PLO that accepted Resolution 242 would no longer be the PLO."[6] Thus began the U.S. effort to persuade the PLO to accept 242 in order to facilitate Palestinian representation at Geneva and to pave the way for a dialogue between the PLO and the United States. The process continued even after the Begin government refused to consider dealing with the PLO under any circumstances. Egypt, Saudi Arabia, and Syria were all to become involved in this enterprise in various ways.[7]

Sadat's approach to the problem of Palestinian representation was to encourage a political accommodation between Jordan and the PLO that dealt with the nature of their relationship in a settlement. The solution that he envisaged, he told Vance, was a Palestinian state constitutionally linked to Jordan. He made it clear that in his view "the Palestinian issue, not Sinai or the Golan Heights, should be at the top of the negotiating agenda."[8]

When the PLO Central Council decided in late January that the question of ties to Jordan could be decided only by a previously established independent Palestinian state, Sadat countered that Egypt was ready to begin negotiations without Palestinian participation in the early stages of a conference.[9] Syria and Jordan joined Egypt in declaring their willingness to begin negotiations without the PLO. Then, in their first face-to-face encounter since 1970, Hussein and Arafat met in Cairo in mid-March to discuss Jordanian-PLO relations and the possibility of future links between them. A high-water mark of Arab cooperation had been reached: It seemed as if the decision taken at Riyadh to work for a united negotiating front was bearing fruit.

The coordinated Arab effort to persuade Jordan and the PLO to agree to a federated Palestinian state was a serious attempt both to meet Israeli security concerns and to get the PLO to the negotiating table.[10] It finally ended over the PLO's steadfast position that only after forming an independent state would it consider federation with Jordan. Meanwhile, Israel, opposed to any form whatever of Palestinian entity, was rejecting the U.S. proposition that a "settlement must include provisions for a Palestinian entity."[11] The unlikelihood of reconciling these positions led the United States to move away from the effort to reach agreement on principles and to focus on developing procedures that would at least permit the Palestinians to be fairly represented at a peace conference.

Once the efforts to work out a PLO-Jordanian accommodation had failed, Jordan was little more than a spectator during the pre-Geneva talks, though not for lack of interest on the part of Hussein. The nature of a Palestinian settlement had important consequences for the stability of his country, for the aspirations of the exiled Palestinians who make up more than half of Jordan's population, and for his own interests and those of the Hashemite Dynasty.[12] But by this time Hussein had learned to be cautious of attempts to draw him into negotiations with the PLO, even by friendly Arab states. He knew from experience that splits in the PLO leadership led to maximalist positions of almost no relation to power realities and that, if serious negotiations actually got under way, Jordan was vulnerable to PLO charges of a sell-out of Arab interests. He also knew that in any test between Jordan and the PLO, the Arabs would as a body side with the PLO. In the summer of 1977, therefore, Hussein agreed to take part in negotiations only if Israel declared itself willing to return all of the West Bank and Gaza.

Hidden Agendas

As consultations continued, the focus turned to forming a unified Arab delegation in which Palestinians acceptable to the PLO could be included. More was at stake, however, than finding a place at the table for the Palestinians. For Egypt and Syria the issue of unified versus separate delegations embodied the rivalries and mistrust that pushed them apart. Just as Egypt was unwilling to be hamstrung by the doctrinaire positions of Syria, Syria was determined to prevent Egypt from concluding a separate agreement that would leave it to face Israel alone. Syria's preoccupation translated into an overriding concern with procedure. To prevent negotiations between the individual Arab states and Israel, it pressed for a joint Arab delegation to open the conference, to be followed by working groups in which united Arab negotiating teams addressed such functional issues as borders, security, and waterways. Israel, for its part, believed that a combined Arab delegation would be incapable of serious negotiations, while the United States favored a single delegation at the initial phase of the conference as the only feasible way of getting Syria and the Palestinians to the table.

Almost all of the Arab differences over procedure masked questions of regional power and prestige. Who, for example, would emerge from the talks as the key negotiator for the Arabs? How would the negotiating process affect each state's influence with the Palestinians? Who would end up with the Saudis on its side? And especially important for the Syrians, who would be perceived, as the result of its positions, to be the guardian of Arab nationalism?

When Sadat turned to the United States in 1973, he envisaged a negotiating process that was managed by Egypt and the United States, with Syria, Jordan, and the PLO following in their wake. His policy not only assumed a dominant place for Egypt but a special relationship between him and the U.S. president. His goals were not frivolous. They were grounded in the hard facts of Egyptian politics, in which Egyptians expected their country to be preeminent in the Arab world and their president to be foremost among Arab leaders.

From time to time, as we have seen, Sadat worried that the United States would come to view Syria as the key to successful negotiations. President Carter's reference to Assad as the "great leader" of Syria within minutes of their first talk in May 1977 did nothing to reassure Sadat. Sadat was also genuinely convinced that a much more flexible policy than Syria's was needed if negotiations for a comprehensive peace were to have any change of success. As time passed and Assad's positions showed little sign of yielding, he concluded that any negotiating process that gave Syria a veto over the outcome was fatally flawed.

The Ba'ath as Vanguard of Arab Nationalism

To be seen as the protector of Arab nationalism was important to all of the Arab participants, but to none more than to Syria. If the ideology of Arab nationalism encouraged an all-or-nothing approach, the dynamics of Syrian politics reinforced the tendency toward rigidity. The most significant constraint to realistic negotiations was the Syrian branch of the Ba'ath party.[13] In the mid-1970s the Ba'ath leadership in Syria was very much involved in policy formulation, especially in Arab and Arab-Israel policy, where the seventeen members of the Ba'ath national command (two of them Palestinians) had special responsibility. With their tendency toward ideological orthodoxy, the national and regional commands of the Ba'ath served as a counterweight to the more pragmatic tendencies of the president.

Once the Ba'ath decided on a policy, that policy was not lightly changed. Even so influential a figure as Foreign Minister Abdel-Halim Khaddam, when isolated at a November meeting of Arab foreign ministers in Tunis, had to concede to his colleagues that he had little latitude as his position had been dictated by the Supreme Council of the Ba'ath.[14] The Tunis meetings illustrate still another reason for Syria's cautious approach to the peace talks. As was customary at Arab conferences, Iraq bitterly criticized Syria for negotiating with the enemy. So long as the rivalry continued between the Damascus and Baghdad branches of the Ba'ath, the Syrian regime would feel vulnerable to Iraqi attacks on its commitment to Arabism and would present the smallest possible target.

By fall 1977 Syria had won agreement to many of the conference procedures for which it had been pressing hardest. A unified Arab delegation to open the conference had been decided on against the wishes of Egypt and Israel, and a way had been found to include Palestinian representatives acceptable to the PLO leadership. Yet at the November meeting, Damascus pressed for an early Arab summit so that, in the words of the Egyptian foreign minister, "extreme and far-reaching decisions [might be adopted], thus destroying any chance for reconvening the Geneva Conference at the end of December."[15]

Sadat believed that the Ba'athists' hostility to the very concept of negotiating with Israel would in the end undermine the possibility of accommodation. Soon after returning from Jerusalem, he remarked to Vance that although Assad wanted to join the peace process, he was always opposed by the Ba'ath.[16] And in an interview at about the same time with the Cairo magazine *October*, he singled out the party as the ultimate source of his frustration with Arab policy:

The Syrian Baath will not go to Geneva; and if it did the picture would be as follows. The Soviet Union has put Syria in its pocket, and Syria has put the Palestinians in hers. In Geneva, we would get bogged down in what we have completely freed ourselves from, legalistic and semantic quibbling, and procedures and the titles of the functional, positional, geographical and historical committees . . . and the whole bag of tricks we know so well from the Syrian Baath party. . . . I am convinced that the Syrian Baath and its hangers-on don't want peace.[17]

The Contest for Saudi Support

Of the various audiences before which the Arab confrontation states played their parts in preparing for Geneva, Saudi Arabia was for all of them one of the most important. Each needed Saudi support to maintain its position relative to the others. Sadat, in particular, sought increasingly to engage the Saudis in the negotiating process; he obviously believed that with the Saudis behind him, the Arabs who opposed his policies could do Egypt no serious harm. It would have been a rash observer in October 1977 who predicted that Sadat would turn away from the Geneva scenario without so much as informing the Saudis in advance.

Unlike the political and strategic connection, the economic side of the relationship between Egypt and Saudi Arabia remained prickly. Egyptians continued to chafe at what they regarded as Saudi stinginess in the light of Egypt's sacrifices for the Arabs and the petrodollars that flowed from the October War. At a meeting in Riyadh in early 1977 to consider Gulf aid, Fahmy walked out within the first half hour when it became apparent that the conference was unwilling to provide the level of assistance that Egypt had requested.[18] Ultimately the conference pledged $1.4 billion a year to the Arabs for 1977 and 1978, of which $570 million was designated each for Egypt and Syria, $200 million for Jordan, and $28 million for the PLO.

As these figures show, Jordan, Syria, and the PLO had by the late 1970s become as dependent on Gulf aid as Egypt. Syria and the PLO knew that any move to break with Egypt and abandon the peace process could jeopardize their financial stability unless undertaken for reasons the Saudis deemed good and sufficient. Yet there was another side to the aid that was less helpful to the negotiations. Especially in the case of Syria, Saudi financial support may have served as a disincentive to compromise, for it was clear that with a resolution of the Palestinian problem the main justification for continuing the subsidies would disappear.[19]

Saudi influence was reinforced by the dynamics of inter-Arab politics. Other conservative Arab governments hesitated, in the absence of respectable Arab company, to take a forthright stand in favor of a negotiated settlement.

The Saudis provided that company. In Arab councils they furnished the cover that made it possible for Morocco, Tunisia, the Sudan, and the Gulf sheikhdoms to take the positions that were in their natural interests.

Arab Rivalries and the PLO

The mixed motives that govern relationships between Arab states and the PLO were never so apparent as during the pre-Geneva consultations on Palestinian representation. Each of the Arab governments involved believed it had the best interests of the Palestinians at heart, and each saw those interests as identical to its own. That realpolitik and principle both play a part in foreign policy is nothing new; that they are so difficult to disentangle in the minds of the participants themselves is unusual.

The issue over which the Geneva preparations finally broke down is a case in point. The question was whether the PLO should be referred to by name in a working paper that the United States had prepared on October 4 in an attempt to settle the remaining procedural problems. (The issue was complicated, as we shall see, by the impression that Israeli pressure had caused the deletion of an earlier reference to PLO representatives.)[20] At first the Egyptians insisted that the PLO be specifically mentioned in the document, no doubt reasoning that if the PLO would in fact have representatives at the negotiations, it made no sense not to say so. But Cairo must also have been influenced by the need to guard against Syrian efforts to curry favor with the PLO at its expense.

Assad saw the issue in a different light. He had already made it clear to Vance that an explicit invitation to the PLO was important to him as a way of ensuring that its leaders could not later claim that peace had been negotiated over their heads.[21] He must also have been concerned that failing to back the organization on a principle of importance to it could undermine Syria's tenuous dominance in the PLO Central and Executive Committees. Although the considerations for Damascus and Cairo were different, for each the overriding motivation was to strengthen its influence within the PLO and enhance its role in any solution of the Palestinian problem.

Syria's overall relationship with the PLO in 1977 is an example of the tangled Arab interests and motives toward the Palestinians. On the one hand fighting to gain control over the Palestinian movement in Lebanon, on the other demanding that the PLO be invited to Geneva by name, Syria was engaged in a high-wire act that would have fazed less self-confident governments. To the matter-of-fact Egyptians, the Syrian posture was pure and simple hypocrisy. Yet for the Syrians there was no contradiction between support for Palestinian rights and opposition to actions of the PLO that jeopardized Syrian state interests. Historically Palestine was part of Greater

Syria; from that relationship, as Syrians saw it, flowed responsibilities for the Palestinian people that transcended the personalities of the Palestinian leaders of the moment.

Syria's lack of day-to-day contact with the Palestinians under Israeli occupation affected its approach to the Palestinian problem and helped to distinguish its policies from those of Jordan and Egypt. Whereas the latter countries had first-hand experience with the administration of the West Bank and Gaza and were in close touch with their residents, Syria looked at the problem through the eyes of Palestinians who had moved to Syria thirty years before, after partition. Without a realistic prospect of returning to their homes, the diaspora Palestinians were more interested in gaining international acceptance of the principles of self-determination and the right to an independent state than in working out practical arrangements for the withdrawal of Israeli troops. They found it hard to believe that many Palestinians in the West Bank and Gaza at this time regarded pragmatic attempts to end the military occupation as more relevant than the abstract principles to which they had dedicated their lives.[22]

Syria's identification with the Palestinians living on its soil led to policies that were not only at odds with those of Egypt and Jordan but more doctrinaire than those of the PLO itself. The PLO had no option but to represent the interests of the West Bankers and Gazans, as well as the exiled Palestinians, if it was to stay in the diplomatic picture. And if necessary to maintain its primacy in negotiations on the Palestinian issue, the PLO was prepared to consider a process that involved it with Jordan, Egypt, and Israel and left Damascus without a voice in the settlement.

For the Syrians this was an unnerving point of view.[23] It reinforced their determination to nurture their assets in the radical wing of the PLO and, if possible, to establish control over the organization. In August, for example, at meetings of the PLO's Executive and Central Committees that were held in Damascus Syria used its weight to kill a U.S. proposal to open talks with the PLO in exchange for its acceptance of Resolution 242.[24] (Egypt and Saudi Arabia did their best to persuade the PLO to agree to the U.S. proposal but did not have the kind of influence in the Executive and Central Committees that Syria had as the residence of a large proportion of the committee members.) One reason for Syria's position clearly was a reluctance to see the Palestinians negotiate for themselves; had the PLO accepted 242, there would have been no need for Damascus or anyone else to broker its relationship with Washington.

Things Fall Apart

One of the more intriguing questions of modern Middle Eastern history is whether the search for a peace conference had reached a hopeless impasse by November 1977 and was past salvaging, or whether Sadat took advantage of the inevitable problems of a complex negotiation to begin working toward a separate peace with Israel. The question has three facets to it. The first concerns the objective status of the talks at the time of Sadat's decision— the positions of the parties and the facts of the international environment as everyone involved understood them. The second has to do with Sadat's approach during the consultations to the question of a comprehensive settlement and to the heart of that problem, the place of the Palestinian issue in the process. There is finally the question of why, of all possible responses to a bleak negotiating prospect, Sadat chose to go to Jerusalem and address the Knesset. This part of the puzzle will be considered in Chapter 8 on Jerusalem and Chapter 9 on Camp David, for Sadat's initiative opened a new era in Middle East diplomacy, distinct in its issues and in the relationships among the parties from those preceding it.

The status of the main issues in the pre-Geneva talks at the time of Sadat's initiative can be briefly stated.[25] After many false starts the problem of Palestinian representation seemed close to resolution. Both Israel and the Arabs were in virtual agreement by early October that a unified delegation comprising Egyptians, Syrians, Jordanians, Lebanese, and Palestinians could represent the Arab side. The harder question of *which* Palestinians should take part had almost, but not quite, been settled. Two approaches were on the table. Dayan had privately agreed that the Palestinian contingent could include PLO representatives from the West Bank and Gaza; at about the same time Sadat seems to have persuaded Arafat to let two U.S. professors of Palestinian origin, Edward Said and Ibrahim Abu Lughod, speak for the PLO.[26]

For the PLO, however, the assurance that it would as a practical matter be fully represented at the negotiations was not enough. It also demanded formal recognition of its right to a place at the table, leading to the dispute over the October 4 working paper that has already been touched on. The working paper controversy—as much because of the political circumstances of its origin as the substantive issues involved—is central to the question of whether the talks could have been saved.

The document grew out of a discussion between Carter and Dayan following Israeli complaints that a communiqué of October 1 summarizing points of agreement between the United States and the Soviet Union had been issued without Israel's agreement or consultation. Because of the firestorm of criticism from Israel and the U.S. Jewish community that attended its creation, the working paper inevitably came to be seen by the Arabs as a retreat by Carter in the face of pressure. For Sadat especially the episode seems to have been the final straw in settling his opposition to an international conference. Before the incident the only reason that was left for having a conference, in his view, was the prospect that the

United States would stand firm in its own views at Geneva. Carter's apparent retreat plainly shook his faith that this would happen.

Some of those most closely involved in the consultations believe that the remaining problems could have been resolved had Sadat been more patient.[27] Although that may be so objectively, there is little question that in Sadat's mind, and indeed in Carter's, an impasse had been reached. Carter had concluded that Assad was "adamant" in his insistence that the U.S. working paper be rewritten and was just as certain that any such rewriting would be unacceptable to Israel.[28] Sadat was equally persuaded that Assad would not budge. Later in the fall he told Vance that he had decided to go to Jerusalem because "the U.S. working paper had caused a big quarrel with the Syrians and [he wanted] to break the impasse."[29] Although he might more accurately have described the Syrian reaction to the paper as "a big sulk" rather than "a big quarrel" and although his motives for going to Jerusalem were much more complex than his remark would suggest, he was certainly right about Syria's deep unhappiness with the process as it was unfolding.

Given the profound policy differences that stood in the way of a comprehensive agreement in late 1977, the controversy over whether or not the pre-Geneva consultations had reached a dead end seems academic. Even if it had been possible to convene the conference, Sadat is almost certainly right in concluding that the negotiations were doomed to fail. By going to Jerusalem he hoped to breathe new life into an otherwise lifeless negotiating process and to regain what he could of the momentum that had seemed so promising a few months earlier. That he fell short of his goal does not diminish the boldness of his vision or the lasting importance of the course that he set.

The question remains whether Sadat foresaw that his initiative would bring forces into play that would lead inevitably to a separate peace between Egypt and Israel. The evidence suggests that he did not. From the meeting in September between Dayan and Tuhamy he learned—if he had not known perfectly well before—that he could take back the Sinai in exchange for a peace treaty with Israel. Yet as we have seen from Dayan's memoirs, he rejected Israeli overtures for bilateral negotiations unless assured in advance that Israel would withdraw from all occupied Arab territory and settle the Palestinian problem. In numerous talks with U.S. officials throughout 1977 he insisted that no permanent Middle East settlement could be achieved without the recognition of legitimate Palestinian rights.[30] His public declarations all made the same point. The Jerusalem trip, it seems clear, was meant to break through the indecision, the posturing, and the fears that had stood in the way of reasonable discussion of the Palestinian problem during the preparations for a peace conference.

8

The Road to Jerusalem

Why Go to Israel?

In fall 1977, Sadat began to cast about for ways to revive the search for peace. He had reached a point of total frustration with the Geneva conference, having concluded that it either would not convene or, if it did, that lowest-common-denominator Arab politics and Israeli rigidity in the face of maximalist demands would block any chance of progress.[1] In this frame of mind he made plans to visit Bucharest and Tehran. Late that summer Romania's President Nicolae Ceauşescu had met with Begin and Iran's shah had received Dayan; Sadat wanted to know if they believed the Begin government was serious about a peace settlement and strong enough to deliver it.

On October 28, in a meeting outside Bucharest, Ceauşescu assured Sadat that this was the case. There is no question that Ceauşescu's assurances precipitated the decision to go to Jerusalem.[2] Yet the idea of visiting Israel and appealing directly to the people had been in Sadat's mind at least since early September, when he broached the topic to Hassan Tuhamy in a discussion of ways to break the deadlock.[3] Ceauşescu himself was a strong believer in direct talks between Egypt and Israel and had tried since 1972 to set up a meeting between Sadat and various Israeli leaders. He doubtless put the most optimistic interpretation on Begin's remark that "everything is open to discussion in negotiations." At the same time, Ceauşescu's appraisal of Likud policies was based on an intensive probing of Begin's views on the nature of a Palestinian settlement and the possibility of Israeli withdrawal from the occupied territories. When he told Sadat that Begin was in earnest about peace, he meant a comprehensive peace, and that is how Sadat understood him.

For all his efforts to bring Sadat and Begin together, Ceauşescu was probably as surprised as anyone to learn that Sadat planned to visit Israel. Begin himself never seems to have expected more than a private meeting, perhaps on the margins of the Geneva conference. It was one thing for

Sadat to decide to work directly with the Israeli government, another entirely for him to decide to go to Jerusalem and address the Knesset.

In fact, however, the two decisions were closely related. Once he had determined to do business with Israel, Sadat naturally used the style and the diplomatic techniques that had worked for him in the past. In the Jerusalem initiative these all came together: There was the taste for theatrics and the unexpected; the mastery of mass-media techniques and the willingness to spend time shaping public opinion in countries important to Egypt; the shrewd sense of the psychological effect of seeming to ask for nothing; and, most effective because most unusual, a faith in the good sense and potential power of the common man.

Many who opposed the Jerusalem initiative saw it as motivated by Sadat's love of the limelight and desire to be at the center of the international stage. Certainly Sadat reveled in the drama of the trip and the world attention it brought him. Yet one small incident just before the initiative demonstrates that these personal drives were a secondary factor. In late October, trying to divert the president from the Jerusalem trip, Fahmy made an alternative proposal. His suggestion was that Egypt invite to east Jerusalem the heads of state of the five permanent members of the Security Council, along with Arafat, the leaders of the confrontation states, and the UN secretary-general, in order to frame a "master plan" to settle the Middle East conflict. Sadat agreed to the idea and even claimed parentage.[4] It may be hard to imagine Israel welcoming Arafat to occupied Jerusalem, the Arabs consenting to the venue, or the great powers agreeing in two or three days on a solution to the conflict. The point, however, is that Sadat approved the proposal and commended it to Carter. Had the United States agreed and the summit taken place, Sadat would have played a distinctly secondary part, a prospect that does not seem to have bothered him.

The Jerusalem Initiative and Foreign Policy Theory

Because the trip to Jerusalem is so clearly a turning point in history, students of modern Egypt and the Middle East have concentrated on the motivation and process behind the decision. Sadat's initiative serves as a case study of sorts in contemporary approaches to foreign policy decision-making, helping to clarify some of the theoretical assumptions that underlie the analyses of historians and political scientists and perhaps shedding light on their usefulness.

A study of the circumstances leading to Sadat's initiative shows that "process" may be too grand a word for what went on in the making of the decision. On one side of the equation were the peace talks and their changing prospects, on the other was Sadat—his objectives for his country, his interest in political survival, and his innermost ambitions. Consultation with his advisers was haphazard; institutional constraints, like the parliament, the foreign affairs bureaucracy, and even the military, were largely ignored; and external pressures—from the Arabs or from the great powers—played virtually no part in the decision.

The extraordinary maneuverability Sadat enjoyed in making the decision is underscored by a look at those procedures he did follow. He heard out his foreign minister and at first altered the initiative on his advice. But in the end, when determined on his course, he accepted with equanimity not only Fahmy's resignation but those of the minister of state for foreign affairs and, at Camp David, of the succeeding foreign minister. The two countries whose support was most important to him at the time were the United States and Saudi Arabia. He consulted with neither for the simple reason that he knew both would object.

Most striking of all is the apparent nonchalance with which Sadat treated the military. At a meeting of the Egyptian National Security Council on November 5, he casually mentioned his readiness to go to Jerusalem and address the Knesset. Minister of Defense Mohammed Abdel Ghany Gamasy is said to have cried, "No Knesset, no Knesset. This is unnecessary."[5] Without comment Sadat passed on to other matters. It is true that the armed forces had since 1973 consistently supported his moves toward a permanent peace with Israel, and he doubtless knew he could continue to count on them. Yet it is hard to imagine more telling evidence of presidential autonomy in foreign policy than Sadat's failure to consult with his one indispensable base of support on this seminal decision.

What conclusions for foreign policy analysis can one draw from the decisionmaking process that led to the Jerusalem trip? Does that process bear out the "psychologistic approach" to developing countries' foreign policies, which views policy formulation as a function of the leader's drives and idiosyncrasies?[6] In one sense, it does, for the Jerusalem decision accords with the underlying emphasis of that approach, on the weakness of political institutions in most developing countries and the need to focus on the ruler's motives. In Egypt especially, as we have seen, the long tradition of personal political authority allows the president exceptional latitude in foreign affairs—probably more than in any other influential Arab state.[7] Can one then generalize that domestic and international constraints do not much matter and that a close knowledge of the ruler is all that is needed to understand a country's foreign policy? Of course one cannot, largely because of the limitations of models, theories, and analytical frameworks in the study of foreign policy.

For the Jerusalem initiative was defined by its time and circumstances, and by the complex character of its originator, in an infinitely variable combination that would be impossible to duplicate. At another time, the early 1970s, for example, when Sadat was consolidating his power, not only would he have consulted closely with the military and other domestic centers of power but he would have heeded the views of the key conservative Arab states. Moreover, Sadat involved himself deeply in some foreign policy decisions and not at all in others; and those in which he took an interest varied over time and according to the international situation. The great majority of issues were handled by the foreign affairs bureaucracy, which, Third World foreign policy theories notwithstanding, is a highly developed institution in Egypt.

Focusing on the leader's interests and motivation in less pluralistic societies serves a purpose. It is a useful corrective to theories that place undue emphasis on economic forces (*dependencia* analysis, for example), on Third World responsiveness to external pressures (the "great powers" theory), or on domestic political and economic influences. All of these theories have their insights; the difficulty is that they intend a scientific quality, a likeness to "laws," that cannot be sustained. In their attachment to one hypothesis or another, they run the risk of ignoring inconvenient facts. It is the facts themselves, the challenges and responses that occur from one day to the next, that generally reveal most clearly the motives and sources of foreign policy decisions.

Two theories about the Jerusalem initiative deserve a special look. The first assumes a close relationship between Egyptian domestic and foreign policy and accordingly concentrates on the most traumatic domestic event of the period, the massive food riots of 1977. The second looks to economic considerations as the principal source of Egyptian foreign policy. It views the peace initiative as an effort to cure Egypt's financial ills by reducing defense expenditures and encouraging western aid and investments.

On January 18, 1977, demonstrations spread to every major Egyptian city following price increases, announced the day before, on such basic commodities as rice, sugar, and cooking gas. The army restored control the next day, but not before more than seventy people had been killed. Sadat blamed the riots on communists and other leftist elements, but there is no doubt he understood that deeper economic and social grievances were at work. The theory that the food riots led directly to the Jerusalem trip rests on the argument that the demonstrations showed Sadat he had come to the end of the line with his experiments in political and economic liberalization: that "with no recourse to the interior, there was only the exterior"[8] that he could turn to in order to break out of the impasse. Peace with Israel would solve the country's economic and social problems and at the same time silence the political opposition.

The difficulty with this theory is not that it misrepresents the importance of the riots to Sadat but that it offers no evidence of a cause and effect relationship between the violence in January and the Jerusalem trip in November. In the ten months between the two events Sadat had ample opportunity to move toward separate negotiations with Israel had he felt impelled to do so. He was under no serious internal pressure; according to his foreign minister Sadat "was firmly in control and the opposition was negligible."[9] Moreover, a study of the give-and-take of the Geneva preparations shows that the Jerusalem initiative was prompted by a different set of considerations that, rightly or wrongly, led Sadat to conclude that an international conference was bound to fail.

Egypt's perennial financial troubles make it natural to seek economic explanations for major foreign policy initiatives, and for the Jerusalem trip in particular. Proponents of the direct cause-and-effect relationship between economic pressures and the peace initiative argue that Sadat had decided that the only way to obtain the massive financial help that he urgently needed from the United States was to take a dramatic step toward direct negotiations with Israel. They point out that by 1977 the economy was in particularly desperate straits: Defense expenditures were 37 percent of GNP, inflation was running at over 20 percent a year, and debt servicing for the year had reached $1 billion, representing 35 percent of all visible export earnings. Moreover, Sadat is said to have concluded in spring 1977 that the Arabs could not be counted on to provide the sums required over the long term and hence to have stopped worrying about offending them.[10]

But long before his Jerusalem visit Sadat was aware that the economy could not sustain the costs of further conflict with Israel. He had taken to saying that after peace he hoped to shift at least one third of the defense budget into economic development. And every Egyptian negotiation since the first disengagement agreement was driven by the need to move toward a permanent settlement. The issue therefore is not whether Egypt needed peace but whether the economic plight of the country was sufficiently worse before the Jerusalem decision to warrant the hypothesis that economic considerations caused the change in direction. There is no evidence that this was the case. If inflation was high and debt servicing a serious problem, revenues were also increasing. Foreign exchange earnings were up sharply from Suez Canal tolls, remittances from Egyptian workers abroad, and income from the rapidly expanding oil fields along the Red Sea and in the western desert. By 1977 U.S. aid had already reached the plateau of about $1 billion a year that was to last for several years.[11] That level of funding was based on Kissinger's apparent promise to Sadat during the disengagement negotiations that aid to Egypt would remain roughly on a par with that to Israel. There was no question in 1977 of the Carter administration's sharply increasing this amount. Indeed, as the Egyptians knew, U.S. aid officials feared that the Egyptian economy could not absorb such high levels of aid and were having trouble finding enough sound projects on which to spend the money. But the most compelling argument against the theory that Sadat's initiative was designed to increase U.S. aid levels is that the

United States was totally committed to negotiations for a comprehensive settlement. The last thing it wanted was a move that could derail those negotiations.

Nor is there reason to believe that Sadat had given up hope of further large-scale assistance from the Arabs, even though that aid relationship was at one of its periodic low points. The problem at this juncture stemmed from the demands of Egypt's Arab creditors that consumer subsidies be cut back and other actions taken to stabilize the economy. Cairo, for its part, resisted such measures more strongly than ever in the wake of the January riots. Whatever the irritants, both sides needed each other. The Gulf Arabs recognized their interest in preventing economic disorder in Egypt and a possible return to a radical and aggressive foreign posture. And Egypt, which from 1973 to 1976 had received some $5.1 billion in bilateral assistance from Saudi Arabia, Kuwait, the United Arab Emirates, and Qatar, and about $400 million more in multilateral Arab funds,[12] could hardly afford to give up Gulf financial aid out of pique. The result of this mutual dependency was a decision by Arab oil producers to establish a consortium that would enable Egypt to overcome its balance-of-payments problems. Egypt grudgingly agreed to work with its creditors to put its economic house in order.

In considering the relationship between economics and foreign policy in Sadat's Egypt, two distinctions need to be kept in mind. First is the difference between what was economically desirable at the time and what was imperative. For Sadat, whose credo was that freedom of action and unpredictability were the keys to an effective foreign policy, there were few absolute economic imperatives. In 1973 he conducted a war against Israel despite the country's virtual bankruptcy. The economic situation before the Jerusalem initiative was hardly so desperate as to have forced him to make a major decision that he considered unwise in other respects.

It may also be useful to distinguish between long-range objectives and the strategy and tactics needed to achieve them. Sadat's ultimate goal was economic: Throughout his presidency he worked for a durable peace that would enable Egyptians to develop their country and rise above privation. Getting there, however, was a matter of politics. Bored by the abstractions of economics but fascinated by the problems of influencing governments and peoples, Sadat was a political animal. It was natural that his decisions should hinge more on the political means to the end, which is what interested him, than on the economic end itself.

If the Jerusalem initiative was largely the result of Sadat's personality and policy objectives interacting with those of the other main diplomatic actors, it does not follow that the values and foreign policy orientation of the Egyptian people were of no importance. Sadat was a product of his country's history and culture and shared with his compatriots a distinctive view of Egypt's place in the world. Like Nasser, he shared even the ambivalence of that vision, moving from identification with the common values of Arabism to emphasis on the uniqueness and sufficiency of the Egyptian experience. His foreign policy cannot be understood in isolation from Egypt's historical role in the region and its continuing search for national identity.

The Speech to the Knesset and the Response in Egypt

In a country with such wide differences in social class and economic interests, foreign policy attitudes naturally vary from group to group. Intellectuals have one view of Egypt's proper role in the region, middle class entrepreneurs another, and the army, the bureaucracy, and the *fellahin* still others. The legitimacy of a foreign policy rests on that policy's rootedness in values that span the classes and the interest groups. The manner in which Egyptians reacted to the Jerusalem trip provides a glimpse into the ways that foreign policy attitudes form, shift, and spread from one group to another.

After four wars and thirty years of hostility toward Israel, the first reaction of Egyptians to their president's journey was wonder and fascination. As Sadat stepped from his aircraft onto Israeli soil November 19 to a fanfare of trumpets and applause, the millions watching on television throughout Egypt had to ask themselves if a new era of peace and prosperity might really be at hand. The spectacle and the drama combined with pride in Sadat's courage to create a wave of enthusiasm among the mass of Egyptians. And the masses were an important audience for Sadat: Not only was he one of them, but he drew emotional and political support from them.

As the visit progressed it became clear that Sadat had several audiences in mind. The speech to the Knesset, in particular, can best be understood in the context of the groups it was intended to influence. First were the Israelis—the Knesset and the government, of course, but even more the ordinary people of Israel who bore the pains of war and the tensions of uncertain peace. The message was that Egypt wished to live in peace with Israel but that the only road to peace was a just Palestinian settlement. The language was plain and direct, though with strong religious overtones,[13] in its appeal to the deepest feelings of a people that had never known real security:

> Any life that is lost in war is a human life, be it that of an Arab or an Israeli. A wife who becomes a widow is a human being entitled to a happy family life, whether she be an Arab or an Israeli.

Innocent children who are deprived of the care and compassion of their parents are ours. They are ours, be they living on Arab or Israeli land. . . .

Allow me to address my call from this rostrum to the people of Israel. I pledge myself with true and sincere words to every man, woman, and child in Israel. . . . I convey to you the message of peace of the Egyptian people . . . a message of security, safety, and peace to every man, women, and child in Israel; I say, encourage your leadership to struggle for peace.[14]

The heart of the speech, the message directed to Egyptians and other Arabs as well as to Israelis, was that although peace was within reach, it could not be built on the sufferings of the Palestinians. There was no attempt to sugarcoat the message to please the audience. The Knesset, in fact, seems to have been shaken by the directness of Sadat's demand for complete withdrawal from all of the Arab territories, including Jerusalem, that Israel occupied in 1967. (Defense Minister Ezer Weizman passed a note to Dayan saying, "We've got to prepare for a war.") But for Egyptians and, more begrudgingly, other Arabs as well,[15] nothing could have been clearer than Sadat's description of the kind of settlement that Egypt sought:

Frankness makes it incumbent upon me to tell you the following: First, I have not come here for a separate agreement between Egypt and Israel. This is not part of the policy of Egypt. The problem is not that of Egypt and Israel.

An interim peace between Egypt and Israel, or between any Arab confrontation state and Israel, will not bring permanent peace based upon justice in the entire region.

Rather, even if peace between all the confrontation states and Israel were achieved in the absence of a just solution of the Palestinian problem, never will there be that durable and just peace upon which the entire world insists.

Second, I have not come to you to seek a partial peace, namely to terminate the state of belligerency at this stage and put off the entire problem to a subsequent stage. This is not the radical solution that would steer us to permanent peace.[16]

Israeli sources indicate that Sadat, both in private talks with Begin and in public, stressed that he had come to Jerusalem not to make a separate agreement but to discuss the Palestinian issue.[17] To Weizman he said that Arab land was sacred and that he would not be able to look a single Egyptian in the eye if he allowed Israel to remain in the occupied lands.[18] Meanwhile, the same points were being made in talks with senior Israelis by Acting Foreign Minister Boutros Boutros-Ghali, Arab Socialist Union First Secretary Mustapha Khalil, and others in the Egyptian delegation.

On his return to Cairo Sadat was greeted by one of the great mass demonstrations of modern Egyptian history. There is no doubt that support for the Jerusalem initiative by the ordinary people of the country was "massive and surprisingly unsolicited."[19] The reaction of educated Egyptians, on the other hand, was more complicated and took longer to develop. In a reversal of the usual pattern of group interaction in the molding of public opinion, Egyptian intellectuals were much influenced in the immediate aftermath of Jerusalem by the spontaneous enthusiasm of the masses. A leading Egyptian journalist, for example, had planned to write an article against the trip to Jerusalem; after talking with a number of ordinary Egyptians, however, he changed his mind, for he "found that the men in the streets wanted peace. They had changed their views and were quite happy."[20] These changing attitudes reflected a deep-rooted shift in orientation in much of Egyptian society in the mid-1970s. For the first time in twenty-five years, Egyptians were returning to the sense of an Egyptian national destiny that had animated Mohammed Ali, Mohammed Abduh, Colonel Ahmad Bey Urabi, and Saad Zaghloul. And if Sadat's trip to Jerusalem traded on the resurgence of "Egyptianism" and hastened its progress, it did not cause it.

The swing of the pendulum back to Nile-River nationalism was partly the result of changing economic interests among a number of groups. The expanding, business-oriented upper middle class needed peace to prosper, and its members were vocal in extolling the advantages of peace with Israel. The army had redeemed its honor in 1973, and its leaders were well aware that as Egypt shifted its source of weapons supply from east to west, the country was in no shape to fight another war with Israel. (On the day that Sadat left for Jerusalem, Gamasy sent him a telegram pledging the military's support.)[21] And the peace-loving *fellahin*, brought up in the ordered rhythms of the village and the river, felt that they had sacrificed enough for the Arab and Palestinian causes.

In the months after the Jerusalem trip, Egyptian propaganda made the most of the attitudinal changes taking place in Egyptian society. The period in this respect was similar to the first months of 1955. Whereas in 1955 an abrupt change in propaganda themes signaled Nasser's decision to transform the ideological basis of foreign policy from Egyptian nationalism to pan-Arabism, in late 1977 and early 1978 an equally sudden shift in the official line marked Sadat's determination to revert to a narrower sense of national identity.

The media began to feature such slogans as "Egypt first and last" and "Egypt is and always has been Egypt." A recurrent theme became the ingratitude of Egypt's Arab critics. On December 13, for example, Mustapha Amin, writing in *al-Akhbar*, described the five rejectionist leaders who had just met in Tripoli as follows: "Those five angry, furious ones want us to fight alone, to die alone, to go bankrupt alone, to starve alone, to suffer alone. . . . Egypt's great crime is that Egypt has become Egypt again and that Egyptians have again become Egyptians." The treatment of Israel also changed: Israel became "the adversary" rather than "the enemy," and Radio Cairo's "Sounds of the Battlefront" gave way to "The Flags of Peace." Throughout the country, on the walls of schools and clinics, murals portraying Egyptian soldiers locked in combat with the enemy were painted over to show prosperous farmers working in the shadow of doves of peace.

The Arab Response to Jerusalem

It is an interesting question whether Sadat was driven to emphasize Egyptian nationalism by Arab censure or whether, as some argue,[22] he deliberately sought to stir up Egyptian chauvinism and polarize the Arab world in order to pave the way for a separate agreement with Israel. The answer lies in the unfolding Egypt-Arab relationship after Jerusalem—the challenges and responses that led to new directions for Egypt and, ten months later, to the Camp David accords.

As soon as he returned from Jerusalem, Sadat briefed Prince Fahd about his trip and its purposes. It was too late: The Saudis had been sorely offended by his failure to bring them into his thinking before the visit. Moreover, they believed that the slight had been deliberate; for although Sadat had visited the kingdom just a few days before he told the Peoples' Assembly of his readiness to go to Jerusalem, he had said nothing in Riyadh about his plans. It was not that he had not thought about doing so. On the way to Riyadh, Fahmy urged him to consult with the Saudi leadership. He dismissed the idea, however, saying that "they are not of the standard or caliber to digest or understand such moves."[23]

In fact Sadat's main reason for leaving out the Saudis was probably a sense that, if told beforehand, they would feel bound to speak out against the initiative to protect their Arab flanks. He may even have concluded that they would prefer not to be consulted. National pride also doubtless played a part: A move of such importance was not something about which an Egyptian leader consulted with other Arabs. As it turned out, the Saudis were annoyed not only because they had not been consulted but also because the initiative coincided with the yearly pilgrimage to Mecca. To the pious, gathered at Islam's holiest site, Sadat's trip to Jerusalem was a bitter reminder of Israel's occupation of the other city sacred to their religion and an act that seemed to recognize implicitly that occupation. As one Saudi official put it, "Moslems from all over the world were coming to the holy places and there was Sadat going to the Knesset."[24]

The only serious discussion about his Jerusalem initiative that Sadat had with another Arab leader took place with Assad three days before the visit.

Despite their deep-seated personal and policy differences, Sadat spent four hours in Damascus explaining to Assad the purposes of his initiative. Neither man changed his views, but Sadat's effort to explain his objectives argues against any intention to goad the militant Arabs into a confrontation. On November 17 Syria declared a national day of mourning. Thus began a Syrian drive to isolate Egypt and capture the leadership of the confrontation states that dominated Arab politics during the next four years and survived Sadat's death. Syria's swing from strategic cooperation with Saudi Arabia, Egypt, and Jordan to energizer of the rejectionist block was as momentous as it was sudden. With Syria's defection, the militant Arab states and the radical Palestinian groups acquired new weight and credibility.

Before breaking definitively with Egypt, Assad held discussions with Kings Hussein and Khalid. It may be that he would have preferred to form a block with Saudi Arabia and Jordan had they been willing to join him in organizing sanctions against Egypt.[25] The Saudis, however, had decided not to alienate Sadat or drive him toward a separate peace with Israel, and Hussein admired Sadat's courage and (at least at first) refused to have anything to do with efforts to punish him.[26]

What was left for Syria were awkward bedfellows: the committed rejectionists who opposed in principle any effort to negotiate with Israel. Damascus was in no position to fight another war with Israel and had no wish to be drawn into the confrontational politics of the ultra hard-line states. At the same time Assad clearly had concluded that a watershed had been reached—that Sadat's trip to Jerusalem would lead inevitably to a separate Egypt-Israel agreement in which Syria would be left with neither a credible option for war nor bargaining chips for peace. Whether this would have in fact happened had Assad not assured its coming to pass by breaking irrevocably with Egypt is open to debate. Certainly Sadat had no intention at this point of abandoning the search for a comprehensive peace. After returning from Jerusalem he continued to speak of going to Geneva, arguing that the climate for negotiations had been improved by the psychological impact of his trip on the Israeli people.

Whatever qualms Assad may have had about his new allies, within two weeks of the Jerusalem trip he had joined Libya, Algeria, South Yemen, the PLO, and (at first) Iraq in a "Front of Steadfastness and Resistance." The purpose of the alliance apparently was not only to isolate Egypt but to create a new eastern front with at least a theoretical capability of going to war against Israel without Egypt. As Syria set about organizing the Steadfastness Front's conference in Tripoli, it also did its best to undermine a Cairo meeting that Sadat had called for to continue the preparations for Geneva. Partly in response to Syrian urging, Jordan, Lebanon, and the PLO refused to attend the so-called Mena House conference on December 14. With only Egypt, Israel, the United States, and the UN participating, the Cairo meetings served only to demonstrate the depth of the chasm that had opened between Egypt and the other involved Arabs.

The Tripoli summit in early December, and a similar meeting two months later in Algiers, were the battlegrounds on which the rejectionist Arabs strove to bury their differences and reach an effective common front against Egypt. It proved an impossible task; not until nine months later, after the signing of the Camp David Accords, were Sadat's opponents able to achieve a near-consensus on sanctions against Egypt. The problem for the Arabs at Tripoli was not just that a substantial number of moderate Arab states opposed any action that might drive Sadat to a separate peace, but that the rejectionists disagreed among themselves on what to do.

The most violent disagreement, inevitably, was between Syria and Iraq. Syria needed to bring Iraq into the rejectionist alliance to give depth and military credibility to the eastern front, and to do so it seems to have been prepared to suspend the Ba'athist rivalry. The Iraqis, however, were not interested in an alliance in which they would have to take a backseat to Damascus. To frustrate Syria, they called for a rejectionist summit of their own in Baghdad. After their invitations had been declined, the Iraqi foreign minister briefly attended the Tripoli meeting, walking out after the leaders failed (at Syrian insistence) to reject Resolution 242 and the principle of a negotiated peace with Israel.[27] What was left of the Steadfastness Front lacked power, significance, and cohesion. Syria became the odd man out, eager to punish Sadat but unwilling to close doors finally to a negotiated settlement. At the Algiers summit in February it had to fight the other four conferees for a simple reference in the comuniqué to a "just peace."

Those attending the Tripoli and Algiers meetings pledged to frustrate Sadat's policies, to study Egyptian membership in the Arab League, and to "freeze" diplomatic relations with Egypt. On December 5, the day after the Tripoli summit closed, Sadat formally broke diplomatic relations with the rejectionist governments. A calmer leader of a less proud nation might have reacted differently, but Sadat cannot be said to have provoked the confrontation.

By early 1978 Sadat's peace initiative had divided the Arabs into four groups. At one end of the scale were the Tripoli participants and, at the other, the three Arab states that supported Sadat—Morocco, the Sudan, and Oman. Egypt's supporters were motivated by different considerations. King Hassan had long encouraged direct Egyptian-Israeli contacts as a matter of principle; President Numeiry had been helped by Egypt to put down a number of coup attempts; and Sultan Qabus, dependent on Iranian troops for the internal stability of his country, apparently followed the shah's advice in supporting Sadat.[28] A third group, less determined than the rejectionists to punish Sadat but hoping to isolate him temporarily, consisted of Tunisia, Kuwait, and later Jordan. Saudi Arabia and the Gulf kingdoms that followed Saudi guidance composed the fourth group. Because they were central to Sadat's strategy both at this time and after Camp David, their policies and objectives need a closer look.

Saudi Arabia's overriding strategic interest lay in regional stability; its leaders—annoyed as they were by Sadat's failure to consult them—tended to sympathize with Sadat's active search for a negotiated settlement.[29] They were, however, in a difficult position. They could not afford to alienate Syria because of its pan-Arab credentials and centrality to the conflict with Israel; indeed, they needed Syria as much as Syria needed them. In the end they were mildly critical of the Jerusalem initiative in public, reproaching Sadat for breaking Arab ranks and for dealing alone with Israel on matters that concerned the whole region. Of most practical concern to Egypt, Saudi Arabia and its Gulf allies continued their economic aid for another year and a half. Sadat seems to have understood the kingdom's position and to have concluded that its balancing act was the best that Egypt could expect.[30]

The last of Egypt's important Arab relationships in the post-Jerusalem period was with the PLO. Popular Egyptian sentiment toward the Palestinians had taken an angry turn, and the government's relations with the PLO had also reached a new low. The PLO's association with the hard-liners at Tripoli annoyed Egyptians, but the heat of Egyptian anger rose with a series of violent acts by radical Palestinian groups. During the Jerusalem trip alone, Palestinians stormed the Egyptian embassy in Athens, attacked the chancery and staff housing in Beirut, called for Sadat's assassination, and promised to send troops to help overthrow Sadat.[31]

The real falling-out, however, resulted from the February 1978 murder by two Palestinian gunmen of Yusuf al-Sibai, the chairman of al-Ahram and a friend of Sadat. After the assassination, fifteen Egyptian commandos were killed at Larnaca Airport by Cypriot national guardsmen as they attempted to capture the terrorists. At the commandos' funeral in Cairo the crowd called for vengeance, and the press warned that the blow aimed at Egypt would in fact be dealt to Palestine. In the press and on television Arafat's likeness appeared with blood dripping from his hands. Palestinian stereotypes engaged the cartoonists. Rose al-Youssef, for example, portrayed a nattily dressed Palestinian "rejectionist" standing outside a nightclub and saying to a friend, "Excuse me while I go in there and do some struggling."[32]

Before the Sibai murder Sadat responded to PLO criticism with relative restraint. Although he closed the PLO's Cairo office after the Tripoli summit, he did not deny the PLO's right to represent the Palestinians. He toyed at the time with the idea of developing an alternative Palestinian leadership. In late November, for example, the Egyptian Arab Socialist party invited leaders from the occupied territories to Egypt. None of consequence came, although earlier a group of prominent West Bank mayors and politicians had responded to the Jerusalem initiative by praising Sadat's courage and vision.[33] For the pragmatic politicians of the West Bank and Gaza—and indeed for moderates within the PLO—terrorism was a constant threat. In January 1979 the PLO's London representative, Said Hamami, was murdered for opposing a total break with Egypt. Hamami's assassination, apparently by the Abu Nidal group of Palestinian fanatics based in Iraq, was a warning to Arafat and leaders in the West Bank and Gaza not to even think about working with Sadat.

The indignation of Sadat, and of Egyptians generally, toward the PLO after the Sibai murder had important consequences. In the critical year ahead Egypt was to promote Jordan and the indigenous Palestinians as the proper negotiators of a settlement, despite the reluctance of both to assume the task without ironclad assurances of full Israeli withdrawal. In March 1978, Sadat told Weizman: "The test for both of us is the Palestinian problem. I have excluded the PLO from my lexicon. By their own behavior, they have excluded themselves from the negotiations. But . . . I have to be able to tell the Arabs, 'The Arabs of the West Bank and Gaza will be able to shape their future, and the Israelis will leave.'"[34] Sadat knew, of course, that the PLO would try to wreck any negotiations that left them out. But without Saudi Arabia and Jordan to back them he believed the PLO would have a hard time succeeding, and that is what he counted on as he worked to revive the peace process.

9

Camp David
and Its Consequences

Arab Olive Branches Before Camp David

By the spring of 1978, after several fruitless meetings between Egyptian and Israeli representatives had taken place in Ismailiya and Jerusalem, Sadat recognized that the bilateral talks would not elicit serious concessions on the Palestinian issue. Throughout the winter he had pressed Begin for a statement acknowledging (as previous Israeli governments had) that Security Council Resolution 242 applied to all fronts of the 1967 war. He declared that if Israel accepted this principle he would be prepared to negotiate a first-stage bilateral agreement on the Sinai, although he insisted that Egypt would not sign a peace treaty until the Palestinian issue had been settled.[1] In the face of Begin's continued refusal to accept the principle of West Bank withdrawal, Sadat's frustration grew and, with it, his willingness to consider a return to Arab ranks.

The other Arabs, seeing the stalemate in the bilateral talks, stepped up their efforts to persuade Sadat to abandon his initiative. In early May Numeiry appeared in Damascus, where he reportedly tried to forge a reconciliation between Syria and Egypt—although there is no evidence of Sadat's having sanctioned the mission. According to the Syrian press, Numeiry proposed that, in return for Egypt's ending the negotiations with Israel, Assad acknowledge that Sadat had acted honorably in the pursuit of Arab interests. Nothing came of Numeiry's efforts, and the Arab pressure continued. In late July, after the foreign ministers of Egypt, Israel, and the United States had met—and made little progress—at Leeds Castle in England, President Carter wrote in his diary: "The Arabs are really pushing Sadat and, [in order] not to stay vulnerable in the long run, I think he is wanting either to come back to them or to some resolution of the question."[2] Sadat said as much himself. On July 30 he told Ambassador Hermann Eilts and Ambassador-at-Large Alfred Atherton that the Saudis were pressing him to break off the negotiations entirely. That same day Carter made up his mind to invite Sadat and Begin to Camp David.

Sadat and the Issue of Palestinian Autonomy

This is not the place for a detailed account of the Camp David negotiations. Not only have Egyptian, Israeli, and U.S. participants exhaustively examined the talks[3] but, for the thirteen days in which they took place (September 5–17, 1978) most of the Arabs were bystanders. Yet Arab support was critical to the success of the arrangements that were being negotiated for the West Bank and Gaza. Without the active participation of Jordan and the local Palestinians, the proposed self-governing authority would have neither the legitimacy nor the vitality to govern effectively. And unless Saudi Arabia could be persuaded at least to acquiesce in the new arrangements, the major forces in the Arab world would coalesce against Camp David and Egypt would lose its latitude to work with Israel and the United States toward an overall settlement.

Before turning to the Arab response to Camp David, it may be worth recalling why Egypt and the United States chose to negotiate an interim self-government arrangement for the West Bank and Gaza instead of trying for a more permanent resolution of the problem. A key factor was the perception that even if the Begin government would never relinquish sovereignty over the West Bank while it was in power, it might be brought to accept an interval of self-rule that did not prejudge the question of ultimate sovereignty. The transitional period was thus conceived of partly as a way of getting beyond Begin to an Israeli government that accepted Resolution 242 in its original sense. But it was also seen as having the potential, over time, of building both sides' confidence in the possibility of living next to each other in peace. Finally, as a negotiating tactic, the concept was designed to extract as much movement as possible from Israel on the Palestinian issue in return for the bilateral treaty that Israel badly wanted.

Before Camp David, Egypt and the United States had consulted with King Hussein on the nature of interim arrangements for the West Bank, the assumption being that both the self-governing authority and the final agreement would be negotiated by Jordan and the local Palestinians, as well as by Egypt and Israel.[4] In May Mubarak briefed the king on discussions about an interim arrangement and returned to Cairo optimistic that Hussein would take part.[5] As time passed, however, and Israel indicated its reluctance to relinquish control of the land and water or to withdraw its military to a few security outposts, Hussein became skeptical that the self-rule proposal could be developed into full autonomy.

It is clear in retrospect that the unusual circumstances at Camp David led to serious miscalculations about Jordanian and Saudi attitudes and the need for further consultations. The difficulty of the negotiations, the pressure of time, and the deep desire for an agreement all combined to discourage any thought of outside consultations that would compound the problems. But the root of the dilemma was that Sadat and Carter had persuaded each other that Saudi Arabia had no choice but to follow the U.S. lead—and that Hussein was certain to take part in the autonomy negotiations if that was what the Saudis and the United States wanted. As it turned out, the Saudis tended to defer to Jordan on issues relating to the West Bank rather than the other way around.

The framework for the West Bank and Gaza, as it emerged from Camp David, retained most of the elements of the original concept of an interim Palestinian self-government that prepared the way for negotiations on a final settlement. To succeed, however, the plan required not only the participation of Jordan and the Palestinians but the full commitment of Israel. As the occupying power and a negotiator of the arrangement, Israel had the means either to deny or to grant the self-governing authority important responsibilities. Carter seems to have assumed that Israel's treaty commitment "to provide full autonomy to the inhabitants," combined with continuing U.S. involvement during the autonomy negotiations, would ensure the establishment of an authority with substantial responsibilities. Sadat, for his part, put his faith in Carter and in the U.S. commitment to play the role of a "full partner" in the autonomy negotiations.

If Sadat, like Carter, attached too little importance to the problems that lay ahead—both with Israel and with the Arabs—he nevertheless had a clear conception of how the West Bank/Gaza framework was meant to work and why it served Palestinian interests better than any feasible alternative. He described this conception to Foreign Minister Mohamed Kamel near the end of the Camp David meetings. First, to Kamel's argument that the agreement would perpetuate Israel's illegal occupation of the West Bank and Gaza, Sadat replied:

> The autonomy project would lead to the abolition of the Israeli military government in the West Bank and Gaza and will put an end to the suffering of the Palestinians. President Carter has insisted on adding the adjective "full" to the word "autonomy," despite strong opposition by Begin, so the powers of the autonomy authority will be fully comprehensive, say for such things as security. The Palestinians will not be alone. They will have Egypt and Jordan with them during the period of transition. Were the Palestinians to disapprove of the solution to end the transitional period, they would have the right to veto it, because they will vote on this solution. President Carter has told me that the language and formulation of the project may be vague

but this is unimportant. What matters is that he is going to be with us as a full partner in the negotiations on self-rule.

Sadat went on to say that Israel's occupation would be prolonged not by the Camp David agreements but by the alternative of going back to the Arabs in order to create a solid front against Israel:

> You know nothing of the Arabs. I know them only too well. If they are left to themselves, they will never solve the problems and Israeli occupation will be perpetuated. Israel will end by engulfing the occupied Arab territories, with the Arabs not lifting a finger to stop them, contenting themselves with bluster and empty slogans as they have done from the very beginning. They will never agree on anything.

Finally, Sadat argued that linking Israeli withdrawal in the Sinai to progress on the West Bank and Gaza would not only stand in the way of the peace Egypt needed but weaken the position of the Palestinians:

> How can there be a separate agreement, when I am committed to the process of self-rule in the West Bank and Gaza during the five year transitional period and a solution to the Palestinian question in all its aspects? And what sense is there in keeping Sinai under Israeli domination until a solution is reached to the Palestinian problem so that Israel may cover it with new settlements with every day that passes? Wouldn't that be foolish? You are talking like this because you know nothing of the internal situation in Egypt. Nasser left me a heritage encumbered with worries and problems. Our economic and social conditions are extremely bad and the public utilities are in a state of collapse. Egypt will be unable to deal with the deteriorating situation unless it achieves peace and devotes all its resources to development. Egypt will then be in a stronger position to assist the Palestinians in solving their problems.[6]

Jordan and Saudi Arabia Opt Out

Immediately after the Camp David Accords were signed, a procession of visitors met with the Saudi leadership. On September 17 a high-level PLO delegation arrived in Riyadh for discussions with Prince Fahd. Later in the week Secretary of State Vance spent two days in the kingdom seeking Saudi support. Assad arrived for talks with Fahd on September 26, and on the same day Egyptian Deputy Prime Minister Tuhamy, accompanied by an adviser to King Hassan, flew to Geneva to meet with King Khalid. Last in line was King Hussein, who visited Riyadh on September 30.

By early October Saudi Arabia had concluded, with Jordan, that the framework agreement had little chance of success in the absence of commitments from Israel to withdraw from the West Bank and cease its settlement activity.[7] Both governments believed the agreement was flawed on its merits, but each also had strategic reasons for distancing itself from Camp David.

For the Saudis, a separate peace between Egypt and Israel meant a fall from the ascendancy in inter-Arab affairs that they had enjoyed since 1974. No longer would the kingdom be the pivotal point between moderates and hard-liners, the "sober, sagacious . . . arbiter and consensus-finder of inter-Arab disagreements."[8] Of particular concern was the accommodation that seemed likely to take place between Syria and Iraq in opposition to Egypt. Iraq's return from the margin to a place of Arab centrality was, from the Saudi perspective, an ominous development. As the Saudis watched the two radical contenders for regional dominance mend fences, they must have sensed that a policy of outright support for Egypt would leave them very exposed indeed. All the while, in Iran, a revolution was taking place, sending a cautionary message to conservative monarchies closely tied to the United States.

King Hussein had as much, if not more, reason than the Saudis to worry about an Iraqi-Syrian rapprochement, with its inevitable ties to the most radical Palestinians. He may also have concluded that the Camp David framework was not likely to promote the Hashemite dream of ultimate union between the East and West Banks in one Jordan. For it could be argued that Camp David would either lead to indefinite Palestinian self-government under Israeli sovereignty or result in unrestricted self-determination and an independent state under the PLO. Finally, Jordan's traditional sense of vulnerability in the Arab world, and the balance of power politics that flowed from it, must have played a role in the decision to part ways with Egypt.

Jordan did not at first, however, totally reject the Camp David Accords. On September 20 the government issued a statement expressing surprise that Jordan's name appeared in the agreement and stating that "it did not consider itself morally or legally bound."[9] A few days later it sent the United States a letter requesting clarification of a number of provisions.[10] In an effort to meet Jordanian concerns (as well as those of the PLO, which had also sought clarifications), the United States promised to use its full influence to conclude the negotiations successfully. Israel, however, immediately rejected a number of the U.S. interpretations, so that, on balance, the exchange did more to keep Jordan out of the process than to bring it in.

The people most directly addressed in the framework, the West Bankers and Gazans, did not at first unanimously oppose the accords. On the West

Bank initial reactions mirrored the political divisions that characterized the region during the 1970s. The urban mayors who generally favored a pragmatic approach to Israel showed considerable interest in the practical implications of self-government. On the other hand, the increasingly influential group of politicians who identified with the PLO viewed the framework as a denial of Palestinian national rights and rejected it from the start.[11] Without Jordan's involvement or the tacit acquiescence of the PLO, even the most pragmatic West Bankers could do no more than express polite interest. In November the opposition hardened with the establishment of a national guidance committee to orchestrate the resistance to Camp David.

The Baghdad Summit and Its Aftermath

When the Baghdad summit convened in early November, the major Arab countries were united in opposition to Egypt and prepared for the first time to take steps to punish it for breaking Arab ranks. The galvanizing change that brought about this unity was the short-lived accommodation between Syria and Iraq.

The prospect of a peace treaty that allowed Israel to turn its full attention to the north was enough to make Syria swallow its pride and accept a junior partnership with Iraq. Yet the accommodation not only returned Iraq to a pivotal position in Arab politics but had little military value for Syria, given the unstable political base of the relationship. Iraq emerged the clear winner in this rapprochement. With Cairo ostracized and Damascus vulnerable, Baghdad seemed on the verge of playing "an influential role in Arab affairs such as it [had] not enjoyed since the overthrow of Nuri al-Said and the Hashemites 21 years [before]."[12] Less than a year later, however, the kaleidoscope shifted once again: Iraq had invaded Iran, and for the next eight years its energy would be directed eastward.[13]

At the Baghdad summit, the critical dynamic centered on efforts of the rejectionists to draw Saudi Arabia and Jordan into their orbit and dictate the outcome of the conference. It was not at all certain that they would be able to do so. At a preceding meeting of Arab foreign ministers, the Saudi delegate, Prince Saud, had successfully prevented the Iraqi-Syrian axis from dominating the proceedings. Until the last moment, Sadat, although angered by Riyadh's public criticism of Camp David, believed that Prince Fahd would protect Egypt from the imposition of serious sanctions. Indeed, the Saudis appear to have assured him before the summit of their power to do so.[14]

Sadat firmly believed that Prince Fahd was largely responsible for the rejectionist victory at Baghdad—and often said so publicly despite pleas from his senior advisers that he not aggravate the situation.[15] There was in fact only weak opposition by the moderates to the militants' demands at Baghdad that Egypt refrain from signing a peace treaty with Israel or face a range of political and economic sanctions. When Egypt signed the peace treaty on March 26, 1979, the sanctions went into effect. Egypt was suspended from the Arab League, the league's seat was transferred from Cairo to Tunis, Egyptian companies doing business with Israel were boycotted, and diplomatic relations were broken with all Arab countries except the Sudan, Somalia, and Oman.

If Sadat viewed Fahd's behavior at Baghdad as a personal betrayal, he reacted with disdain to Hussein's alignment with the rejectionists. The summit had pledged Jordan $1.25 billion in subsidies over a ten-year period, "the assumption [being] that Jordan would reject any role in negotiations over the West Bank and Gaza foreseen in [the] Accords."[16] Sadat's response to this largesse was to charge the Saudis with buying protection from the radical Arabs by paying others to break their ties with Egypt.[17]

The sanctions imposed at Baghdad were damaging to Egypt's economy and its national pride, but they were by no means disastrous. As Egyptians often pointed out in the years to come,[18] informal, transnational relations continued and even increased after the Baghdad sanctions. Private Arab capital still flowed into Egypt, thousands of Arab students studied in Egyptian universities, Cairo remained a favorite destination of Arab tourists, and the Egyptians working in Arab countries continued to send home their remittances (estimated at about $2 billion in 1978). At the same time, more than a billion dollars of annual economic and military aid from the Arab states dried up. The Saudis, for example, decided (after one of Sadat's public attacks on Fahd) not to pay some $500 million for F-5 aircraft that Egypt had bought on the understanding that the kingdom would bear the cost. Kuwait asked Egypt to return about $1 billion in bank deposits, and Gulf financing for the nascent Egyptian arms industry was suspended. Some of the damage was, of course, offset by U.S. aid.

Egyptians reacted ambivalently to the Arab efforts to punish Egypt for making peace. On the one hand, they regarded the sanctions as unwarranted interference in their affairs and tended to close ranks against Arab critics. On the other, many educated Egyptians were troubled by the intensity of the Arab opposition and especially by its extension to Egypt's former allies. A survey of 131 fourth-year students at Cairo University, taken about a year after the Baghdad summit, illustrates the ambivalence. The survey found that 46 percent of the students still favored the peace treaty as against 36 percent who did not and 18 percent who were undecided. Seventy-nine percent said that although they were frustrated by the policies of the Arab regimes, they identified with an Arab nationality.[19]

Over the next three years the steady drumbeat of Arab criticism reinforced the concerns of intellectuals that Egypt had failed in its Arab responsibilities.

The unease deepened as Israel accelerated its settlement of the West Bank, extended Israeli law to the Golan Heights, and, in June 1982, sent troops into Lebanon in order to expel and disperse the PLO. There were few Egyptians who did not believe that Israel was using the peace with Egypt to damage the interests of other Arabs.

Arab Issues at the Blair House Talks

In the five months between the Baghdad summit and the Egyptian-Israeli peace treaty, the continuing Arab diatribes against Egypt had two seemingly contradictory effects on Sadat. Publicly he remained on the offensive, pouring contempt on the "dwarfs" of the Arab world whose interest was in "auctioneering" rather than in finding practical ways to end the war with Israel. Privately he badly wanted to prove the Arabs wrong— to show that the Camp David framework was a realistic path to Palestinian rights. During the peace treaty negotiations at Blair House this attitude manifested itself in a hardened Egyptian stand on two issues central to Egypt's Arab relations.

The first was the question of linkage, the Egyptians insisting that the first phase of the Egyptian-Israeli treaty be tied to the holding of elections for Palestinian self-government. Later, as it became clear that Begin attached great importance to the exchange of ambassadors, Egypt tried to link that exchange to the establishment of a self-governing authority. In the end the most that could be extracted from Begin was a commitment to a target date, the parties setting for themselves a goal of one year for completing negotiations on the powers and responsibilities of the self-governing authority.

The second Arab-related issue was the question of which Egyptian treaty obligations had priority in the case of a conflict between them: those in the peace treaty with Israel or those in the Arab League covenant and in Egypt's defense agreements with Arab states. Sadat wanted it made clear that if Israel attacked an Arab country allied to Egypt, nothing in the peace treaty prevented him from going to that country's aid. Israel, on the other hand, pressed for an explicit statement that the parties' commitments under the peace treaty superseded all others.[20] The U.S. position, communicated to Egypt during the negotiations, was that "nothing would prevent Egypt from honoring its commitments under other treaties in the event of armed attack against one of its allies."[21] Both sides realized that the wording would not determine what happened in the event of a future Arab-Israeli confrontation. But for Sadat the language was central to his contention that the peace treaty did not conflict with Egypt's Arab obligations.

The Collapse of the Autonomy Talks

The Palestinian autonomy talks began in August 1979 and continued intermittently for three years. President Carter's continuing personal involvement, which Sadat had counted on heavily, did not materialize. Preoccupied by the Iran hostage crisis and the 1980 election campaign, Carter was unable to engage himself in the problem in the same way that he had at Camp David.

Egypt's stance at the autonomy talks tended toward caution and rigidity, partly, no doubt, to avoid Arab charges of negotiating away Palestinian rights. But the fundamental reason for the failure of the negotiations lay in Israeli politics. Influenced by the extreme hawks in his cabinet, Begin became fearful that Palestinian self-government would indeed generate a dynamic "that would inevitably lead to the emergence of a sovereign Palestinian state."[22] The result was a series of Israeli positions designed to neutralize this risk and freeze the status quo. The nature and powers of the self-governing council were defined in the narrowest terms, the Arabs of East Jerusalem were excluded from the council, and a large, continuing Israeli military presence was envisaged. Within months Dayan and Weizman resigned from the cabinet in disgust.[23] The negotiations nevertheless dragged on, an exercise in frustration for everyone involved, until they were finally suspended by Egypt after the Israeli invasion of Lebanon in June 1982.

The impasse in the autonomy talks ended Sadat's seven years of momentum in foreign policy. From the October War through Camp David he had kept in the air the two balls of Egyptian and Palestinian interests, an impressive juggling act in view of the efforts of allies and adversaries alike to upset the performance. There had never been any question that the recovery of Egyptian territory came first, but that did not lessen the importance, either to Sadat's self-esteem or to his political legitimacy, of progress toward Palestinian self-determination. When that path was blocked, the sense of movement and purpose in his foreign policy came to an end as well.

The last year of Sadat's life was marked by futile attempts to regain the lost momentum of his foreign policy. In November 1980 he offered to divert 1 million cubic meters of Nile water a day to irrigate Israel's Negev Desert in exchange for a resolution of the Palestinian and Jerusalem questions. Not only did Israel briskly dismiss the offer, but Egyptians were angered by their president's presumption in using the country's lifeblood as a bargaining chip. Then in August 1981, while embarked on a "second pilgrimage of peace" to Europe and the United States, he suddenly and without apparent consultation proposed the establishment of a Palestinian government in exile.

The clearest signs of capriciousness and lost direction, however, appeared on the domestic front. A month before his death, Sadat sent to prison more than 1,500 perceived opponents of his regime, mainly from the militant Islamic right but including about 250 of the most prominent intellectual and political figures in the country.[24] Among those jailed was the brother of Khaled Islambouli, Sadat's assassin.

Khaled Islambouli was a committed fundamentalist whose decision to kill Sadat was motivated by the grievances of militant Islam against a secular state and ruler. If his brother's arrest galvanized him to action, his underlying purpose was to exact retribution for the "persecution" of the Islamic movement since the 1952 revolution.[25] There is little evidence in the testimony of Islambouli (or of his fellow conspirators) of any interest in Egyptian foreign policy or the Camp David Accords. Yet one cannot help but feel that a connection exists between Sadat's inability to achieve a Palestinian settlement and the atmosphere of frustration that pervaded Egypt at the time that he was assassinated.

In the brief moment between the murder and his arrest, Islambouli cried, "I have killed the pharaoh." It is hard to imagine a more apt comment for a Muslim fundamentalist in the circumstances. The pharaoh appears in the Koran "as the ultimate example of the irreligious and oppressive ruler whom it is the believer's duty to disobey and if possible to overthrow."[26] Yet Egyptian children have been taught in modern times to look upon the ancient pharaohs not as despots but as exemplars of Egypt's splendor in its golden age. In a few short words Islambouli rejected the nation state in which he lived, specified the punishment due to a leader who rules by laws alien to Islam, and made clear which political community he considered legitimate.

10

The Making of a
New Arab Coalition

As the economic and political balance among Arab nations has shifted since the 1967 War, as alliances have come and gone and attitudes toward Israel have moved from confrontation toward negotiation, periodic summit meetings have been called to confirm the changes and turn them into common policy. These meetings are the mileposts of modern Arab diplomatic history. At Khartoum in 1967, Rabat in 1974, Baghdad in 1978, and Fez in 1982, new bearings were set in inter-Arab relations and the conflict with Israel. More recently, in Amman in 1987 and Algiers in 1988, summits were held that illuminated the changes that have occurred in Arab relationships since Camp David.

The meetings in Amman and Algiers were important not simply because they returned Egypt to a position of Arab centrality, showed a solid front to Iran in the last stages of the Gulf War, and pledged support to the Palestinian uprising but because they signaled the emergence of a new dynamic in inter-Arab relations. On all of the controversial issues, the decisionmaking process was controlled by a new coalition, led by the conservative states that had backed the quest for a negotiated settlement before Sadat's trip to Jerusalem, and joined on most issues by Iraq.

The appearance of this coalition raises a number of questions. What issues does the moderate consensus embrace and what are its limits? How strong are the underlying bilateral relationships, especially those among Egypt and Saudi Arabia, Jordan, and Iraq? Is the enhanced sense of common interest likely to long survive the Gulf War? Finally, how will the Arab-Israeli peace process be affected, and what impact will the Palestinian uprising have on the move toward the center?

Changes in the Strategic Landscape

The summit in Amman that opened the way for Egypt's Arab reintegration took place exactly nine years after Egypt was threatened with suspension

from the Arab League at Baghdad. There had been little significant collective
Arab activity during most of the period in between; indeed, except for
Fez in 1982, it had been impossible to convene a summit because of the
intensity of inter-Arab quarrels. Yet the meetings in Amman were as
effectively controlled by the Arab moderates as the Baghdad summit had
been dominated by the militants.

This turnabout in inter-Arab dynamics was partly a movement toward
realism and away from the ardent ideologies of the past (to be discussed
in the next chapter). But equally important was a transformation taking
place in the relative power positions of the principal Arab actors. Before
turning to the summits of 1987 and 1988, let us look at some of the
changes that had taken place since Baghdad in the strategic landscape of
the Middle East.

Three developments in particular had altered the Arab nations' perception
of their regional interests. First was the two-pronged challenge from
revolutionary Iran—to the political legitimacy and to the territorial integrity
of Arab governments; second was the PLO's dispersal from Beirut in 1982
and the relative quiescence of the Palestinian problem before the *intifadah*
(uprising) began in December 1987; and third was the staying power of
the peace treaty that followed Camp David, with its impact not only on
Egyptian-Israeli relations but also on Israel's interaction with the other
Arabs. Still another important event was Hosni Mubarak's accession to
power: By removing from the inter-Arab equation the element of personal
bitterness toward Sadat, it opened the way for Egypt to take advantage of
the first three developments.

The Impact of Revolutionary Iran

There is no doubt that Iran's proprietary interest in its Gulf neighbors
served to concentrate Arab attention on what was important to the common
interest and what was not. Because of the challenge to Arab-wide interests
that the Gulf war posed, a trend already under way in the Arab community—
a trend toward greater realism, less rhetoric, and a more serious search
for common ground—gathered steam. Nor did the impact of the war end
with the cease-fire. Arab views about the long-term threat from militant
Iranian Shi'ism have not changed substantially, and Iraq spares no effort
to ensure that they do not.

The nature of the Iranian threat has been perceived by different Arabs
in different ways. For Saudi Arabia the very existence of another Islamic
state that claims to represent all true believers—be it Sunni or Shi'ite—
is a challenge to the legitimacy of the regime. That Iran's revolutionary
Islamic republic is five times the kingdom's size in population and much
superior in military power underlines the danger. Of greatest concern to
some of the smaller Arab countries that face Iran across the Gulf has been

the threat of internal subversion from pro-Iranian Shi'ite minorities. The chief Palestinian worry during the war was that the other Arabs would become so preoccupied with Iranian ambitions that they would lose interest in the Palestinian problem. As Arafat put it at the Amman summit, the Arab leaders were intent on closing ranks because of "the danger of this fireball rolling closer to the oil wells."[1]

The most complex Arab attitude toward Iran has been that of Syria. Hostility toward Iraq and cheap oil from Iran no doubt help account for the Syrian tilt. But beyond that, the isolation of the Syrian Alawite regime in a sea of Sunni orthodoxy has led Damascus to support states on the Arab periphery like Iran and the Shi'ite minority in Lebanon. Syria's highly authoritarian regime has also made the most of an atmosphere of threat from abroad, either from Israel or from enemies within the Arab world. Finally, by backing the outs and taking unpopular positions, Syria has so far avoided being drawn into a moderate Arab consensus on the peace process while it remains in an unfavorable military situation relative to Israel. Its nonconformist policies are not, however, cost-free: In the face of a forceful, well-coordinated Arab opposition it runs the risk of breaking the consensus tradition in Arab councils and, ultimately, of being isolated and ignored.

The paramount concern in Egypt during the Gulf War was the impact of Iranian expansionism on the regional balance of power. At the same time, however, legitimacy considerations affected Egyptian policy in contradictory ways. On the one hand, an overly belligerent posture toward Iran could have inflamed Egypt's own militant Islamic groups—even though mainstream organizations like the Muslim Brotherhood were generally supportive of Egypt's pro-Iraq stance. On the other hand, an Iranian military victory would have galvanized the Islamic movement within Egypt and posed a much greater threat to the regime.

Egypt's strategic interests clearly lay in halting the expansion of Iranian power and influence. The overthrow of conservative regimes in the Gulf and their replacement by radical, pro-Iranian governments would have pushed Egypt back to the defensive posture from which it had just emerged. Yet Egyptians do not need to be reminded that their historic competitor in the Middle East has been not Iran, but Iraq. Not only has the rivalry persisted for more than three thousand years, but it had sunk to one of its more venomous moments in the late 1970s after Camp David. The war had its perils, but from the Egyptian standpoint Iraq's dependence on the moderate Arabs was not one of them.

Quiet on the Palestinian Front

If the challenge from revolutionary Iran was the driving force behind the Arab world's new alliances, the relative quiet on the Palestinian front from 1982 to late 1987 opened the way for a return to more pragmatic, interest-driven Arab politics. Several reasons explain the diminished attention given the Palestinian issue before the uprising in the occupied territories: First, the scattering of the main body of the PLO through the Middle East (much of it in the Maghreb, far from the confrontation with Israel) led to a sharp reduction in the PLO's physical power. Then the breach between Syria and the PLO after Arafat's second exit from Lebanon in December 1983 meant that the PLO had less leverage with the moderate Arab states. Finally, a widening rift between Fatah and the Damascus-based PLO elements tended to fragment the PLO and lessen its impact on Arab policies.

Arab attitudes toward the PLO were also changing. As respect grew for leaders who spoke plainly and provided a better life for their people, there was a sense that the PLO was hamstrung by the need for consensus and that its leadership was becoming more interested in preserving its own position than in achieving an attainable agreement for the Palestinians. Contributing to the PLO's tarnished image in Arab eyes was its inability to defend its people in the Lebanese refugee camps from attacks by the Shi'ite Amal. But the war of the camps did more than damage the PLO's prestige. It was a major factor in the near-total break with Syria, as the radical Palestinian groups of Naef Hawatmeh and George Habash joined Arafat in opposition to Damascus because of Syrian support for Amal. And it meant that Syria's already hard-pressed economy was drained further as it struggled in Lebanon with the PLO and then with the Iranian-backed Hizbollah. The upshot was a further erosion of radical Arab weight in inter-Arab councils, already being hastened in the mid-1980s by Libya's reverses in Chad and domestic strife in Democratic Yemen.

In February 1985, Hussein and Arafat (aided by the active diplomacy of Egypt) reached agreement on principles for a Jordanian-PLO relationship in the negotiating process. The hope was that Arafat—without the radical PLO elements—would move toward negotiations on the basis of Resolution 242.[2] It was not to be. At a meeting of the Palestine National Council in Algiers in April 1987, the hard-line factions insisted that Arafat formally disavow the agreement with Hussein. A resolution was also passed denouncing Egypt and the Camp David Accords, to which Egypt responded by closing the PLO office in Cairo and severing contact with all high-level PLO officials. Seven months later, amid the scramble of Arab states to reopen their embassies, Egypt quietly let the PLO return to its Cairo office.

Just when the Palestinian question began to look like a sterile exercise in which exiled politicians maneuvered for power and foreign ministers issued white papers, the Palestinians of Gaza and the West Bank brought the problem back to life. The political inexperience of the young people in the forefront gave the uprising a spontaneity that caught the Arab imagination. And its emotional impact, especially on Arab youth and religious elements, continued to grow in the absence of movement toward a Palestinian settlement.

The Palestinian uprising began three weeks after the Amman summit ended. Its timing may have been affected by the frustration of West Bank and Gaza Arabs at the indifference to their concerns shown at the summit, although there is no clear evidence that this was the case. Whatever their initial motives, the insurgents returned the Palestinian issue to the priority it had lost on the Arab agenda.

The Mixed Legacy of Camp David

The settlement between Egypt and Israel negotiated at Camp David is one of the most important, and one of the most complex, factors shaping inter-Arab relations. The durability of the peace treaty has had one set of consequences, the failure of the Palestinian autonomy negotiations another. And as Egyptians and Israelis have responded to events and to each other, their emerging attitudes and policies have also influenced the views of the other Arabs.

The dominant fact, however, is that the peace treaty has endured. It survived the assassination of the man who flouted the Arab world to make it, the concerted efforts of the Arabs to punish Egypt for its conclusion, and the Israeli invasion of Lebanon and bombardment of Beirut in 1982 over Egypt's strong protests. It weathered the freezing of the normalization process and the recall of the Egyptian ambassador after the Phalangist massacre of Palestinian refugees in the Sabra and Shatila camps with the knowledge of the Israeli army.[3] And it withstood the public outcries in Israel and Egypt in the mid-1980s following three attacks on Israeli diplomats by an Egyptian terrorist group with which Nasser's eldest son was associated. Arab recognition that the peace between Egypt and Israel is here to stay despite these strains has been a psychological watershed in Middle East politics. More than anything else, it has helped to shift the Arab center of gravity toward acceptance of the need for a negotiated final settlement that recognizes Israel's right to live in peace within secure boundaries.

Since Camp David basic Egyptian policy toward Israel has followed a steady and consistent path throughout the rocky periods in bilateral relations. At the heart of Egypt's policy is the goal of bringing the Arab world with it into a peace with Israel. This requires constant attention to the often flickering interest of Arabs and Israelis alike in the negotiating process. Like Sadat before him, Mubarak has kept Arab concerns before the Israelis, just as he has tried to keep serious negotiating proposals on the Arab agenda.

An example of this kind of Egyptian diplomatic activity occurred in the spring of 1988: After reports of Saudi Arabia's purchase of Chinese missiles prompted Israeli officials to advocate their removal by force, *al-Ahram* carried an official announcement that "Egypt would consider any Israeli aggression on Saudi Arabia as an attack on Egypt, to which it would respond with force and determination."[4] Ten days later, after Israel had moderated its tone, Field Marshal Mohammed Abd al-Halim Abu Ghazala publicly expressed satisfaction at Israel's "appropriate reaction" to Egyptian and U.S. diplomatic representations. The episode was doubtless seen in Cairo as a helpful reminder to the Saudis of the usefulness of the Egyptian connection with Israel.

There is no way of knowing how much attention Israel pays to Egypt; indeed the question has become part of a longstanding Israeli debate on the relative importance of the states on the Middle East's periphery versus those at its core. Some Israelis maintain that the peace treaty with Egypt should change the old theory that Israel's interest lies in cultivating the periphery (Iran, Turkey, and Ethiopia, for example) in order to balance the hostility of the core. They argue that the peace with Egypt proved the possibility of better relations with the core at the same time that the Iranian revolution perplexed relations with the periphery. Israel can exploit the opportunity, they say, by taking serious account of Cairo's views.[5]

Israelis are also divided about the implications for them of Egypt's return to a central position in Arab affairs. Some fear that the process could radicalize Egypt, causing it to reintegrate militarily with the other Arabs, whereas others believe that Arab acceptance of the one Arab nation that negotiated peace with Israel can only be to Israel's advantage. A related debate concerns the significance of an emerging centrist Arab bloc. Some, like former Foreign Minister Abba Eban, believe that a revolutionary change is taking place in the Arab world in which the Arabs "may be on their way to changing their struggle with Israel from one about legitimacy to a pragmatic argument about interests and territory."[6] Eban considered the Amman summit a continuation of the process that began when Sadat visited Jerusalem; he feared, however, that Israel would fail to grasp the nature of the process and miss an historic opportunity to move toward peace.

The stabilizing effect of the peace treaty and the parties' commitment to it is offset by the failure of the Camp David Accords to stimulate a negotiating dynamic on the Palestinian issue. That failure not only undercuts the forces working for Israel's acceptance by other Arab moderates but saps the Egyptian-Israeli relationship of its vitality. There is no other issue that has the same potential to turn Egypt and Israel back to a position of belligerency.

Sympathy for Palestinian aspirations has been, as we have seen, a persistent current in Egypt since 1936, when a cross section of society pressed the Wafd government to support the Palestinians in their uprising against the British. Egypt's Islamic groups have been especially supportive of the

Palestinians, and Mubarak has no intention of ignoring those groups. He has on the contrary tried to draw them into the country's established political institutions, to the point that members of the Muslim Brotherhood now dominate the opposition in the People's Assembly.

Signposts on the Road
to Egypt's Arab Reintegration

As these broad changes were occurring in the Arabs' perception of their strategic interests, a number of specific developments in the Arab world helped pave the way for Egypt's return. Three signposts in particular pointed the way to the Amman summit and its decision that one Arab state's peace with Israel need not rule out good relations with the others.

The first event was Jordan's resumption of diplomatic relations with Egypt in September 1984. The move cost Jordan little. With the exception of Syria's response, there was hardly a ripple in the Arab world. The close relationship that developed between the two countries nudged the regional balance of power further toward the center. And because of Egyptian support, Hussein was able to pursue an independent policy on the peace process that was considerably ahead of the Arab consensus.

A second sign of growing self-confidence among the moderates was the decision by Morocco's King Hassan to meet with Israeli Prime Minister Shimon Peres in July 1986. The meeting was consistent with Hassan's longstanding, behind-the-scenes efforts to encourage an Arab-Israeli accommodation, but this time Morocco openly acknowledged its role. Syria was alone in breaking relations with Morocco.

The third signpost was Egypt's return to full membership in the Islamic Conference Organization at a summit held in Kuwait in January 1987. At the opening of the meeting, Syria challenged Egypt's participation but was overwhelmingly defeated. The large number of participants from Africa, where Egyptian diplomacy had been extremely active in the post–Camp David period, contributed to the pro-Egyptian atmosphere. Mubarak arrived early at the summit to consult with other heads of state and when it was over made a brief, but triumphal, tour of the Gulf.

Egypt's Arab Policies Under Mubarak

Mubarak's use of the Islamic summit to cement Egyptian bilateral relations was one example of Egypt's versatile diplomacy in the mid-1980s. If the goal of Egyptian diplomacy was the swift resumption of sound economic and political relations with the moderate Arabs, its style was to project a correct, aloof, almost detached public posture. It was a mix that encouraged the trend toward centrism already under way.

Beneath the surface, the policies of Mubarak and Sadat had much in common. They shared an assumption that the rest of the world had no choice but to follow Egypt's lead. But whereas Sadat nursed a sense of personal grievance that boiled over into public recrimination, Mubarak approached the differences with the Arabs with the dispassion and plain speaking that have marked his style on most issues.

Four more-or-less distinct lines of strategy are discernible in Egypt's pursuit of Arab reintegration.[7] First was the creation of special relationships with the countries critical to Egyptian objectives—Jordan, through strong support for Hussein's initiative for an international peace conference and cooperation in military and strategic matters; Saudi Arabia, through consultations on Gulf defense and outspoken support for the kingdom's handling of the July 1987 Iranian demonstrations in Mecca; and Iraq, through unqualified backing in the Gulf War and the provision of advisers for its army, manpower for its farms, and about $1 billion a year in arms sales for its military forces.

A second, related strand of Egyptian policy was the systematic development of a network of mutually beneficial relations with the great majority of Arab states, gradually isolating the handful that remained opposed to Egypt's reintegration. Egypt also toned down public criticism of its two main antagonists, Syria and Libya, although bilateral relations with both countries remained poor before the Amman summit.

The third element of strategy was to put Egypt squarely into the Arab mainstream on matters of Arab-wide importance. Vigorous support for the Gulf states against Iran was the most striking example. Also important, however, were Cairo's defense of the PLO leadership against attempts to divide the organization and diplomatic efforts throughout the mid-1980s to bring Jordan and the moderate Palestinians into the peace process.

The fourth ingredient was not so much a strategy as a facet of the Egyptian temperament. To a marked degree, national pride governed the making of foreign policy: Egypt consistently declined to apologize for Camp David or the peace treaty with Israel. Later, Mubarak's refusal to make the least concession in exchange for Egyptian participation in the Algiers summit was to slow the pace of reintegration. But Egypt returned to the Arab community with its obligations intact and its peace with Israel an accepted fact of international life.

Egypt's regional policies not only hastened its return to the Arab world but seemed to accord generally with popular attitudes. Certainly that was true of the tilt toward Iraq. It seems there has been little sympathy in Egypt for the Iranian revolution, except among the more radical Islamic fringe groups. Yet it would be wrong to assume that there was any inclination during the war to aid Iraq militarily. Opposition to the use of Egyptian armed force outside the country, except in the defense of vital national interests, has become a central element of Egyptian foreign policy and popular opinion. For the current generation of military leaders, in particular, Nasser's ineffectual intervention in Yemen was a formative experience, reinforcing the general aversion to fighting other peoples' battles for them and to undertaking military adventures outside the country.

If there is one point on which all Egyptians appear to agree, it is that the country's first priority is to build a healthy, prosperous society at home. It is because Mubarak's Arab policies are driven largely by practical economic and financial considerations that they appear to be widely accepted, even by much of the opposition. And the benefits have been tangible. From 1986 to 1989 Arab tourism to Egypt increased by more than one third; financial aid from Saudi Arabia and Kuwait again began to flow in substantial amounts; and some two million Egyptians working in other Arab countries continued to send home their remittances, amounting in 1987 to about $2 billion in hard-currency earnings. Despite falling oil revenues in the Gulf states, the anticipated forced return of large numbers of Egyptian workers did not occur, although there was a very substantial drop in new hiring.

The extraordinary network of economic and social connections that has developed between millions of Egyptian individuals and the Arab oil-producing states has changed the complexion of Egypt's Arab relations. Indeed, these links have brought to the Arab world a level of socioeconomic unity unprecedented in modern history.[8] As personal and business contacts have multiplied, the views of Egyptians about the appropriate political relationships between their country and other Arab states have naturally also evolved. The trend, as we shall see in the next chapter, has been toward greater acceptance of the differences in temperament and outlook between Egypt and the other Arabs and a desire for closer government-to-government relations. Although some of this sentiment stems from the increased economic and social linkages, some of it also comes from a renewed sense of identification with Arab-wide political causes. Since the early 1980s, when Israel invaded Lebanon and Iraq went to war with Iran, the two have gone hand in hand.

The days of an Egyptian mission to unite the Arab world or singlehandedly bring peace to the Middle East have passed. The government's pursuit of tangible national interests both reflects popular sentiment and reinforces it. Yet there is nothing isolationist about the current climate of opinion; Egypt's pragmatic self-interest is seen to include a leadership role that is commensurate with its weight in the region and its interest in a stable political and economic environment.

Dynamics at the Amman Summit

By November 1987, when the Arab leaders met in Amman, Cairo had through careful spadework developed reasonably good informal relationships with every Arab state except Syria, Libya, Democratic Yemen, and Algeria. The absence of formal diplomatic relations with most Arab countries as a result of the Baghdad decisions did not cramp the growth of busy Arab interest sections in Cairo or large Egyptian missions in the Arab capitals. Of the smaller Arab states, the Gulf sheikhdoms, led by the UAE, were the most active in seeking close ties with Egypt. The UAE was the first of the Arab oil producers to rejoin the Egypt-based weapons-manufacturing complex, the Arab Organization for Industrialization. The driving force behind Egypt's reintegration of the Amman summit was provided by Jordan, Saudi Arabia, and Iraq. As host Jordan played an especially critical role, both at the conference itself and during the months of preparation, when the broad lines of the decisions were negotiated. Jordan's support for Egypt followed three years of increasingly close cooperation; bilateral ties had come to span a broad range of activities, including a growing number of joint business ventures and trade links that gave depth to the relationship. From the Jordanian standpoint, the alliance with Egypt fulfilled a cardinal principle of balance-of power diplomacy: Of the four major eastern Arab powers (Egypt, Saudi Arabia, Syria, and Iraq) at least two, and if possible three, must be friendly to Jordan.

After Hussein withdrew from his constitutional role in the West Bank in July 1988, he and Mubarak continued to work together to moderate the positions of the PLO. The most conspicuous example was their joint meeting with Arafat before the Palestine National Council met in Algiers in fall 1988. Supported by Saudi Arabia and Iraq, the meeting strengthened the hand of PLO moderates before the PNC debate on Resolution 242 and the renunciation of terrorism. It was an example of the centrist Arab coalition in action.

The support of Saudi Arabia was less obvious than Jordan's activity but equally important to Egypt. Although careful to avoid outright confrontation with Syria and Lybia, the Saudis were in the forefront of the movement to overturn the Arab League's ban on diplomatic relations with Egypt. Saudi Arabia's active role at Amman (after several years of less than enthusiastic support for Egyptian reintegration) was the first sign of a resumption of the relatively dynamic Saudi diplomacy of 1976 and 1977. With its great wealth, political stability, and relative social cohesion, the Saudi potential for leadership in bringing the Arabs together is greater than ever. The kingdom's return to a position of major influence in Arab affairs manifested itself most clearly in the pivotal role it played in late 1989 in the difficult negotiation of an agreement on Lebanon.

Egypt's third important Arab relationship, with Iraq, has been most closely tied to the war in the Gulf and will undoubtedly continue to be affected by the extent to which Iraq sees itself threatened over the long term by Iran. If the Gulf cease-fire does not lead to verifiable arms limitations and the dispute between Iraq and Iran over navigation of the Shatt al-

Arab is not resolved, Baghdad will hesitate to alienate its conservative Arab supporters by reasserting its claims to Arab leadership. After eight years of fighting, the Iraqi regime may also be compelled by popular sentiment to concentrate on internal reconstruction and development. Having emerged from the war victorious and self-confident, with the largest and best-equipped army in the Arab world,[10] Iraq is nevertheless likely to remain deeply engaged in inter-Arab politics.

In the past few years Baghdad has moved away from total rejection of Israel.[11] Iraqi President Saddam Hussein's statements and the positions taken by Iraq at Arab meetings are close to predominant Arab policy favoring a negotiated settlement on the basis of the land-for-peace formulation in UN Security Council Resolution 242—although Iraq has not formally accepted that resolution. Saddam Hussein has made it clear that Iraq would not oppose any solution that the PLO accepted, including confederation with Jordan. Indeed, soon after the Palestinian uprising began, he and Mubarak met with Arafat in Baghdad for talks concerning the coordination of Palestinian policy. If Iraq continues to work with Egypt and Saudi Arabia to strengthen the mainstream elements of the PLO, the long-term prospects of the centrist coalition will improve.

Syria spearheaded the opposition to Egypt at the Amman summit, with Libya and Democratic Yemen in its train. Before the meeting, as Jordan tried to lay the foundation for an international peace conference, Syria contested Egypt's right to participate in such a conference.[12] In Amman Syria asserted that Egypt had forfeited its right to normal Arab relations by agreeing, in Article 6 of the peace treaty with Israel, to give its obligations under that treaty priority over its commitments under the Arab League covenant. (Egypt's supporters pointed out that the agreed minute interpreting Article 6 stated that the peace treaty did not prevail over other treaties or commitments.)[13] Although Syria finally acquiesced in the resolution lifting the Arab League injunction against diplomatic relations with Egypt, for the next eighteen months it continued to oppose any action that tended to legitimize the peace between Egypt and Israel.

The Algiers Summit and the Palestinian Uprising

In early June 1988, Arab heads of state met in Algiers to coordinate support for the Palestinian uprising. Because the conference was concerned with the issue that speaks most directly to Arab emotions, it provided a different perspective from the Amman summit, where the focus was on practical measures to counter a common threat.

To almost everyone's surprise, the Algerian hosts did not invite Egypt to the summit. Six months after Amman, Algeria was alone with Libya, Syria, and Lebanon (the latter following Syria's lead in foreign policy) in not having reestablished relations with Egypt. Algeria could not have relished the prospect of its summit serving as a launching pad for Egypt's return to the Arab League, yet Egypt's absence seems to have been less a matter of policy than of unwillingness by either country to make the least concession to the other.

Before the summit, the Algerians asked that Egyptian Foreign Minister Ismat Abdel Meguid pay a visit to Algiers, after which the two governments would announce the resumption of relations.[14] Egypt viewed the request as a condition to renewed relations and refused to consider it. Various efforts to break the impasse failed as neither party would bend. When the summit got under way, Mubarak flew to Baghdad to consult with Saddam Hussein on matters of Gulf security. If Egypt intended the trip as a message, it probably was not lost on the conferees in Algiers.

At the conference, the evolution of the power competition between centrists and militants came to light in two controversial questions: who should disburse financial aid to the insurgents and how the U.S. initiative for renewed negotiations for a Palestinian settlement should be treated. The PLO's apparent goals were to win Arab endorsement of its exclusive right to distribute funds and to obtain a commitment of $300 million to $400 million a year to sustain the uprising. King Hussein vigorously opposed Arafat's bid for power over the West Bank Palestinians. His case was helped by the main donors' desire to retain some control over how their aid was used and through whom it flowed. In the end the PLO was treated as one of several channels for the distribution of funds.[15] And to assure a continuing moderate voice in support of the uprising, a policy guidance committee was set up, comprising Algeria, Syria, the PLO, Jordan, Saudi Arabia, Qatar, and Bahrain, the last four constituting a majority.

Arafat reportedly mounted a major campaign to have the summit reject outright the U.S. peace proposal, which Secretary of State George Schultz had that same week been pressing in Israel, Jordan, and Syria. Clearly the PLO had concluded that the plan diminished its status by emphasizing the roles of Jordan and the indigenous Palestinians in the negotiating process, rather than treating the PLO as the Palestinians' sole legitimate representative. The summit criticized the U.S. initiative by inference, mildly in the communiqué, more harshly in the resolution. There was no consensus that the United States should disengage from the peace process; in fact the centrist states seemed to regard U.S. involvement as reinforcing their position, even if they disagreed with parts of the U.S. proposal.

Although the PLO did not attain its major objectives in Algiers, this by no means represented a lessening of its influence in the occupied territories. The summit reflected inter-Arab relationships and conference dynamics, not the state of relations between the PLO and the insurgents. In fact, by mid-1988 the PLO—helped by Israel's policy of deporting emerging leaders from the West Bank and Gaza—had already captured the allegiance of much of the indigenous leadership. This growing PLO influence in the West Bank led Hussein, a month after Algiers, to announce his withdrawal from active engagement in the search for a Palestinian settlement.

Moderates and hard-liners alike were brought together at the Algiers summit by a common sympathy for the Palestinian cause and for those struggling to advance it in the occupied territories. On the controversial issues, however, the moderates held their ground; the movement toward a centrist coalition appeared, if anything, to gain impetus from the conference. It seemed clear that the moderate Arabs were moving beyond the collective security requirements of the Gulf war to cooperation in other areas of common concern, including, as we shall see, the Middle East peace process.

11

Foreign Policy and the Search for National Identity

Sources of Change and Continuity

In a country as old and as rich in experience as Egypt, the relationship of the past to the present has more than the usual implications for national policy. Sadat addressed the issue in *The October Working Paper of 1974*, a declaration outlining the philosophical basis of his "Corrective Revolution":

> The real challenge confronting peoples with deep-rooted origins who are facing the problem of civilizational progress is precisely how to renovate their civilization. They should not reject the past in the name of the present and should not renounce the modern in the name of the past, but they should take of the new without losing sight of their origins.[1]

The passage was intended primarily as a criticism of Nasser's domestic policies—of the efforts during the 1960s to modernize the economy while neglecting the values, relationships, and institutions needed to turn the reforms into productive tools. But it was also an implicit criticism of Nasser's foreign policy. For if Nasser assumed that money could buy modernization, his foreign policy was designed to bring in the money—by thrusting Egypt to leadership among the Arabs and the nonaligned and then playing off East against West for the privilege of financing Egypt's economic development. By 1974 Sadat had concluded that the domestic and foreign policy failures of Nasser's last years stemmed in part from too close an alignment with socialist states whose values were at odds with Egypt's conservative traditions.

Both Nasser and Sadat devoted an unusual amount of their time and attention to foreign affairs. The paths that led to this emphasis were remarkably similar. Each began his administration with a period of about three years when sovereignty concerns were paramount: Nasser had to bring about the evacuation of the British, Sadat to set in motion the process of recovering the Sinai. Each devised a highly successful foreign policy to accomplish his objective, leading in both cases to wide popularity at home and the consolidation of power. These early triumphs had lasting consequences. Both men learned that they were good at foreign policy and that they liked it; indeed, in its coalitions and maneuvering between allies and enemies, international politics must have brought back the adventure of their conspiratorial youth. It is hardly surprising that both men gravitated to foreign affairs in the face of internal problems that offered no clear-cut victories.

President Mubarak, on the other hand, with no experience in the struggle for power and little taste for the world stage, adopted a pragmatic approach to foreign affairs that parted ways with both his predecessors. Mubarak, of course, faced a very different situation from theirs when he came to power. With the country's independence and territorial integrity secure, his only compelling foreign policy problem was to bring normalcy to Egypt's Arab relations. This problem did not lend itself to theatrics, and Mubarak was in any case well aware that Egyptians had had enough of the highly charged policies of the past thirty years. He seized the opportunity to break with the past. By developing a foreign policy that emphasized the change from earlier heroics, he fostered the legitimacy that stems from being seen as having a leadership style of one's own.

Neither Nasser nor Sadat, nor Mubarak after them, ever doubted that one object of Egyptian foreign policy must be to help provide a decent, humane life for their people in the face of limited resources and heavy population pressures. Nor did they question the need for substantial foreign assistance to achieve that goal; all three in fact explained their foreign policies partly in terms of the economic benefits to society. The need for outside assistance has been one of the main constants in Egyptian policy, as enduring in its way as the strategic imperatives that have shaped Egypt's regional relations. Yet equally important as a source of policy continuity has been the persistent effort to maintain independence from the regional and great-power patrons who have provided the aid.

Egypt has had its successes and its failures in this effort. The most conspicuous example of political linkage to foreign aid since the revolution was Nasser's abandonment of Egypt's "cold war" against the conservative Arabs in 1967 in return for reconstruction aid from the oil-producing states. After October 1973 Sadat also relied heavily on Gulf subsidies, but his foreign policy goals were largely congruent with those of the Arab monarchies. When strategy or tactics differed, he followed his own instincts. The nature of the relationship with the United States was often deceptive. At times Sadat deliberately magnified the extent of Egyptian dependence on the United States in order to generate in U.S. leaders a sense of indebtedness and commitment to the peace process. In the end Sadat failed to achieve the comprehensive peace he sought, yet he succeeded in fully engaging two U.S. administrations in the negotiations for a Middle East settlement—and that is what he set out to do.

Where sovereignty concerns were involved, Sadat drew a firm line. In 1980, for example, after the Soviet invasion of Afghanistan, Egypt and the United States discussed the possibility of U.S. military use of the Egyptian Red Sea base of Ras Banas in the event of a Soviet move into the gulf. Sadat promised to help the United States deter any Soviet attack that threatened the Arab countries of the region. At the same time, he refused to accord automatic rights of access to Ras Banas in the event of Soviet aggression: The opposition to extraterritorial rights is one of the most deep-seated strands of continuity in Egyptian policy, its roots grounded in centuries of foreign rule and the struggle with the British over sovereignty in the Suez Canal Zone.

The experiences of Egypt's last three presidents suggest strong forces at work for both change and continuity in Egyptian foreign policy. Contributing to change are the differing temperaments and backgrounds of Egypt's leaders, the need of each to establish his own political legitimacy, and the evolving power relationships and changing problems in the region. Even the "deep-rooted origins" that Sadat invokes—the cultural values and historic experiences Egyptians share—contribute not only to continuity but to change as well. For in Egypt history has often been used to justify different courses of action. When Sadat speaks of respecting the past, he means his particular vision of the past. The richness and diversity of Egypt's history also evoke other visions.

Recurring Patterns from the Past

In our brief look at pharaonic history, we saw how geography turned Egypt in upon itself and helped to create the most enduring, self-contained civilization in history. Some features of this highly distinctive culture disappeared after the Persian conquest, and many others died out later. In a few areas, however, the land and its early history continue to influence Egyptian attitudes and behavior. In foreign policy, as we have noted, Sadat's decision to go to Jerusalem followed a tradition of absolute authority whose roots lie in pharaonic administration. And in matters outside the ruler's immediate interest, the legacy of the heavy bureaucracy needed to extend the pharaoh's authority has contributed to policy continuity. But the historic pattern most important in shaping the nation's identity and spirit has been the alternating pull on Egyptian loyalties of the Nile, the Mediterranean basin, and Asia. This pattern has had significant consequences for Egypt's relations with the Arabs.

The Nile has always been the symbol of Egyptianness, standing for the uniqueness of the civilization and coloring the attitudes of Egyptians toward their neighbors. For nearly 3,000 years the Nile valley was Egypt; protected by geography from conquest and lasting foreign influence, Egyptians had no need for outside support and no reason to relate to any alien people except as conqueror. The tension began with the Mediterranean orientation imposed by Persia and maintained by Greece, Rome, and Byzantium. A small number of Egyptians benefited from the wars and the trade and came to equate their interests with those of the maritime empires. Those living inland along the river could have had scant sense of national community. They nevertheless seem to have recognized the Mediterranean civilizations as alien to theirs and to have rejected them.

From Asia the Arabs brought a religion and an all-embracing social code that for the first time led Egyptians to identify with the people and culture of the East. Unlike the religion of the pharaohs, Islam sank deep roots into the masses. It shared with pharaonic culture a vision of the world divided between regions of revealed wisdom and of unenlightenment, *dar al-Islam* and *dar al-harb*. The Islamic belief-system brought Egypt great learning and the benefits of political and social cohesion. But because its norms were grounded in revelation, a new cycle of tension inevitably followed in the nineteenth century upon the collision with rationally grounded science, technology, and political organization. By the early twentieth century many educated Egyptians had come to believe that the religious precepts of Islam were one thing, the political and economic principles needed to run an effective, progressive state a different matter entirely.

As Egyptian nationalists came to see Western democracy as the path to independence and a liberated society, it became necessary to plant the new ideas in Egyptian soil. One solution was to reach back behind Islam to Egypt's other distinctive culture under the pharaohs. Ahmad Lutfi al-Sayyid was the main proponent of the notion that during its first three millennia Egypt had developed a "pharaonic core," an identity so unique and so right for Egypt that it could not be altered even by extensive borrowing from the West.[2]

To many Western-oriented intellectuals who sought an alternative to Asia and Islam, the ancient culture of the Nile was not a realistic answer for the twentieth century. In the late 1930s Taha Hussein gave a new turn to Lutfi al-Sayyid's theory. He argued that the essential Egyptian spirit that had evolved before Islam was Mediterranean, as rational and open to new ideas as the post-Enlightenment Western mind.[3] In view of Egypt's traditional inward orientation, it may seem curious to link the Egyptian spirit to Mediterranean culture, but the theory reflects a psychological truth about the way Egyptians perceive their identity as a nation. To some Egyptians— at certain times in history—the Mediterranean has seemed more relevant to Egypt's needs and values than has Asia.

The Mediterranean orientation reached its height during the Sadat regime. As an eminent Arab scholar put it, "The old dream of turning Egypt into a piece of Europe that had tantalized some Egyptians came to be revived in Sadat's Egypt."[4] In 1972 Tawfic al-Hakim published a critique of Nasserist policy, *The Return of Consciousness*, in which he argued that the time had come for Egypt to stop fighting the Arabs' battles and return to its Mediterranean roots.[5] Writers like Nagib Mahfouz, Anis Mansour, and Hussein Fawzi contended that Egypt's civilization was not only older than that of the Arabs but "more attached to Greco-Roman traditions than Arab-Islamic values—in short, Egypt [was] part of Europe and Western civilization."[6] Even at the height of Sadat's popularity, however, this evocation of the Mediterranean past seems to have had less appeal to most Egyptian intellectuals than did Arab nationalism.

In Mubarak's Egypt, as we have seen, popular attitudes and foreign policy alike have moved toward an increased sense of identification with the interests of other Arabs. The new Arabism, however, is of a remarkably nonideological kind. For if many Egyptians favor greater Arab solidarity,[7] the unity that they have in mind is for the most part linked closely to Egyptian economic and political interests. The approach extends to much of the Arab world. Not only has it transformed Arab nationalism but it has deeply affected the other ideologies that propelled Arab politics not long ago. Let us look briefly at these changes and consider their implications for the foreign policies of Egypt and the Arabs.

The Eclipse of Ideology

Pan-Arabism

The passing of ideology as a driving force in Arab foreign relations has been apparent for more than a decade. Pan-Arabism, Ba'athism—even pan-Islam in the midst of an Islamic religious revival—have not only ceased to shape foreign policy but have lost even their mythic function of justifying policies based on state or personal power. Nationalism alone remains, and for most Arab countries it is increasingly a pragmatic, economically oriented nationalism without much sentimental overlay.

Contemporary Arab attitudes toward pan-Arabism are instructive. If Arab unity is dead as a serious political objective—and there is no doubt that it is—there is nevertheless more real interest in policy coordination, among a broader spectrum of Arab countries, than there was at the height of pan-Arab fervor. This is partly because Arab solidarity no longer necessarily means doing things Egypt's way. A leveling of the main components of power in the last two decades has fostered cooperation. The huge growth in oil revenues in what had been the poorer Arab states led to a leap forward in literacy, higher education, and governmental and diplomatic expertise. And while this was going on, Egypt increasingly turned inward, striving to break out of the vise of burgeoning population and limited irrigable land. There has never been a question of Egypt's bowing out of Arab politics; it could hardly do so if it wished. Yet it is not the regional colossus it once was, attracting or repelling its neighbors by sheer weight and dynamism. The door has opened to a search for common ground among partners, based on realism and mutual self-interest.

In Egypt pan-Arabism lives on in the vision of Nasser as the voice of all Arabs and protector of the dispossessed. If only as a dream of what might have been, it grows brighter as the years pass, especially to the masses. And although pan-Arabism has long ceased to have a practical effect on Egyptian foreign policy, it is still publicly proclaimed as a long-term objective.

The resurrection of Nasser's reputation can be seen in the recent formation of two active Nasserist groups, the Alliance of the People's Working Forces party and the Nasserist Arab Socialist party, both of which have begun the process of securing government approval to compete in elections.[8] Populist and left-wing, they attract people who are repelled by the atheism of the traditional left. The Cairo press has been joined by a Nasserist weekly, *The Voice of the Arabs*. Despite its name, its message is based on a mix of Nasserist economic socialism and anti-Westernism rather than on any serious program for Arab unity.

For many thoughtful Egyptians, some form of partial integration persists as a realistic long-term goal for countries with economies as complementary as those of the Arabs. Egypt's growing ties with its neighbors are seen as building blocks that could lead to association into larger economic units and perhaps, over time and with careful preparation, to political federation. As a former Egyptian foreign minister put it, "Where there is capital in the Middle East, there's no know-how, and where there is know-how, as in Egypt, there's no capital. The real hope of the region is a marriage of the two—not for ideological, but for practical, reasons."[9]

Other Egyptians maintain that a compelling reason for Arab integration is the imbalance in demographics and resource distribution between Egypt and its immediate neighbors. Libya and Sudan have the irrigable land, Egypt the people to farm it; whatever the obvious obstacles to close political association, some sort of economic federation among the three states seems to make sense. Moreover, as growing numbers of landless *fellahin* pour into the already overcrowded Egyptian cities, finding them work becomes as critically important to the social and political health of the country as to its economic prosperity. One safety valve already in place is the migration of farm labor to the region's other great river valley: Hundreds of thousands of Egyptian farmers now work the fields of Iraq.

The pragmatic drift of Egyptian thinking is evident not only in the remaking of Nasserism but in changing attitudes toward Sadat and his policies. If there is little desire to return to Nasser's pan-Arab activism, neither is there much bitterness left toward Sadat's pursuit of Egyptian interests at the expense of Arab solidarity—except, still, from the extreme left and the religious right. One frequently hears the observation in Cairo that although it is too soon to judge Sadat's place in history, Egyptian grievances against him had more to do with his actions at home than his foreign policies. The desire to become the center of Arab action again is great; but few would trade for it a return to the time when Israel occupied the Sinai and war seemed the only way to get it back.

Pan-Islam

What happened to the secular ideology of pan-Arabism has also happened to pan-Islam. A unifying force throughout much of Arab history, Islam today keeps the Arab and Islamic states apart more than it pulls them together. Iranian expansionism has of course been a major centrifugal force, widening the historic breach between Sunni and Shi'ite Islam. But the eclipse of pan-Islamic ideology occurred before the Iranian revolution. Most striking now is that, as the fundamentalist wave gathers force and threatens to engulf a number of Arab governments, no active pan-Islamic movement aims to break down the barriers among Arab and Islamic states.

One reason for the absence of such a movement is that nowhere in the Arab world are the clerics in power. Even in opposition, however, the *ulama* and the lay Islamic groups are not normally hesitant to express their views, yet few have called for serious steps toward Islamic unity. A number of characteristics of contemporary Islam explain their diffidence. First is the difficulty of reconciling the different Islamic styles and points of view that exist from one Arab country to another. It is as hard to imagine the Wahabi clerics of Saudi Arabia forming a government with the Egyptian divines of al-Azhar as it is to envision a harmonious coalition of born-again Baptists and Anglo-Catholics. Similarly divisive are the competing interests and rivalries among national Islamic organizations—the Egyptian and Syrian branches of the Muslim Brotherhood being a notable example.[10] Finally, because Islam has for so long been used by Arab governments to further their secular interests, the clerics have become wary of efforts to involve them in cooperative enterprises with other Islamic nations.

If there is no serious movement toward pan-Islamic unity, the religious revival nevertheless affects Arab relations in other ways. Often the impact is subtle and indirect, submerged in the overall worldview of people who are both Muslim and Arab. The strands of Arabism, Islam, and patriotism are in fact so interwoven in the national consciousness that frequently no one of them can be separated out as *the* motive for a particular foreign policy. In Egypt the place of Islam has been central to the question of Egyptian identity: Was one a Muslim first, then an Arab, and then an Egyptian, or did the claims of one identity rule out the others? Most Egyptians think of themselves as all three, and see nothing unreasonable in doing so.

One indirect way in which Islam affects Arab foreign policy is in its impact on policies toward the Palestinians. For the devout, the expulsion of Muslims from Palestine by nonbelievers from the West is a repetition of the Crusades, a humiliation that calls not only for Arab solidarity but for religious retribution. The intensity of this commitment to the Palestinians, reiterated in sermons and Islamic books and periodicals, cannot help but influence the views of Arab policymakers.

For regimes whose main internal opposition comes from the religious right (as in Egypt, Syria, Algeria, and Tunisia), the Islamic approach to the Palestinian problem has a more direct impact. In Syria, for example, the fundamentalist uprising of the late 1970s was partly a reaction to the regime's fierce attacks on the PLO in Lebanon; the government, responding to Islamic protests, drew dack from its confrontation with the Palestinians.

Ba'athism

Of all the ideologies that have shaped Arab foreign policies, Ba'athism has come the closest to being completely eclipsed. For twenty years, beginning with the 1958 Egyptian-Syrian merger and ending with the abortive federation between Syria and Iraq, Ba'athism was a driving force in inter-Arab relations. Its commitment to the destruction of the artificial borders the West had imposed on the Arab world after World War I was for many Arabs, especially those in the Fertile Crescent, a blueprint for action. Today the institution of the Ba'ath party remains, but the ideology has become a tool for mobilizing mass opinion and preserving the status quo.

In Iraq, even before the war with Iran, the subordination of Ba'athist ideology to the interests of the state was well under way.[11] The war accelerated the process. One casualty was the Ba'athist practice of choosing allies according to their political principles—a taste that could no longer be indulged in light of the need for financial help from the Gulf Arabs. At the beginning of the war the pan-Arab component of Ba'athism provided a means of assailing Syria for siding with Iran against the interests of the Arab nation. Later, the simple need to preserve the state became the dominant propaganda theme.

In Syria, as in Iraq, the decline of Ba'athist ideology paralleled a growing attention to more traditional state interests. Three developments contributed to the change in Syrian priorities. First, President Assad came to power with a down-to-earth approach to foreign affairs that focused on achieving a reasonable fit between goals and capabilities—at least in operative policy, if not in rhetoric.[12] Assad's contempt for ideologically based policy stemmed in part from his experience as defense minister during the June war, when the Ba'athists propelled Syria into a conflict it could not win. Second was the changing dynamic of inter-Arab relations. After Nasser's humiliation in 1967 and his death three years later, no Arab state remained with both the interest in Arab unity and the weight to move toward its achievement.

Finally, in Syria as elsewhere in the Arab world, a new generation that finds the old belief systems inappropriate to its problems has reached maturity. Concerned with the hard realities of state-building, this generation has psychological needs that are no longer met by the old political ideologies. Nor are its members obsessed with the problems of the past. After nearly seventy years they have become used to living in the ministates carved out of the eastern Arab world; indeed, they have a stake now in their preservation. As the injusticies that followed the breakup of the Ottoman Empire have merged with the others of history, so the frustration has passed away that was the driving force behind Ba'athism.

The growing irrelevance of the secular ideologies of the past has practical implications for the Middle East negotiating process. No longer are the centrist Arab states forced to posture for the benefit of powerful, ideologically driven constituencies in their own and other countries. As the quarrel with Israel has come to focus on territory rather than legitimacy, the balance of power in the Arab world has passed to the countries that are committed to bringing about a territorial settlement. Increasingly, the rejectionist minority is being forced to choose between a fair balance of Palestinian, Israeli, and Arab state interests and a future of growing isolation and irrelevance.

12

Arab Politics
and the Peace Process

Everything that has happened since Israel signed armistice agreements with its Arab neighbors in 1949 bears out the judgment that a durable Middle East peace depends on territorial compromise. Indeed, the chances for successful negotiations can be measured largely by the willingness of both sides to give up their claims to all of the land in dispute that stem from legitimacy and ideology. Using this benchmark, let us consider the implications for the peace process of the recent developments and trends in inter-Arab politics.

As efforts to revive the negotiating process move ahead, Arab policy seems likely to be determined mainly by four sets of relationships: first, the relations of the most involved Arab states with each other and with the PLO; second, the interaction between the PLO and the Arabs of the West Bank and Gaza; third, the attitudes of the Arabs toward Israel and its policies, whether through direct diplomatic communication (as in Egypt's case) or indirectly through third parties; and, finally, the relations of the PLO and the key Arab nations with the major powers (principally, for the sake of this analysis, the United States).

New Elements in Inter-Arab Dynamics

The situation today is similar in many respects to that of the failed negotiations for a peace conference in 1977, but three developments have occurred since then that change the dynamics and prospects of the next round. The first is Egypt's peace with Israel, with its impact on Arab power, attitudes, and diplomatic strategy; the second is the Palestinian uprising and, related to it, the PLO's acceptance of UN Security Council Resolution 242 in December 1988; and the third is the increased power and centrality of the moderate Arab States.

In the mixed legacy of Camp David, the dominant fact, we have argued, is the durability of the peace between Egypt and Israel and the recognition by Arabs of every persuasion that the peace treaty is a permanent part of the Middle East scene. That recognition is a psychological watershed; it has helped to shift the Arab center of gravity toward acceptance of a negotiated settlement assuring Israel's right to exist in the region in peace and security.

Militarily, the peace treaty has had far-reaching consequences for both sides. For the Arabs, it has meant that war as it was once waged against Israel is no longer a realistic option, any more than the threat of force to achieve political ends is a credible posture. For Israel, peace with Egypt has meant that Israel's military security has been greatly enhanced, not only because it need no longer fear a two-front war but because its right to exist within secure boundaries has ceased to be a matter of dispute among Arabs of weight and authority. The policy implications are apparent. As the threat to security recedes, the advantages to Israel of a settlement that trades military occupation for peace and an end to the festering grievances of its neighbors grow in proportion.[1] This assumes, of course, that the object of Israeli policy is security rather than territorial expansion or fulfillment of the claims of religion and ideology.

The second principal change in the negotiating scene, the PLO's acceptance of Resolution 242, was largely the result of efforts by the centrist Arab powers to moderate PLO policy and bring the organization into the negotiating process. In 1977 Egypt and Saudi Arabia, with U.S. encouragement, had made a major effort to persuade the PLO to accept 242, but they were frustrated in the end by Syria and the radical Palestinian groups. Eleven years later the main protagonists were the same. Egypt and Saudi Arabia put heavy pressure on Arafat to renounce terrorism and respect Israel's right to live in peace; at the same time they urged the United States to open a dialogue with the PLO. Syria, which had earlier pressed the PLO not to declare an independent Palestinian state (with its implication of sharing the territory of mandated Palestine with Israel),[2] failed in that effort as well as in blocking the PLO's acceptance of the UN resolution. The one active new player on the scene, Iraq, used its influence to support Arafat against the PLO militants.

A critical new element in the situation was the PLO's need to show the West Bank and Gaza Arabs that it could act as a viable representative for them in negotiations. Yet if the impact of the *intifadah* on Palestinian dynamics was one important change from 1977, the other was the increased power of the bloc of centrist Arab states on the issue where the lines were most clearly drawn, that of PLO acceptance of Resolution 242, and, with it, the principle of territorial compromise.

At the Arab summit in Casablanca in May 1989, Egypt was formally readmitted to the Arab League, and within months Cairo recovered its traditional leadership position. The radical members of the league have had to scramble for respectability. Libya and Syria have sought to reestablish diplomatic relations with Egypt and by March 1990 appeared on the verge of doing so.

A price may have been attached. Qadhafi has reportedly confined to base the Palestinian terrorist group of Abu Nidal, and Assad has toned down his attacks on Arafat. Nowhere has the influence of the moderate Arabs been so evident as in Egypt's emerging role in the effort to bring Israel and the Palestinians to the negotiating table. In August 1989, as Israel appeared to back away from its proposal for elections on the West Bank and Gaza, Egypt advanced a simple five-point plan that has remained the centerpiece of discussion. With its lines to Israel, the PLO, and the United States, Egypt is well placed to assume the critical task of building bridges among the parties.

Not only in the peace process but also in bilateral and regional affairs, common interests have continued to draw the moderates together. The most conspicuous example of cooperative action carrying over from the Gulf war is the new economic association of Egypt, Iraq, Jordan, and North Yemen, signed into being in February 1989. Known as the Arab Cooperation Council (ACC), the association hopes to remove trade barriers and encourage investment among the four nations. It follows an emerging pattern of regional relationships, such as the Gulf Cooperation Council made up of Saudi Arabia and its neighbors, and the Arab Maghreb Union of the North African Arab states. The ACC has been active during its first year, sponsoring at least a dozen agreements ranging from simplified visa requirements to expanded airline flights. Politically, the association is significant for the one country in the region that does not belong—Syria—as much as for the four that do. Egypt and Jordan have played down the importance of Syria's exclusion, Cairo maintaining that the door is open to Syria and South Yemen and, when conditions permit, to Lebanon and Sudan.[3]

Syria and the War in Lebanon

If Egypt's public statements about Syria have softened, its opposition to Syria's involvement in Lebanon has not. At the May 1989 Arab summit, Cairo sought to achieve a consensus on the replacement of Syrian troops in Lebanon with an Arab peacekeeping force. The effort failed, partly because the delegates' first concern was to block Syrian efforts to condemn the PLO's conciliatory moves toward Israel. It also appears that neither Egypt nor anyone else involved in the peace process wanted a confrontation with Damascus so divisive as to jeopardize the chances of progress toward a settlement.

Indeed, the war in Lebanon has great potential for disruption. Within weeks of its announcement, one of the last serious plans for settling the Palestinian issue, the Reagan initiative of September 1, 1982, was pushed aside by the assassination of Bashir Gemayel, the horrors of Sabra and Shatila, and the subsequent urgent U.S. efforts to work out an agreement for the withdrawal of Israeli and Syrian forces. The escalation brought about by Iraq's arming of the Lebanese Christian forces under Michel Aoun has made the conflict even more unpredictable and threatening to the peace process.

One of the few hopeful signs in the Lebanese tragedy has been the agreement of Lebanese parliamentarians on a new constitution increasing the governmental power of Lebanon's Muslims to reflect changes in the demographic balance. Signed at Taif on October 24, 1989, the accord acknowledged, but somewhat restricted, Syria's role in Lebanese affairs. The result of active Saudi mediation, the accord dramatized the kingdom's return to its traditional role of Arab conciliator.

The *Intifadah,* the Arabs, and Israel

Syria's relationship with the radical Palestinian groups continues to be an important and potentially disruptive part of the inter-Arab dynamic. Although the objectives of Damascus and the Palestinian radicals differ (the return of the Golan Heights for the one, the return of all Palestine for the other), the two have in the past joined forces in opposing plans that have tried to leave them both out. The new element in the equation is the insistence of the Palestinians inside the occupied territories that those outside adopt realistic positions if they want to be part of the negotiating process. That is powerful leverage, influencing not only the PLO mainstream but the radical factions, which have their own constituencies to accommodate in the West Bank and Gaza.

The *intifadah* has forced others beside the PLO and Syria to rethink their positions. In focusing attention on the Palestinian dimension of the Arab-Israeli dispute, it has cleared the air of illusions that Jordan or anyone other than the Palestinians themselves can negotiate Palestinian issues. It has opened possibilities to a powerful coalition between the centrist Arab states and the PLO. And in Israel, as the costs of occupation become increasingly apparent, it has brought growing recognition that a political settlement is essential to the country's health and security.

Changing Israeli attitudes and positions on the nature of a settlement fix the boundaries of Arab policy. When Israel has seemed ready to join negotiations that could lead to the return of territory, as in 1974 and 1977, the Arab confrontation states and the PLO have taken steps toward negotiations that, however modest, offended powerful constituencies. When Israel has rejected such negotiations, and little reason remained for Arab leaders to risk their credibility or the unity of party or nation, the result has been a drift toward militancy.

In appraising Israeli policy, the Arabs of course listen to the public pronouncements, but they also watch the politics of the country. They hear Prime Minister Yitzhak Shamir's repeated statements that giving up land is foreign to his vocabulary. But they also see an electorate that polls show is increasingly willing to consider the exchange of occupied territory on all fronts for peace. They know from experience that Israeli governments find it good politics to stand up to outside pressure. But they also know that there are limits, and that it is very bad politics indeed to jeopardize the support vital to the nation's security.

Policy Implications for the United States

The first and most fundamental question that any administration faces in shaping its Middle East policy is how actively to engage itself in the search for a settlement. The issue is partly one of philosophy. Many believe that the parties to a dispute should, as a matter of principle, be left largely to solve their problems on their own. An outside power can perhaps facilitate communications and create a better climate for negotiations. But only the parties can negotiate an agreement, and it is useless to press them to do so until they have decided that the costs of trying to reach a settlement are less than those of living without one.

Another school, however, points out that, in the Middle East at least, leaving the parties to themselves has led historically to radicalization and war. Only when the United States has deeply engaged itself in the process has there been serious progress. The result, for better or worse, is that both sides have come to rely on the United States to take the initiative in starting negotiations and to be a partner in them once begun. In any event, the activists continue, the United States has such a fundamental interest in a peaceful settlement that it has no option but to try to serve as a catalyst to agreement.

No government wants to waste its capital on efforts that seem bound to fail because of the distance between the parties' positions. Yet considerations other than merely the short-term prospects for agreement affect the decision on the level of diplomatic engagement. Are the politics of the region, for example, likely to become more, or less, favorable to negotiations? Could active U.S. involvement change the equation? And how dangerous would the situation be if left to itself, now and ten years from now?

If there is one recurring theme in inter-Arab politics, it is volatility and change. And although the main currents in Arab attitudes and power alignments have been toward the center, there is no assurance that this favorable climate for negotiations will last. The Palestinian uprising is the single most powerful catalyst for change. It has imposed on the Palestinian movement as a whole its pragmatic interest in a settlement based on territorial compromise, but it also has the potential of returning the region to war. There is little reason to believe that the uprising will diminish as a political force in the absence of movement toward a settlement, though Israeli military and economic pressures have unquestionably taken a toll. The self-confidence of the insurgents and the conviction that they are winning; the demographics of the territories, with permanent control of the movement apparently in the hands of young people who find their identity in sacrifice and struggle; the grinding poverty, especially in Gaza, and the constricting opportunities to work abroad; and the coalition form of leadership, comprising militant Islamic groups and radical PLO factions as well as mainstream Palestinian elements—all point toward a turn to the use of increased force in the face of political stagnation.

What can be expected of the Arab states if the violence escalates, with the inevitable incidents involving excessive force and the equally inevitable reprisals? Certainly Egypt and Saudi Arabia would use their influence with the PLO to try to prevent the situation from getting out of hand. But Arafat's ability to hold the organization on its course of negotiation depends on two things, both of which would be absent: the movement toward a political settlement that gives his policies credibility and the pressures for compromise from within the territories that give him leverage over the radical factions. Should the moves to prevent further deterioration fail despite the efforts of the centrist Arabs, the forces at work would be similar to those preceding the four major wars between Israel and the Arabs.

In these circumstances, it would be rash to predict the actions of Egypt and the other centrist states. Perhaps the best that can be done is to recall some incidents of recent history. In 1971 Sadat called for the conclusion of peace with Israel, but the United States decided that he did not mean a binding peace and that the pressures should be allowed to grow. In the summer of 1973 Egypt asked the UN Security Council to draw up principles for a peaceful settlement as a last alternative to the recovery of its territory by force, but the United States assumed it was bluffing and vetoed the resolution. Three months later, Egypt and Syria went to war after years of preparation, without giving the United States or Israel the least advance warning. Today Egypt has its land back, a peace treaty with Israel is in force, and Egyptians want nothing more than to get on with the development of their country. Nevertheless, the experience of the recent past suggests caution in assuming a peaceful future for the Middle East as long as issues of self-determination and the return of territory are at stake.

One reason for believing that time is on no one's side is the proliferation in the region of weapons of mass destruction and their delivery systems. As Iraq expands its arsenal of chemical weapons and hardens its nuclear facilities; as Libya reportedly begins production of mustard and nerve gas at its desert complex near Rabta; as Saudi Arabia buys ballistic missiles from China and other sources of missiles multiply, Israel worries about threats to its security from the Golan Heights and from a Palestinian entity so small and so poor that it would have all it could do to survive. There are powerful historical reasons why Israel—or at least some Israelis—can look at the world in this fashion. The United States, however, cannot afford to do so. No other dispute has a greater potential for escalation into nuclear conflict and no other dispute has been harder for the superpowers to stay out of when it erupts into war. The argument for activism rests finally on the U.S. national interest.

If the last four decades have shown that the substance of a solution lies in territorial compromise, those years have also provided guides to diplomatic style and process. Consistency, staying power, and a readiness by the United States to use its influence with both sides have marked the successful diplomatic efforts of the past. Most important of all has been the demonstration, in words and in action, that the United States is determined to see the conflict through to a just and permanent peace.

United Nations Security Council Resolutions 242 and 338

U.N. RESOLUTION 242, NOVEMBER 22, 1967

The Security Council,

Expressing its continuing concern with the grave situation in the Middle East,

Emphasizing the inadmissibility of the acquisition of territory by war and the need to work for a just and lasting peace in which every State in the area can live in security,

Emphasizing further that all Member States in their acceptance of the Charter of the United Nations have undertaken a commitment to act in accordance with Article 2 of the Charter.

1. *Affirms* that the fulfillment of Charter principles requires the establishment of a just and lasting peace in the Middle East which should include the application of both the following principles:

(i) Withdrawal of Israeli armed forces from territories occupied in the recent conflict;

(ii) Termination of all claims or stages of belligerency and respect for and acknowledgement of the sovereignty, territorial integrity and political independence of every State in the area and their right to live in peace within secure and recognized boundaries free from threats or acts of force;

2. *Affirms further* the necessity:

(a) For guaranteeing freedom of navigation through international waterways in the area;

(b) For achieving a just settlement of the refugee problem;

(c) For guaranteeing the territorial inviolability and political independence of every State in the area, through measures including the establishment of demilitarized zones;

3. *Requests* the Secretary-General to designate a Special Representative to proceed to the Middle East to establish and maintain contacts with the States concerned in order to promote agreement

and assist efforts to achieve a peaceful and accepted settlement in accordance with the provisions and principles of this resolution;

4. *Requests* the Secretary-General to report to the Security Council on the progress of the efforts of the Special Representative as soon as possible.

U.N. RESOLUTION 338, OCTOBER 22, 1973

The Security Council

1. *Calls upon* all parties to the present fighting to cease all firing and terminate all military activity immediately, no later than 12 hours after the moment of the adoption of this decision, in the positions they now occupy;

2. *Calls upon* the parties concerned to start immediately after the cease-fire the implementation of Security Council Resolution 242 (1967) in all of its parts;

3. *Decides that,* immediately and concurrently with the cease-fire, negotiations shall start between the parties concerned under appropriate auspices aimed at establishing a just and durable peace in the Middle East.

President Anwar Sadat's Address
to the Israeli Knesset, November 20, 1977

In the name of God, Mr. Speaker of the Knesset, ladies and gentlemen, allow me first to thank deeply the Speaker of the Knesset for affording me this opportunity to address you. . . .

I come to you today on solid ground to shape a new life and to establish peace. We all love this land, the land of God, we all, Moslems, Christians and Jews, all worship God. . . .

I do not blame all those who received my decision when I announced it to the entire world before the Egyptian People's Assembly. I do not blame all those who received my decision with surprise and even with amazement, some gripped even by violent surprise. Still others interpreted it as political, to camouflage my intentions of launching a new war.

I would go so far as to tell you that one of my aides at the presidential office contacted me at a late hour following my return home from the People's Assembly and sounded worried as he asked me: "Mr. President, what would be our reaction if Israel actually extended an invitation to you?"

I replied calmly: "I would accept it immediately. I have declared that I would go to the end of the earth. I would go to Israel, for I want to put before the people of Israel all the facts. . . ." No one could have ever conceived that the president of the biggest Arab state, which bears the heaviest burden and the main responsibility pertaining to the cause of war and peace in the Middle East, should declare his readiness to go to the land of the adversary while we were still in a state of war.

We all still bear the consequences of four fierce wars waged within 30 years. All this at the time when the families of the 1973 October war are still mourning under the cruel pain of bereavement of father, son, husband and brother.

As I have already declared, I have not consulted as far as this decision

The text has been slightly edited from the version published in the *New York Times*, November 21, 1977.

133

is concerned with any of my colleagues or brothers, the Arab heads of state or the confrontation states.

Most of those who contacted me following the declaration of this decision expressed their objection because of the feeling of utter suspicion and absolute lack of confidence between the Arab states and the Palestine people on the one hand and Israel on the other that still surges in us all.

Many months in which peace could have been brought about have been wasted over differences and fruitless discussions on the procedure of convening the Geneva conference. All have shared suspicion and absolute lack of confidence.

But to be absolutely frank with you, I took this decision after long thought, knowing that it constitutes a great risk, for God Almighty has made it my fate to assume responsibility on behalf of the Egyptian people, to share in the responsibility of the Arab nation, the main duty of which, dictated by responsibility, is to exploit all and every means in a bid to save my Egyptian Arab people and the pan-Arab nation from the horrors of new suffering and destructive wars, the dimensions of which are foreseen only by God Himself.

After long thinking, I was convinced that the obligation of responsibility before God and before the people make it incumbent upon me that I should go to the far corners of the world, even to Jerusalem to address members of the Knesset and acquaint them with all the facts surging in me, then I would let you decide for yourselves. . . .

Ladies and gentlemen, there are moments in the lives of nations and peoples when it is incumbent upon those known for their wisdom and clarity of vision to survey the problem, with all its complexities and vain memories, in a bold drive towards new horizons.

Those who like us are shouldering the same responsibilities entrusted to us are the first who should have the courage to make determining decisions that are consonant with the magnitude of the circumstances. We must all rise above all forms of obsolete theories of superiority, and the most important thing is never to forget that infallibility is the prerogative of God alone.

If I said that I wanted to avert from all the Arab people the horrors of shocking and destructive wars I must sincerely declare before you that I have the same feelings and bear the same responsibility towards all and every man on earth, and certainly towards the Israeli people.

Any life that is lost in war is a human life be it that of an Arab or an

Israeli. A wife who becomes a widow is a human being entitled to a happy family life, whether she be an Arab or an Israeli.

Innocent children who are deprived of the care and compassion of their parents are ours. They are ours, be they living on Arab or Israeli land.

They command our full responsibility to afford them a comfortable life today and tomorrow.

For the sake of them all, for the sake of the lives of all our sons and brothers, for the sake of affording our communities the opportunity to work for the progress and happiness of man, feeling secure and with the right to a dignified life, for the generations to come, for a smile on the face of every child born in our land, for all that I have taken my decision to come to you, despite all the hazards, to deliver my address.

I have shouldered the prerequisites of the historic responsibility and therefore I declared on Feb. 4, 1971, that I was willing to sign a peace agreement with Israel. This was the first declaration made by a responsible Arab official since the outbreak of the Arab-Israeli conflict. Motivated by all these factors dictated by the responsibilities of leadership, on Oct. 16, 1973, before the Egyptian People's Assembly, I called for an international conference to establish permanent peace based on justice. I was not heard.

I was in the position of a man pleading for peace or asking for a cease-fire. Motivated by the duties of history and leadership, I signed the first disengagement agreement, followed by the second disengagement agreement at Sinai.

Then we proceeded, trying both open and closed doors in a bid to find a certain road leading to a durable and just peace.

We opened our heart to the peoples of the entire world to make them understand our motivations and objectives and actually to convince them of the fact that we are advocates of justice and peacemakers. Motivated by all these factors, I also decided to come to you with an open mind and an open heart and with a conscious determination so that we might establish permanent peace based on justice. . . .

Ladies and gentlemen, let us be frank with each other. Using straightforward words and a clear conception with no ambiguity, let us be frank with each other today while the entire world, both East and West, follows these unparalleled moments, which could prove to be a radical turning point in the history of this part of the world if not in the history of the world as a whole.

Let us be frank with each other, let us be frank with each other as we answer this important question.

How can we achieve permanent peace based on justice? Well, I have come to you carrying my clear and frank answer to this big question, so that the people in Israel as well as the entire world may hear it. . . .

Before I proclaim my answer, I wish to assure you that in my clear and frank answer I am availing myself of a number of facts that no one can deny.

The first fact is that no one can build his happiness at the expense of the misery of others.

The second fact: never have I spoken, nor will I ever speak, with two tongues; never have I adopted, nor will I ever adopt, two policies. I never deal with anyone except in one tongue, one policy and with one face.

The third fact: direct confrontation is the nearest and most successful method to reach a clear objective.

The fourth fact: the call for permanent and just peace based on respect for United Nations resolutions has now become the call of the entire world. It has become the expression of the will of the international community, whether in official capitals where policies are made and decisions taken, or at the level of the world public opinion, which influences policymaking and decision-taking.

The fifth fact, and this is probably the clearest and most prominent, is that the Arab nation, in its drive for permanent peace based on justice, does not proceed from a position of weakness. On the contrary, it has the power and stability for a sincere will for peace.

The Arab declared intention stems from an awareness prompted by a heritage of civilization, that to avoid an inevitable disaster that will befall us, you and the whole world, there is no alternative to the establishment of permanent peace based on justice, peace that is not swayed by suspicion or jeopardized by ill intentions.

In the light of these facts, which I meant to place before you the way I see them, I would also wish to warn you, in all sincerity I warn you, against some thoughts that could cross your minds.

Frankness makes it incumbent upon me to tell you the following:

First, I have not come here for a separate agreement between Egypt and Israel. This is not part of the policy of Egypt. The problem is not that of Egypt and Israel.

An interim peace between Egypt and Israel, or between any Arab confrontation state and Israel, will not bring permanent peace based on justice in the entire region.

Rather, even if peace between all the confrontation states and Israel were achieved in the absence of a just solution of the Palestinian problem, never will there be that durable and just peace upon which the entire world insists.

Second, I have not come to you to seek a partial peace, namely to terminate the state of belligerency at this stage and put off the entire problem to a subsequent stage. This is not the radical solution that would steer us to permanent peace.

Equally, I have not come to you for a third disengagement agreement in Sinai or in Golan or the West Bank.

For this would mean that we are merely delaying the ignition of the fuse. It would also mean that we are lacking the courage to face peace, that we are too weak to shoulder the burdens and responsibilities of a durable peace based upon justice.

I have come to you so that together we should build a durable peace based on justice to avoid the shedding of one single drop of blood by both sides. It is for this reason that I have proclaimed my readiness to go to the farthest corner of the earth.

Here I would go back to the big question.

How can we achieve a durable peace based on justice? In my opinion, and I declare it to the whole world, from this forum, the answer is neither difficult nor is it impossible despite long years of feuds, blood, faction, strife, hatreds and deep-rooted animosity. . . .

You want to live with us, in this part of the world.

In all sincerity I tell you we welcome you among us with full security and safety. This in itself is a tremendous turning point, one of the landmarks of a decisive historical change. We used to reject you. We had our reasons and our fears, yes.

We refused to meet with you, anywhere, yes.

We were together in international conferences and organizations and our representatives did not, and still do not, exchange greetings with you. Yes. This has happened and is still happening.

It is also true that we used to set as a precondition for any negotiations with you a mediator who would meet separately with each party.

Yes. Through this procedure the talks of the first and second disengagement agreements took place.

Our delegates met in the first Geneva conference without exchanging a direct word, yes, this has happened.

Yet today I tell you, and I declare it to the whole world, that we accept to live with you in permanent peace based on justice. We do not want to encircle you or be encircled ourselves by destructive missiles ready for launching, nor by the shells of grudges and hatreds.

I have announced on more than one occasion that Israel has become a fait accompli, recognized by the world, and that the two superpowers have undertaken the responsibility for its security and the defense of its existence. As we really and truly seek peace we really and truly welcome you to live among us in peace and security.

There was a huge wall between us that you tried to build up over a quarter of a century but it was destroyed in 1973. It was the wall of an implacable and escalating psychological warfare.

It was a wall of the fear of the force that could sweep the entire Arab nation. It was a wall of propaganda that we were a nation reduced to immobility. Some of you have gone as far as to say that even for 50 years to come, the Arabs will not regain their strength. It was a wall that always threatened with a long arm that could reach and strike anywhere. It was a wall that warned us of extermination and annihilation if we tried to use our legitimate rights to liberate the occupied territories.

Together we have to admit that that wall fell and collapsed in 1973. Yet, there remains another wall. This wall constitutes a psychological barrier between us, a barrier of suspicion, a barrier of rejection; a barrier of fear, of deception, a barrier of hallucination without any action, deed or decision.

A barrier of distorted and eroded interpretation of every event and statement. It is this psychological barrier that I described in official statements as constituting 70 percent of the whole problem.

Today, through my visit to you, I ask why don't we stretch out our hands with faith and sincerity so that together we might destroy this barrier? Why shouldn't our and your will meet with faith and sincerity so that together we might remove all suspicion of fear, betrayal and bad intentions?

Why don't we stand together with the courage of men and the boldness of heroes who dedicate themselves to a sublime aim? Why don't we stand together with the same courage and daring to erect a huge edifice of peace?

An edifice that builds and does not destroy. An edifice that serves as a beacon for generations to come with the human message for construction, development and the dignity of man.

Ladies and gentlemen, to tell you the truth, peace cannot be worth its name unless it is based on justice and not on the occupation of the land of others. It would not be right for you to demand for yourselves what you deny to others. With all frankness and in the spirit that has prompted me to come to you today, I tell you you have to give up once and for all the dreams of conquest and give up the belief that force is the best method for dealing with the Arabs.

You should clearly understand the lesson of confrontation between you and us. Expansion does not pay. To speak frankly, our land does not yield itself to bargaining, it is not even open to argument. . . .

We cannot accept any attempt to take away or accept to seek one inch of it nor can we accept the principle of debating or bargaining over it.

I sincerely tell you also that before us today lies the appropriate chance for peace. If we are really serious in our endeavor for peace, it is a chance that may never come again. It is a chance that if lost or wasted, the resulting slaughter would bear the curse of humanity and of history.

What is peace for Israel? It means that Israel lives in the region with her Arab neighbors in security and safety. Is that logical? I say yes. It means that Israel lives within its borders, secure against any aggression. Is that logical? And I say yes. It means that Israel obtains all kinds of guarantees that will ensure these two factors. To this demand, I say yes.

Beyond that we declare that we accept all the international guarantees you envisage and accept. We declare that we accept all the guarantees you want from the two superpowers or from either of them or from the Big Five or from some of them. Once again, I declare clearly and unequivocally that we agree to any guarantees you accept, because in return we shall receive the same guarantees.

In short then, when we ask what is peace for Israel, the answer would be that Israel lives within her borders, among her Arab neighbors in safety and security, within the framework of all the guarantees she accepts and that are offered to her.

But, how can this be achieved? How can we reach this conclusion that would lead us to permanent peace based on justice? There are facts that should be faced with courage and clarity. There are Arab territories that Israel has occupied and still occupies by force. We insist on complete withdrawal from these territories, including Arab Jerusalem.

I have come to Jerusalem, the city of peace, which will always remain as a living embodiment of coexistence among believers of the three religions. It is inadmissible that anyone should conceive the special status of the city of Jerusalem within the framework of annexation or expansionism. It should be a free and open city for all believers.

Above all, this city should not be severed from those who have made it their abode for centuries. Instead of reviving the precedent of the Crusades, we should revive the spirit of Omar Ibn al-Khattab and Saladin, namely the spirit of tolerance and respect for right.

The holy shrines of Islam and Christianity are not only places of worship but a living testimony of our interrupted presence here. Politically, spiritually and intellectually, here let us make no mistake about the importance and reverence we Christians and Moslems attach to Jerusalem.

Let me tell you without the slightest hesitation that I have not come to you under this roof to make a request that your troops evacuate the occupied territories. Complete withdrawal from the Arab territories occupied after 1967 is a logical and undisputed fact. Nobody should plead for that. Any talk about permanent peace based on justice and any move to ensure our coexistence in peace and security in this part of the world would become meaningless while you occupy Arab territories by force of arms.

For there is no peace that could be built on the occupation of the land of others, otherwise it would not be a serious peace. Yet this is a foregone conclusion that is not open to the passion of debate if intentions are sincere or if endeavors to establish a just and durable peace for our and for your generations to come are genuine.

As for the Palestine cause, nobody could deny that it is the crux of the entire problem. Nobody in the world could accept today slogans propagated here in Israel, ignoring the existence of a Palestinian people and questioning even their whereabouts. Because the Palestine people and their legitimate rights are no longer denied today by anybody; that is nobody who has the ability of judgment can deny or ignore it. It is an acknowledged fact, perceived by the world community, both in the East and in the West, with support and recognition in international documents and official statements. It is of no use to anybody to turn deaf ears to its resounding voice, which is being heard day and night, or to overlook its historical reality.

Even the United States of America, your first ally, which is absolutely committed to safeguard Israel's security and existence and which offered and still offers Israel every moral, material and military support. I say, even the United States has opted to face up to reality and admit that the

Palestinian people are entitled to legitimate rights and that the Palestine problem is the cause and essence of the conflict and that so long as it continues to be unresolved, the conflict will continue to aggravate, reaching new dimensions.

In all sincerity I tell you that there can be no peace without the Palestinians. It is a grave error of unpredictable consequences to overlook or brush aside this cause.

I shall not indulge in past events such as the Balfour Declaration 60 years ago. You are well acquainted with the relevant text. If you have found the moral and legal justification to set up a national home on a land that did not all belong to you, it is incumbent upon you to show understanding of the insistence of the people of Palestine for establishment once again of a state on their land. When some extremists ask the Palestinians to give up the sublime objective, this in fact means asking them to renounce their identity and every hope for the future.

I hail the Israeli voices that called for the recognition of the Palestinian people's right to achieve and safeguard peace.

Here I tell you, ladies and gentlemen, that it is no use to refrain from recognizing the Palestinian people and their right to statehood as their right of return. We, the Arabs, have faced this experience before with you. And with the reality of the Israeli existence, the struggle that took us from war to war, from victims to more victims, until you and we have today reached the edge of a horrible abyss and a terrifying disaster unless, together, we seize this opportunity today of a durable peace based on justice.

You have to face reality bravely, as I have done. There can never be any solution to a problem by evading it or turning a deaf ear to it. Peace cannot last if attempts are made to impose fantasy concepts on which the world has turned its back and announced its unanimous call for the respect of rights and facts. . . .

Direct confrontation and straightforwardness are the shortcuts and the most successful way to reach a clear objective. Direct confrontation concerning the Palestinian problem and tackling it in one single language with a view to achieving a durable and just peace lie in the establishment of that peace. With all the guarantees you demand, there should be no fear of a newly born state that needs the assistance of all countries of the world.

When the bells of peace ring there will be no hands to beat the drums of war. Even if they existed, they would be stilled.

Conceive with me a peace agreement in Geneva that we would herald to a world thirsting for peace. A peace agreement based on the following points:

—Ending the occupation of the Arab territories occupied in 1967.

—Achievement of the fundamental rights of the Palestinian people and their right to self-determination, including their right to establish their own state.

—The right of all states in the area to live in peace within their boundaries, their secure boundaries, which will be secured and guaranteed through procedures to be agreed upon, which will provide appropriate security to international boundaries in addition to appropriate international guarantees.

—Commitment of all states in the region to administer the relations among them in accordance with the objectives and principles of the United Nations Charter. Particularly the principles concerning the nonuse of force and a solution of differences among them by peaceful means.

—Ending the state of belligerence in the region.

Ladies and gentlemen, peace is not a mere endorsement of written lines. Rather it is a rewriting of history. Peace is not a game of calling for peace to defend certain whims or hide certain admissions. Peace in its essence is a dire struggle against all and every ambition and whim.

Perhaps the example taken and experienced, taken from ancient and modern history, teaches that missiles, warships and nuclear weapons cannot establish security. Instead they destroy what peace and security build.

For the sake of our peoples and for the sake of the civilization made by man, we have to defend man everywhere against rule by the force of arms so that we may endow the rule of humanity with all the power of the values and principles that further the sublime position of mankind.

Allow me to address my call from this rostrum to the people of Israel. I pledge myself with true and sincere words to every man, woman and child in Israel. I tell them, from the Egyptian people who bless this sacred mission of peace, I convey to you the message of peace of the Egyptian people, who do not harbor fanaticism and whose sons, Moslems, Christians and Jews, live together in a state of cordiality, love and tolerance.

This is Egypt, whose people have entrusted me with their sacred message. A message of security, safety and peace to every man, woman and child in Israel. I say, encourage your leadership to struggle for peace. Let all endeavors be channeled towards building a huge stronghold for peace instead of building destructive rockets.

Introduce to the entire world the image of the new man in this area so that he might set an example to the man of our age, the man of peace everywhere. Ring the bells for your sons. Tell them that those wars were the last of wars and the end of sorrows. Tell them that we are entering upon a new beginning, a new life, a life of love, prosperity, freedom and peace.

You, sorrowing mother, you, widowed wife, you, the son who lost a brother or a father, all the victims of wars, fill the air and space with recitals of peace, fill bosoms and hearts with the aspirations of peace. Make a reality that blossoms and lives. Make hope a code of conduct and endeavor. . . .

I have chosen to set aside all precedents and traditions known by warring countries. In spite of the fact that occupation of Arab territories is still there, the declaration of my readiness to proceed to Israel came as a great surprise that stirred many feelings and confounded many minds. Some of them even doubted its intent.

Despite all that, the decision was inspired by all the clarity and purity of belief and with all the true passions of my people's will and intentions, and I have chosen this road, considered by many to be the most difficult road.

I have chosen to come to you with an open heart and an open mind. I have chosen to give this great impetus to all international efforts exerted for peace. I have chosen to present to you, in your own home, the realities, devoid of any scheme or whim. Not to maneuver, or win a round, but for us to win together, the most dangerous of rounds embattled in modern history, the battle of permanent peace based on justice.

It is not my battle alone. Nor is it the battle of the leadership in Israel alone. It is the battle of all and every citizen in all our territories, whose right it is to live in peace. It is the commitment of conscience and responsibility in the hearts of millions.

When I put forward this initiative, many asked what is it that I conceived as possible to achieve during this visit and what my expectations were. And as I answer the questions, I announce before you that I have not thought of carrying out this initiative from the precepts of what could be achieved during this visit. And I have come here to deliver a message. I have delivered the message and may God be my witness. . . .

The Camp David Accords, September 17, 1978

A FRAMEWORK FOR PEACE IN THE MIDDLE EAST AGREED AT CAMP DAVID

Muhammad Anwar al-Sadat, President of the Arab Republic of Egypt, and Menachem Begin, Prime Minister of Israel, met with Jimmy Carter, President of the United States of America, at Camp David from September 5 to September 17, 1978, and have agreed on the following framework for peace in the Middle East. They invite other parties to the Arab-Israeli conflict to adhere to it.

Preamble

The search for peace in the Middle East must be guided by the following:

—The agreed basis for a peaceful settlement of the conflict between Israel and its neighbors is United Nations Security Council Resolution 242, in all its parts.

—After four wars during thirty years, despite intensive human efforts, the Middle East, which is the cradle of civilization and the birthplace of three great religions, does not yet enjoy the blessings of peace. The people of the Middle East yearn for peace so that the vast human and natural resources of the region can be turned to the pursuits of peace and so that this area can become a model for coexistence and cooperation among nations.

—The historic initiative of President Sadat in visiting Jerusalem and the reception accorded to him by the Parliament, government and people of Israel, and the reciprocal visit of Prime Minister Begin to Ismailia, the peace proposals made by both leaders, as well as the warm reception of these missions by the peoples of both countries, have created an unprecedented opportunity for peace which must not be lost if this generation and future generations are to be spared the tragedies of war.

—The provisions of the Charter of the United Nations and the other accepted norms of international law and legitimacy now provide accepted standards for the conduct of relations among all states.

—To achieve a relationship of peace, in the spirit of Article 2 of the United Nations Charter, future negotiations between Israel and any neighbor prepared to negotiate peace and security with it, are necessary for the purpose of carrying out all the provisions and principles of Resolutions 242 and 338.

—Peace requires respect for the sovereignty, territorial integrity and political independence of every state in the area and their right to live in peace within secure and recognized boundaries free from threats or acts of force. Progress toward that goal can accelerate movement toward a new era of reconciliation in the Middle East marked by cooperation in promoting economic development, in maintaining stability, and in assuring security.

—Security is enhanced by a relationship of peace and by cooperation between nations which enjoy normal relations. In addition, under the terms of peace treaties, the parties can, on the basis of reciprocity, agree to special security arrangements such as demilitarized zones, limited armaments areas, early warning stations, the presence of international forces, liaison, agreed measures for monitoring, and other arrangements that they agree are useful.

Framework

Taking these factors into account, the parties are determined to reach a just, comprehensive, and durable settlement of the Middle East conflict through the conclusion of peace treaties based on Security Council Resolutions 242 and 338 in all their parts. Their purpose is to achieve peace and good neighborly relations. They recognize that, for peace to endure, it must involve all those who have been most deeply affected by the conflict. They therefore agree that this framework as appropriate is intended by them to constitute a basis for peace not only between Egypt and Israel, but also between Israel and each of its other neighbors which is prepared to negotiate peace with Israel on this basis. With that objective in mind, they have agreed to proceed as follows:

A. West Bank and Gaza

1. Egypt, Israel, Jordan and the representatives of the Palestinian people should participate in negotiations on the resolution of the Palestinian problem in all its aspects. To achieve that objective,

negotiations relating to the West Bank and Gaza should proceed in three stages:

(a) Egypt and Israel agree that, in order to ensure a peaceful and orderly transfer of authority, and taking into account the security concerns of all the parties, there should be transitional arrangements for the West Bank and Gaza for a period not exceeding five years. In order to provide full autonomy to the inhabitants, under these arrangements the Israeli military government and its civilian administration will be withdrawn as soon as a self-governing authority has been freely elected by the inhabitants of these areas to replace the existing military government. To negotiate the details of a transitional arrangement, the Government of Jordan will be invited to join the negotiations on the basis of this framework. These new arrangements should give due consideration both to the principle of self-government by the inhabitants of these territories and to the legitimate security concerns of the parties involved.

(b) Egypt, Israel, and Jordan will agree on the modalities for establishing the elected self-governing authority in the West Bank and Gaza. The delegations of Egypt and Jordan may include Palestinians from the West Bank and Gaza or other Palestinians as mutually agreed. The parties will negotiate an agreement which will define the powers and responsibilities of the self-governing authority to be exercised in the West Bank and Gaza. A withdrawal of Israeli armed forces will take place and there will be a redeployment of the remaining Israeli forces into specified security locations. The agreement will also include arrangements for assuring internal and external security and public order. A strong local police force will be established, which may include Jordanian citizens. In addition, Israeli and Jordanian forces will participate in joint patrols and in the manning of control posts to assure the security of the borders.

(c) When the self-governing authority (administrative council) in the West Bank and Gaza is established and inaugurated, the transitional period of five years will begin. As soon as possible, but not later than the third year after the beginning of the transitional period, negotiations will take place to determine the final status of the West Bank and Gaza and its relationship with its neighbors, and to conclude a peace treaty between Israel and Jordan by the end of the transitional period. These negotiations will be conducted among Egypt, Israel, Jordan, and the elected representatives of the inhabitants of the West Bank and Gaza. Two separate but related committees will be convened, one committee, consisting of representatives of the four parties which will negotiate and agree on the final status of the West Bank and Gaza, and its relationship with its neighbors, and the second committee, consisting of representatives of Israel and representatives of Jordan to be joined by the elected representatives of the inhabitants of the West Bank and Gaza, to negotiate the peace treaty between Israel and Jordan, taking into account the agreement reached on the final status of the West Bank and Gaza. The negotiations shall be based on all the provisions and principles of UN Security Council Resolution 242. The negotiations will resolve, among other matters, the location of the boundaries and the nature of the security arrangements. The solution from the negotiations must also recognize the legitimate rights of the Palestinian people and their just requirements. In this way, the Palestinians will participate in the determination of their own future through:

(1) The negotiations among Egypt, Israel, Jordan and the representatives of the inhabitants of the West Bank and Gaza to agree on the final status of the West Bank and Gaza and other outstanding issues by the end of the transitional period.

(2) Submitting their agreement to a vote by the elected representatives of the inhabitants of the West Bank and Gaza.

(3) Providing for the elected representatives of the inhabitants of the West Bank and Gaza to decide how they shall govern themselves consistent with the provisions of their agreement.

(4) Participating as stated above in the work of the committee negotiating the peace treaty between Israel and Jordan.

2. All necessary measures will be taken and provisions made to assure the security of Israel and its neighbors during the transitional period and beyond. To assist in providing such security, a strong local police force will be constituted by the self-governing authority. It will be composed of inhabitants of the West Bank and Gaza. The police will maintain continuing liaison on internal security matters with the designated Israeli, Jordanian, and Egyptian officers.

3. During the transitional period, representatives of Egypt, Israel, Jordan, and the self-governing authority will constitute a continuing committee to decide by agreement on the modalities of admission of persons displaced from the West Bank and Gaza in 1967, together with necessary measures to prevent disruption and disorder. Other matters of common concern may also be dealt with by this committee.

4. Egypt and Israel will work with each other and with other interested parties to establish agreed procedures for a prompt, just and permanent implementation of the resolution of the refugee problem.

B. Egypt-Israel

1. Egypt and Israel undertake not to resort to the threat or the use of force to settle disputes. Any disputes shall be settled by peaceful means in accordance with the provisions of Article 33 of the Charter of the United Nations.

2. In order to achieve peace between them, the parties agree to negotiate in good faith with a goal of concluding within three months from the signing of this Framework a peace treaty between them, while inviting the other parties to the conflict to proceed simultaneously to negotiate and conclude similar peace treaties with a view to achieving a comprehensive peace in the area. The Framework for the Conclusion of a Peace Treaty between Egypt and Israel will govern the peace negotiations between them. The parties will agree on the modalities and the timetable for the implementation of their obligations under the treaty.

C. Associated Principles

1. Egypt and Israel state that the principles and provisions described below should apply to peace treaties between Israel and each of its neighbors—Egypt, Jordan, Syria and Lebanon.

2. Signatories shall establish among themselves relationships normal to states at peace with one another. To this end, they should undertake to abide by all the provisions of the Charter of the United Nations. Steps to be taken in this respect include:

(a) full recognition;

(b) abolishing economic boycotts;

(c) guaranteeing that under their jurisdiction the citizens of the other parties shall enjoy the protection of the due process of law.

3. Signatories should explore possibilities for economic development in the context of final peace treaties, with the objective of contributing to the atmosphere of peace, cooperation and friendship which is their common goal.

4. Claims Commissions may be established for the mutual settlement of all financial claims.

5. The United States shall be invited to participate in the talks on matters related to the modalities of the implementation of the agreements and working out the timetable for the carrying out of the obligations of the parties.

6. The United Nations Security Council shall be requested to endorse the peace treaties and ensure that their provisions shall not be violated. The permanent members of the Security Council shall be requested to underwrite the peace treaties and ensure respect for their provisions. They shall also be requested to conform their

policies and actions with the undertakings contained in this Framework.

For the Government of the Arab Republic of Egypt:

A. Sadat

For the Government of Israel:

M. Begin

Witnessed by:

Jimmy Carter
Jimmy Carter, President of
the United States of America

FRAMEWORK FOR THE CONCLUSION OF A PEACE
TREATY BETWEEN EGYPT AND ISRAEL

In order to achieve peace between them, Israel and Egypt agree to negotiate in good faith with a goal of concluding within three months of the signing of this framework a peace treaty between them.

It is agreed that:

The site of the negotiations will be under a United Nations flag at a location or locations to be mutually agreed.

All of the principles of UN Resolution 242 will apply in this resolution of the dispute between Israel and Egypt.

Unless otherwise mutually agreed, terms of the peace treaty will be implemented between two and three years after the peace treaty is signed.

The following matters are agreed between the parties:

(a) the full exercise of Egyptian sovereignty up to the internationally recognized border between Egypt and mandated Palestine;

(b) the withdrawal of Israeli armed forces from the Sinai;

(c) the use of airfields left by the Israelis near El Arish, Rafah, Ras en Naqb, and Sharm el Sheikh for civilian purposes only, including possible commercial use by all nations;

(d) the right of free passage by ships of Israel through the Gulf of Suez and the Suez Canal on the basis of the Constantinople Convention of 1888 applying to all nations; the Strait of Tiran and the Gulf of Aqaba are international waterways to be open to all nations for unimpeded and nonsuspendable freedom of navigation and overflight;

(e) the construction of a highway between the Sinai and Jordan

near Elat with guaranteed free and peaceful passage by Egypt and
Jordan; and
(f) the stationing of military forces listed below.

Stationing of Forces

A. No more than one division (mechanized or infantry) of Egyptian
armed forces will be stationed within an area lying approximately
50 kilometers (km) east of the Gulf of Suez and the Suez Canal.

B. Only United Nations forces and civil police equipped with
light weapons to perform normal police functions will be stationed
within an area lying west of the international border and the Gulf
of Aqaba, varying in width from 20 km to 40 km.

C. In the area within 3 km east of the international border there
will be Israeli limited military forces not to exceed four infantry
battalions and United Nations observers.

D. Border patrol units, not to exceed three battalions, will
supplement the civil police in maintaining order in the area not
included above.

The exact demarcation of the above areas will be as decided
during the peace negotiations.

Early warning stations may exist to insure compliance with the
terms of the agreement.

United Nations forces will be stationed: (a) in part of the area in
the Sinai lying within about 20 km of the Mediterranean Sea and
adjacent to the international border, and (b) in the Sharm el Sheikh
area to ensure freedom of passage through the Strait of Tiran; and
these forces will not be removed unless such removal is approved
by the Security Council of the United Nations with a unanimous
vote of the five permanent members.

After a peace treaty is signed, and after the interim withdrawal
is complete, normal relations will be established between Egypt and
Israel, including: full recognition, including diplomatic, economic
and cultural relations; termination of economic boycotts and barriers
to the free movement of goods and people; and mutual protection
of citizens by the due process of law.

Interim Withdrawal

Between three months and nine months after the signing of the
peace treaty, all Israeli forces will withdraw east of a line extending
from a point east of El Arish to Ras Muhammad, the exact location
of this line to be determined by mutual agreement.

For the Government of the Arab Republic of Egypt:

A. *Sadat*

For the Government of Israel:

M. *Begin*

Witnessed by:

Jimmy Carter
Jimmy Carter, President of
the United States of America

LETTER FROM ISRAELI PRIME MINISTER MENACHEM BEGIN TO PRESIDENT JIMMY CARTER, SEPTEMBER 17, 1978

Dear Mr. President:

I have the honor to inform you that during two weeks after my return home I will submit a motion before Israel's Parliament (the Knesset) to decide on the following question:

If during the negotiations to conclude a peace treaty between Israel and Egypt all outstanding issues are agreed upon, "are you in favor of the removal of the Israeli settlers from the northern and southern Sinai areas or are you in favor of keeping the aforementioned settlers in those areas?"

The vote, Mr. President, on this issue will be completely free from the usual Parliamentary Party discipline to the effect that although the coalition is being now supported by 70 members out of 120, every member of the Knesset, as I believe, both on the Government and the Opposition benches will be enabled to vote in accordance with his own conscience.

Sincerely yours,

Menachem Begin

LETTER FROM PRESIDENT JIMMY CARTER TO EGYPTIAN PRESIDENT ANWAR EL SADAT, SEPTEMBER 22, 1978

Dear Mr. President:

I transmit herewith a copy of a letter to me from Prime Minister Begin setting forth how he proposes to present the issue of the Sinai settlements to the Knesset for the latter's decision.

In this connection, I understand from your letter that Knesset approval to withdraw all Israeli settlers from Sinai according to a timetable within the period specified for the implementation of the peace treaty is a prerequisite to any negotiations on a peace treaty between Egypt and Israel.

Sincerely,

Jimmy Carter

Enclosure:
Letter from Prime Minister Begin

LETTER FROM EGYPTIAN PRESIDENT ANWAR EL SADAT TO PRESIDENT JIMMY CARTER, SEPTEMBER 17, 1978

Dear Mr. President:
In connection with the "Framework for a Settlement in Sinai" to be signed tonight, I would like to reaffirm the position of the Arab Republic of Egypt with respect to the settlements:

1. All Israeli settlers must be withdrawn from Sinai according to a timetable within the period specified for the implementation of the peace treaty.

2. Agreement by the Israeli Government and its constitutional institutions to this basic principle is therefore a prerequisite to starting peace negotiations for concluding a peace treaty.

3. If Israel fails to meet this commitment, the "Framework" shall be void and invalid.

Sincerely,

Mohamed Anwar El Sadat

LETTER FROM PRESIDENT JIMMY CARTER TO ISRAELI PRIME MINISTER MENACHEM BEGIN, SEPTEMBER 22, 1978

Dear Mr. Prime Minister:
I have received your letter of September 17, 1978, describing how you intend to place the question of the future of Israeli settlements in Sinai before the Knesset for its decision.

Enclosed is a copy of President Sadat's letter to me on this subject.

Sincerely,

Jimmy Carter

Enclosure:
Letter from President Sadat

LETTER FROM EGYPTIAN PRESIDENT ANWAR EL SADAT TO PRESIDENT JIMMY CARTER, SEPTEMBER 17, 1978

Dear Mr. President:

I am writing you to reaffirm the position of the Arab Republic of Egypt with respect to Jerusalem:

1. Arab Jerusalem is an integral part of the West Bank. Legal and historical Arab rights in the City must be respected and restored.

2. Arab Jerusalem should be under Arab sovereignty.

3. The Palestinian inhabitants of Arab Jerusalem are entitled to exercise their legitimate national rights, being part of the Palestinian People in the West Bank.

4. Relevant Security Council Resolutions, particularly Resolutions 242 and 267, must be applied with regard to Jerusalem. All the measures taken by Israel to alter the status of the City are null and void and should be rescinded.

5. All peoples must have free access to the City and enjoy the free exercise of worship and the right to visit and transit to the holy places without distinction or discrimination.

6. The holy places of each faith may be placed under the administration and control of their representatives.

7. Essential functions in the City should be undivided and a joint municipal council composed of an equal number of Arab and Israeli members can supervise the carrying out of these functions. In this way, the City shall be undivided.

Sincerely,

Mohamed Anwar El Sadat

LETTER FROM ISRAELI PRIME MINISTER MENACHEM BEGIN TO PRESIDENT JIMMY CARTER, SEPTEMBER 17, 1978

Dear Mr. President:

I have the honor to inform you, Mr. President, that on 28 June 1967—Israel's Parliament (The Knesset) promulgated and adopted a law to the effect: "the Government is empowered by a decree to apply the law, the jurisdiction and administration of the State to any part of Eretz Israel (land of Israel–Palestine), as stated in that decree."

On the basis of this law, the Government of Israel decreed in
July 1967 that Jerusalem is one city indivisible, the Capital of the
State of Israel.
Sincerely,

Menachem Begin

LETTER FROM PRESIDENT JIMMY CARTER TO
EGYPTIAN PRESIDENT ANWAR EL SADAT,
SEPTEMBER 22, 1978

Dear Mr. President:
I have received your letter of September 17, 1978, setting forth the
Egyptian position on Jerusalem. I am transmitting a copy of that
letter to Prime Minister Begin for his information.
    The position of the United States on Jerusalem remains as stated
by Ambassador Goldberg in the United Nations General Assembly
on July 14, 1967, and subsequently by Ambassador Yost in the
United Nations Security Council on July 1, 1969.
Sincerely,

Jimmy Carter

LETTER FROM EGYPTIAN PRESIDENT ANWAR EL
SADAT TO PRESIDENT JIMMY CARTER,
SEPTEMBER 17, 1978

Dear Mr. President:
In connection with the "Framework for Peace in the Middle East,"
I am writing you this letter to inform you of the position of the
Arab Republic of Egypt, with respect to the implementation of the
comprehensive settlement.
    To ensure the implementation of the provisions related to the
West Bank and Gaza and in order to safeguard the legitimate rights
of the Palestinian people, Egypt will be prepared to assume the Arab
role emanating from these provisions, following consultations with
Jordan and the representatives of the Palestinian people.
Sincerely,

Mohamed Anwar El Sadat

LETTER FROM PRESIDENT JIMMY CARTER TO ISRAELI PRIME MINISTER MENACHEM BEGIN, SEPTEMBER 22, 1978

Dear Mr. Prime Minister:

I hereby acknowledge that you have informed me as follows:

A) In each paragraph of the Agreed Framework Document the expressions "Palestinians" or "Palestinian People" are being and will be construed and understood by you as "Palestinian Arabs."

B) In each paragraph in which the expression "West Bank" appears, it is being, and will be, understood by the Government of Israel as Judea and Samaria.

Sincerely,

Jimmy Carter

LETTER FROM SECRETARY OF DEFENSE HAROLD BROWN TO ISRAELI DEFENSE MINISTER EZER WEIZMAN, ACCOMPANYING THE DOCUMENTS AGREED TO AT CAMP DAVID, RELEASED SEPTEMBER 29, 1978

September 28, 1978

Dear Mr. Minister:

The U.S. understands that, in connection with carrying out the agreements reached at Camp David, Israel intends to build two military airbases at appropriate sites in the Negev to replace the airbases at Eitam and Etzion which will be evacuated by Israel in accordance with the peace treaty to be concluded between Egypt and Israel. We also understand the special urgency and priority which Israel attaches to preparing the new bases in light of its conviction that it cannot safely leave the Sinai airbases until the new ones are operational.

I suggest that our two governments consult on the scope and costs of the two new airbases as well as on related forms of assistance which the United States might appropriately provide in light of the special problems which may be presented by carrying out such a project on an urgent basis. The President is prepared to seek the necessary Congressional approvals for such assistance as may be agreed upon by the U.S. side as a result of such consultations.

Harold Brown

Notes

Chapter 1

1. See Arnold J. Toynbee, *A Study of History* (London: Oxford University Press, 1934), p. 128. Of the nineteen major societies in history that Toynbee identifies and studies, pharaonic civilization is one of only two with no "affiliation" or "apparentation." In other words, it was not strongly influenced by societies preceding it, nor did it significantly influence those following it.

2. Ellen Churchill Semple, *The Geography of the Mediterranean Region* (New York: Henry Holt & Company, 1931), p. 595.

3. Sir Alan Gardiner, *Egypt of the Pharaohs* (London: Oxford University Press, 1966), p. 36.

4. P. J. Vatikiotis, *The History of Egypt* (Baltimore, Md.: Johns Hopkins University Press, 1980), p. 6.

5. Egypt's conflicts with the Ethiopians to the south, and its subsequent domination by them during the second half of the eighth century B.C., could be considered an exception to the general rule that Egypt's most important relationships were with nations to its east. Even during the period of Ethiopian ascendancy, however, the pharaohs were either half Egyptian or greatly influenced by Egyptian culture. (See George Rawlinson, *History of Ancient Egypt*, Vol. 2 [New York: John W. Lovell, 1880], pp. 233–237). The Twenty-second Dynasty (about 975–750 B.C.) might be thought another exception, but authorities differ as to whether its rulers were Libyans (J. H. Breasted, *A History of Egypt* [New York: Scribners, 1909], Chapter 25), Assyrians (Heinrich Karl Brugsch, *A History of Egypt Under the Pharaohs*, Vol. 2 [London: J. Murray, 1879], pp. 197–206), or native Egytians (Rawlinson, *Ancient Egypt*, pp. 223–224).

6. Gardiner, *Egypt of the Pharaohs*, p. 38.

7. Siegfried J. Schwantes, *A Short History of the Ancient Near East* (Grand Rapids, Mich.: Baker Book House, 1965), p. 57.

8. Quoted in Rawlinson, *Ancient Egypt*, p. 57.

9. *The History of Herodotus* (London: J. M. Dent and Sons, 1912), p. 166.

10. Toynbee complains that the Hyksos occupation—in his scheme a predictable dislocation of a declining empire by a *Völkerwanderung*—should by rights have been succeeded by a new society emerging from the old; instead, history repeated itself in the form of the Eighteenth Dynasty. He concludes that the Egyptians were able to regain their independence because a bond developed between king and rank-and-file through their common hostility to the alien civilization of the interloping Hyksos. Toynbee, *A Study of History*, Vol. 2, p. 41.

11. Quoted in Adeed Dawisha, *Egypt in the Arab World* (New York: John Wiley and Sons, 1976), p. 1.

12. P. L. Shinnie, "The Legacy to Africa," in *The Legacy of Egypt*, edited by J. R. Harris (Oxford: Clarendon Press, 1971), p. 438.

13. Breasted, *A History of Egypt*, p. 579.

14. One difference between the accounts in the Bible and the Koran is that the latter states that the pharaoh's body was saved from the sea (and presumably embalmed, its mummy accorded the rites of the dead) after the Egyptian king had repented and acknowledged "that there is no god Except Him Whom the Children of Israel believe in," that is, the one true God (Sura x, 90 and 92).

15. Bernard Lewis, *The Political Language of Islam* (Chicago: University of Chicago Press, 1988), p. 96.

16. See Abdullah Yusuf Ali, *The Holy Qur-an: Text, Translation and Commentary* (Washington, D.C.: The Islamic Center, 1934 [date of first publication]), Commentary in Appendix 4 to Sura vii, p. 405.

17. *New York Times*, December 24, 1985 ("Science Times," p. 1).

18. Ronald J. Williams, "Egypt and Israel," in Harris, *The Legacy of Egypt*, p. 272.

19. Breasted, *A History of Egypt*, pp. 371-374.

20. Williams, "Egypt and Israel," p. 277.

21. Robert H. Pfeiffer, *Introduction to the Old Testament* (New York: Harper & Brothers, 1941), p. 71.

22. See Bernard Lewis, *The Arabs in History* (London: Hutchinson House, 1950), pp. 22, 28, 33, 154 and 157-159, on the effects of changes in the East-West trade routes on the development of Islam.

23. Ibid., p. 58.

24. Quoted in Tom Little, *Egypt* (New York: Praeger, 1958), p. 47.

25. H.A.R. Gibb, *Mohammedanism*, (London: Oxford University Press, 1949), p. 6.

26. Ibid.

27. Quoted in Lewis, *The Arabs in History*, p. 9.

28. Shimon Shamir, "Egyptian Rule (1832-1840) and the Beginning of the Modern Period in the History of Palestine," in *Egypt and Palestine*, edited by Ammon Cohen and Gabriel Baer (New York: St. Martin's Press, 1984), p. 227).

29. George Kirk, *A Short History of the Middle East* (New York: Praeger, 1955), p. 73.

Chapter 2

1. See Nadav Safran, *Egypt in Search of Political Community* (Cambridge, Mass.: Harvard University Press, 1981), Introduction and Chapters 3 and 4.

2. See Bernard Lewis, *The Political Language of Islam* (Chicago: University of Chicago Press, 1988), pp. 40-41. Lewis traces the changing connotations of the term *watan* as it developed after the French revolution from its original Arabic meaning of "birthplace" or "homeland," to the equivalent of the French *patrie*, with its overtones of sentimental patriotic attachment, to a reflection finally of

modern nationalist concepts of political identity and authority. He notes as well that the word *umma*, charged as it is with religious content, has been adopted by the Arabs to designate the Arab nation. Another, less formal word for "country," *bilad*, has the connotation of "countryside" as distinct from "city," and is used by Arabs (especially Egyptians) in the emotional sense of one's "motherland" or "native soil." Finally, the more literary term for nationalism is *gawmiyya*, as in *al-gawmiyya al-misriyya*, or "Egyptian nationalism."

3. Albert Hourani, *Arabic Thought in the Liberal Age, 1798–1939* (London: Oxford University Press, 1962), p. 79.

4. Safran, *Egypt in Search of Political Community*, p. 63, quoting from an article by Mohammed Abduh published in *al-Ahram* in 1876.

5. Israel Gershoni and James P. Jankowski, *Egypt, Islam, and the Arabs: The Search for Egyptian Nationhood, 1900–1930* (Oxford: Oxford University Press, 1986), p. 17.

6. George Antonius, *The Arab Awakening* (London: Hamish Hamilton, 1938), p. 287.

7. Malcolm H. Kerr, *The Arab Cold War, 1958–1964* (London: Oxford University Press, 1965), p. 33.

8. Safran, *Egypt in Search of Political Community*, p. 58.

9. In its National Charter the Nasser regime blamed the failure of the 1919 revolution on parochial leaders who "were incapable of deducing from history the fact that there is no conflict between Egyptian patriotism and Arab nationalism." Quoted in Adeed Dawisha, *Egypt in the Arab World* (New York: John Wiley and Sons, 1976), p. 35.

10. See Marius Deeb, *Party Politics in Egypt: The Wafd and Its Rivals, 1919–39* (London: Ithaca Press, 1979), p. 39.

11. Malcolm H. Kerr, "Regional Arab Politics and the Conflict with Israel," in *Political Dynamics in the Middle East*, edited by Paul Y. Hammond and Sidney S. Alexander (New York: American Elsevier, 1972), p. 35.

12. See James P. Jankowski, "Egyptian Responses to the Palestine Problem in the Inter-War Period," *International Journal of Middle East Studies* (August 1980), p. 18.

13. Albert Hourani, *Arabic Thought in the Liberal Age, 1798–1939* (London: Oxford University Press, 1962), p. 316.

14. Quoted in Sylvia G. Haim, *Arab Nationalism: An Anthology* (Berkeley: University of California Press, 1962), p. 53.

15. Hourani, *Arabic Thought*, p. 295.

16. British support for the league inevitably led to charges that the organization served the interests of Western imperialism. See Sati al-Husri, "Muslim Unity and Arab Unity," in Haim, *Arab Nationalism*, p. 152.

Chapter 3

1. Gamal Abdel Nasser, *Egypt's Liberation: The Philosophy of the Revolution* (Washington, D.C.: Public Affairs Press, 1956), p. 87.

2. Jean Lacouture, *Nasser* (New York: Alfred A. Knopf, 1973), p. 18.

3. Conversation with the author, November 1987.

4. See Robert Stephens, *Nasser: A Political Biography* (London: Allen Lane, Penguin Press, 1971), p. 141.

5. Gamal Abdel Nasser, *The Philosophy of the Revolution* (Buffalo, N.Y.: Smith, Keynes and Marshall, 1959 [first published in Cairo in 1953]), p. 28.

6. A former member of the Revolutionary Command Council, conversation with the author, November 1987.

7. Conversation with the author, November 1987.

8. See Charles Issawi, *The Arab World's Legacy* (Princeton, N.J.: Darwin Press, 1981), p. 134. Issawi notes that "Egypt's desire to control Syria has been largely, though never solely, motivated by the wish to hold all the Mediterranean exits of the land-bridge. Its power to do so was due [in part] to the fact that it has in historical times almost always been a unified country, in marked contrast to Syria."

9. The opening lines of the first statement by the new regime after the coup d'état of July 23, 1952, underline the impact on the military of the defeat in Palestine: "Egypt has undergone a most critical period of bribery, corruption, and government instability in her recent history. These factors had a great influence on the Army. People who received bribes and those with ulterior motives contributed to our defeat in the Palestine War." Quoted in Hisham B. Sharabi, *Nationalism and Revolution in the Arab World* (Princeton, N.J.: D. Van Nostrand Company, 1966), p. 162.

10. Nasser, *The Philosophy of the Revolution*, p. 31.

11. An incident that rankled nearly as much as the defeat in Palestine was Britain's show of power in February 1942 to enforce its demand that the king install a Wafd government. Nasser dates the beginning of his own sense of revolution to this incident. Nasser, *The Philosophy of the Revolution*, p. 29.

12. Tom Little, *Egypt* (New York: Praeger, 1958), p. 202.

13. See R. Hrair Dekmejian, *Egypt Under Nasir: A Study in Political Dynamics* (Albany: State University of New York Press, 1971), pp. 94 and 95.

14. Malcolm H. Kerr, *Egypt Under Nasser* (New York: Foreign Policy Association [Headline Series, Number 161], 1963), p. 37.

15. Nasser, *The Philosophy of the Revolution*, p. 71.

16. Georges Vaucher, *Gamal Abdel Nasser et Son Equipe* (Paris: René Juillard, 1960), p. 61.

17. Nissim Rejwan, *Nasserist Ideology: Its Exponents and Critics* (New York: John Wiley and Sons, 1974), p. 51.

18. The difficulty in appealing directly to the Arab people over the heads of their governments was that it often undermined the traditional state-to-state diplomacy that was being pursued at the same time. The Nasser regime was reluctant to curb the propaganda to protect its governmental relationships, regarding ideological propaganda as the natural function of a revolutionary state. See Khaled Mohieddin, "Foreign Policy Since 1952: An Egyptian View," in *Egypt Since the Revolution*, edited by P. J. Vatikiotis (New York: Praeger, 1968), pp. 135–139, written in response to Malcolm Kerr's paper entitled "Egyptian Foreign Policy Since the Revolution."

19. Little, *Egypt*, p. 268.

20. P. J. Vatikiotis, *Nasser and His Generation* (London: St. Martin's Press, 1978), p. 249.

21. David Ben-Gurion, *My Talks with Arab Leaders* (New York: Third Press, 1973), p. 273 and passim.

22. Malcolm H. Kerr, *The Arab Cold War, 1958–1964* (London: Oxford University Press, 1965), p. 42.

23. Gamal Abdel Nasser, *The Palestinian Problem (Correspondence Exchanged between Nasser and John F. Kennedy on the Palestinian Problem)* (Cairo: UAR Information Department, 1961), p. 15.

24. In March 1957, for example, Anwar Sadat wrote in *Al-Ahram* that "there was nothing behind our coup other than Arab nationalism." Quoted in Adeed Dawisha, *Egypt in the Arab World* (New York: John Wiley and Sons, 1976), p. 16.

25. Quoted in Kerr, *The Arab Cold War*, p. 216.

26. Quoted in Dawisha, *Egypt in the Arab World*, p. 32.

27. See Kerr, *The Arab Cold War*, for a detailed account of the negotiations and their results.

28. William B. Quandt, "United States Policy in the Middle East: Constraints and Commitments," in *Political Dynamics in the Middle East*, edited by Paul Y. Hammond and Sidney S. Alexander (New York: American Elsevier, 1972), p. 513.

29. Anwar Sadat, *In Search of Identity: An Autobiography* (London: Collins, 1978), p. 172.

30. Quoted in P. J. Vatikiotis, "The Politics of the Fertile Crescent," in Hammond and Alexander, *Political Dynamics in the Middle East*, p. 245.

Chapter 4

1. Raymond A. Hinnebusch, Jr., *Egyptian Politics Under Sadat* (Cambridge: Cambridge University Press, 1985), p. 80.

2. W. S. Gilbert and Sir Arthur Sullivan, *Iolanthe*.

3. Anwar Sadat, *In Search of Identity: An Autobiography* (London: Collins, 1978), p. 3.

4. Hamed Ammar, *Growing Up in an Egyptian Village* (New York: Octagon Books, 1966), p. 16. Ammar attributes the relative meagerness of Egyptian folk literature in part to the "puritanism of Islam," which frowns on other-than-cautionary storytelling.

5. Winifred S. Blackman, *The Fellahin of Upper Egypt* (London: Frank Cass and Co., 1968 [first published in 1927]), p. 23.

6. Ibid., p. 129. Blackman's observations about village disputes may be somewhat less applicable to the Delta than to Upper Egypt, which is the principal focus of her study. By conventional stereotype, at least, the Saidis of Upper Egypt are more quarrelsome than the peasants of the Delta.

7. See John Waterbury, *The Egypt of Nasser and Sadat* (Princeton, N.J.: Princeton University Press, 1983), pp. 309–312 and 379–383, for a discussion of corporatism and its practice under Sadat.

8. Sadat, *In Search of Identity*, p. 139.

9. Mohamed Hasaneyn Heikal develops this argument in *Autumn of Fury: The Assassination of Sadat* (New York: Random House, 1983), pp. 10–13. Written after Sadat's death, Heikal's account of Sadat's last years is informative and often perceptive,

if hostile in the extreme. The rancor evidently stems mainly from Heikal's imprisonment in September 1981 along with more than 1,500 Muslim fundamentalists and other critics of Sadat. Although Heikal's anger is understandable, Sadat remains a complex figure capable of courage and magnanimity as well as self-deception and vindictiveness. To balance Heikal in 1983 one might quote Heikal in 1978: "as we know now, Anwar Sadat was to prove a much more resourceful and original President than anyone expected." (Mohamed Hasaneyn Heikal, *The Sphinx and the Commissar* [New York: Harper and Row, 1978], p. 217.)

10. Anwar Sadat, *Revolt on the Nile* (New York: John Day, 1957), p. 42.

11. See P. J. Vatikiotis, *Nasser and His Generation* (London: St. Martin's Press, 1978), p. 173 (Note 9). Speaking to Feisal in 1965 about the war in Yemen, Nasser reportedly pointed to Sadat and said, "He brought us into this."

12. Sadat, *In Search of Identity*, p. 239.

13. Sadat, *Revolt on the Nile*, p. 60.

14. Mohamed Hasaneyn Heikal, *The Road to Ramadan* (New York: Quadrangle, 1975), p. 81.

15. R. Michael Burrell and Abbas R. Kelidar, *Egypt: The Dilemmas of a Nation* (Beverly Hills, Calif.: Sage Publications, 1977), p. 16.

16. See Michael Handel, *The Diplomacy of Surprise: Hitler, Nixon, Sadat* (Cambridge, Mass.: Harvard University Center for International Affairs, 1981), passim.

17. Heikal, *The Road to Ramadan*, p. 31.

Chapter 5

1. H. M. Sachar, *Egypt and Israel* (New York: Richard Marek Publishers, 1981), p. 213. See also Anwar Sadat, *In Search of Identity: An Autobiography* (London: Collins, 1978), p. 259.

2. Quoted in Insight Team of *The Sunday Times, Insight on the Middle East War* (London: Andre Deutsch, 1974), p. 41.

3. Walter Z. Laqueur, *Confrontation: The Middle East War and World Politics* (London: Wildwood House, 1974), pp. 98 and 148. Laqueur comments that among the "sacred cows" the war proved false was the notion that Israeli settlements in the Golan Heights would contribute to Israel's defense, the settlements having been immediately evacuated at the onset of hostilities. And, he adds, because "Jordan effectively stayed out of the war, Israel was spared yet another bitter lesson, that the settlements which had been established in the Jordan Valley would have to be evacuated too."

4. Mohamed Hasaneyn Heikal, *The Road to Ramadan* (New York: Quadrangle, 1975), p. 269. Heikal provides an interesting and detailed account of Egypt's changing posture on the use of Arab oil in wartime and its efforts to influence the politics of the Gulf states.

5. Henry A. Kissinger, *White House Years* (Boston: Little, Brown, 1979), p. 1299.

6. Henry A. Kissinger, *Years of Upheaval* (Boston: Little, Brown, 1982), p. 967. From the context it is clear that Sadat meant that he would in such circumstances join Syria in renewed hostilities.

7. Kissinger, *Years of Upheaval*, Chapters 13, 18, and 21, passim.

8. Quoted in Abba Eban, *An Autobiography* (New York: Random House, 1977), p. 562.

9. William B. Quandt, *Decade of Decisions: American Policy Toward the Arab-Israeli Conflict, 1967-1976* (Berkeley: University of California Press, 1977), p. 246.

10. Matti Golan, *The Secret Conversations of Henry Kissinger* (New York: Quadrangle, 1976), p. 227.

11. Quoted in Edward R. F. Sheehan, *The Arabs, Israelis and Kissinger* (New York: Reader's Digest Press, 1976), p. 196.

12. Ibid.

13. The first three assurances are recounted by Sheehan, *The Arabs, Israelis and Kissinger*, p. 194, the last one by *The New York Times*, September 17, 1975.

Chapter 6

1. Quoted in R. Michael Burrell and Abbas R. Kelidar, *Egypt: The Dilemmas of a Nation* (Beverly Hills, Calif.: Sage Publications, 1977), p. 17.

2. Quoted in John Waterbury, *The Egypt of Nasser and Sadat* (Princeton, N.J.: Princeton University Press, 1983), p. 128.

3. The figures are based on the lower of the two estimates in Mohamed Hasaneyn Heikal, *Autumn of Fury: The Assassination of Sadat* (New York: Random House, 1983), p. 79. They are rough approximations.

4. Quoted in Adeed Dawisha, *Egypt in the Arab World* (New York: John Wiley and Sons, 1976), p. 188.

5. *The New York Times*, July 17, 18, and 20, 1976.

6. *The New York Times*, September 12, 1976.

7. Heikal, *Autumn of Fury*, p. 95.

8. In *Years of Upheaval* (Boston: Little, Brown, 1982), p. 793, Henry A. Kissinger cites Algerian Prime Minister Abdelaziz Bouteflika as acknowledging "that the problem of the Palestinians was complicated by the fact that each country of the region supported its own group of Palestinians."

9. Quoted in Waterbury, *The Egypt of Nasser and Sadat*, p. 417.

10. *The New York Times*, June 10, 1976.

11. Henry Tanner, writing in *The New York Times*, October 23, 1976.

Chapter 7

1. Detailed accounts of this period and of the negotiations that followed at Camp David have been written from the perspectives of the United States, Israel, and Egypt. The major accounts by policymakers and participants in the talks are: William B. Quandt, *Camp David: Peacemaking and Politics* (Washington, D.C.: Brookings Institution, 1986); Cyrus Vance, *Hard Choices: Critical Years in America's Foreign Policy* (New York: Simon and Schuster, 1983); Zbigniew Brzezinski, *Power and Principle: Memoirs of the National Security Adviser, 1977-1981* (New York: Farrar, Strauss, Giroux, 1983); Jimmy Carter, *Keeping Faith: Memoirs of a President* (New York: Bantam Books, 1982); Moshe Dayan, *Breakthrough: A Personal Account of the Egypt-Israel Peace Negotiations* (New York: Alfred A. Knopf, 1981); Yitzhak

Rabin, *The Rabin Memoirs* (Boston: Little, Brown, 1979); Ezer Weizman, *The Battle for Peace* (New York: Bantam Books, 1981); Ismail Fahmy, *Negotiating for Peace in the Middle East* (Baltimore, Md.: Johns Hopkins University Press, 1983); and Mohamed Ibrahim Kamel, *The Camp David Accords: A Testimony by Sadat's Foreign Minister* (London: Routledge and Kegan Paul, 1986).

2. Quandt, *Camp David*, p. 66.

3. Vance, *Hard Choices*, p. 178.

4. Dayan, *Breakthrough*, p. 110.

5. Ibid., p. 49.

6. Vance, *Hard Choices*, p. 171.

7. See Quandt, *Camp David*, Chapters 3, 4, and 5, for a detailed account of the efforts during 1977 to persuade the PLO to accept Resolution 242.

8. Vance, *Hard Choices*, p. 170.

9. *The New York Times*, January 26, 1977.

10. See Fouad Ajami, "Stress in the Arab Triangle," *Foreign Policy* (Winter 1977–1978), p. 90 and passim. Writing in the fall of 1977, shortly after the joint Arab effort to bring Jordan and the PLO together, Ajami argued that a "trilateral order has come to prevail in Arab politics," in which Egyptian military power, Syrian dominance on the eastern front, and Saudi wealth joined in a common "commitment to stability and political order." It was a conclusion that at the time seemed justified by the circumstances.

11. Quandt, *Camp David*, p. 80.

12. See Arthur R. Day, *East Bank/West Bank: Jordan and the Prospects for Peace* (New York: Council on Foreign Relations, 1986), Chapter 6, and Arthur R. Day, "Hussein's Constraints, Jordan's Dilemma," *SAIS Review* (Winter–Spring 1987), pp. 81–93.

13. See Adeed Dawisha, "Syria and the Sadat Initiative," *The World Today* (May 1978), pp. 192–198.

14. Fahmy, *Negotiating for Peace*, p. 152.

15. Fahmy, *Negotiating for Peace*, p. 269. Fahmy, who as Egyptian foreign minister managed to frustrate the Syrian maneuver, argues that the road to Geneva remained open despite Syria's attempts to block it. As will become apparent in later chapters, many of the main players differed on this critical question.

16. Quandt, *Camp David*, p. 152.

17. Quoted in David Hirst and Irene Beeson, *Sadat* (London: Faber and Faber, 1981), p. 288.

18. *The New York Times*, January 10 and 13, 1977.

19. Harold H. Saunders, *The Other Walls: The Politics of the Arab-Israeli Peace Process* (Washington, D.C.: American Enterprise Institute, 1985), p. 86.

20. See Quandt, *Camp David*, pp. 127–131, for an analysis of this issue and its impact on the preparations for Geneva.

21. Vance, *Hard Choices*, p. 170.

22. See Saunders, *The Other Walls*, pp. 87–88 and Chapter 4, for an analysis of the implications for the negotiating process of the different goals of the West Bankers and Gazans as contrasted to those of the Palestinians living in Syria and Jordan.

23. Vance recalls that PLO-Syrian relations had in 1977 reached so low a point that Assad "with some reluctance . . . acknowledged that he and the PLO were hardly on speaking terms." Vance, *Hard Choices*, p. 170.

24. Quandt, *Camp David*, p. 91. See also *The New York Times* of August 7, 1977, reporting the PLO's Salah Khallaf's comments on PLO-Syrian cooperation at the time of the Executive Committee meeting.

25. Detailed accounts of the meetings, letters, proposals, and counterproposals that filled the critical six weeks before Sadat's November 9 announcement of his willingness to visit Jerusalem can be found in Quandt, *Camp David*, pp. 122–146, and Fahmy, *Negotiating for Peace*, pp. 233–267.

26. *The New York Times*, December 4, 1977.

27. See Fahmy, *Negotiating for Peace*, Chapters 12 and 13, and Vance, *Hard Choices*, p. 194. Vance believes, as does Fahmy, that the preparations for Geneva were still on track, if barely so, and that "Syria's position was slowly evolving toward a satisfactory resolution."

28. Carter, *Keeping Faith*, p. 295.

29. Quandt, *Camp David*, p. 153.

30. See Hermann F. Eilts, "Improve the Framework," *Foreign Policy* (Winter 1980–1981), p. 11. Also, in "The Mideast: Impressive Achievements and Sober Hopes," *Worldview* (December 1979), p. 14, Eilts makes the same point even more strongly: "Over the past five years, I can personally attest, [Sadat] has consistently and strongly fought for a comprehensive peace and Palestinian rights. He has never wavered on these points."

Chapter 8

1. As mentioned in the previous chapter, what little remained of Sadat's faith in the Geneva process had been shaken by Carter's apparent retreat in the face of Israeli pressure. The impression that the U.S. effort was losing its drive and that something needed to be done to revive the process may have been strengthened by the wording of a letter from Carter on October 21, 1977, containing a "personal appeal for your support." In his autobiography Sadat cites this letter as first directing his thinking to the need for a dramatic new initiative. In fact, Carter's letter is nothing more than an appeal for Egyptian help in clearing away the remaining obstacles to a peace conference. It was most probably Sadat's own mood of despair that made him interpret Carter's appeal as a *cri de coeur* requiring a spectacular initiative on his part—which he had in any case already been considering. See Anwar Sadat, *In Search of Identity: An Autobiography* (London: Collins, 1978), pp. 301–305, and William Quandt, *Camp David: Peacemaking and Politics* (Washington, D.C.: Brookings Institution, 1986), pp. 138–143, the latter containing the text of Carter's letter.

2. See Sadat, *In Search of Identity*, p. 306, and Ismail Fahmy, *Negotiating for Peace in the Middle East* (Baltimore, Md.: Johns Hopkins University Press, 1983), pp. 253–260. Fahmy recounts in detail the circumstances of Sadat's decision to visit Jerusalem after meeting with Ceaușescu—as well as the arguments that he and other senior Egyptian officials advanced against the initiative. The two main points of

difference between Sadat and his advisers were, first, the latters' more sanguine view of the prospects for a successful peace conference and, second, their conviction that the Begin government would not reciprocate Egyptian magnanimity with flexibility on the core Palestinian issues. On the second point they of course turned out to be right.

3. See Eitan Haber, Zeev Schiff, and Ehud Yaari, *The Year of the Dove* (New York: Benniton Books, 1979), p. 5. Because he had chosen Tuhamy to be his point man in exploratory talks with the Begin government, it is perfectly credible that Sadat should have talked to him about ways to get through to the Israelis before mentioning the Jerusalem idea to his foreign minister. (Later, one of Tuhamy's chores was to keep in touch with members of the Israeli press in Cairo, one of whom was one of the authors of *The Year of the Dove*.) While Tuhamy's talks with Dayan in Morocco were evidently the main substantive contact with the Israelis in the pre-Jerusalem period, Sadat also used his old friend and counselor, Sayed Marei, to try to get a sense of Israeli intentions. On August 25, 1977, during Begin's visit to Romania, Marei and Begin met secretly to explore the possibility of a meeting between the Egyptian and Israeli leaders. See Robert Springborg, *Family, Power and Politics in Egypt: Sayed Bey Marei—His Clan, Clients, and Cohorts* (Philadelphia: University of Pennsylvania Press, 1982), p. 241.

4. See Fahmy, *Negotiations for Peace*, p. 259, and Sadat, *In Search of Identity*, p. 306.

5. Fahmy, *Negotiating for Peace*, p. 266. Fahmy notes that four days later, after Sadat's speech to the People's Assembly publicly declaring his willingness to go to Jerusalem, Gamasy whispered to him, "He said it again." The clear implication is that Sadat never discussed his intentions with his minister of defense.

6. See Bahgat Korany and Ali E. Hillal Dessouki, editors, *The Foreign Policies of Arab States* (Boulder, Colo.: Westview Press, 1984), p. 5. The first two chapters of this work, discussing contemporary theories of foreign policy formation in the Arab world, contain many useful and provocative insights.

7. Ibid., p. 3, and Bahgat Korany, "The Cold Peace, the Sixth Arab-Israeli War, and Egypt's Public," *International Journal* (Autumn 1983), p. 655.

8. Mark N. Cooper, *The Transformation of Egypt* (Baltimore, Md.: Johns Hopkins University Press, 1982), p. 251. A direct link between the January riots and the Jerusalem initiative is asserted not only by Cooper (p. 247) but also by Mohamed Hasaneyn Heikal, *Autumn of Fury: The Assassination of Sadat* (New York: Random House, 1983), p. 93; Saad Eddin Ibrahim, "Anatomy of Egypt's Militant Islamic Groups; Methodological Note and Preliminary Findings," *International Journal of Middle East Studies* (December 1980), p. 424; and Afaf Lutfi al-Sayyid Marsot, *A Short History of Modern Egypt* (Cambridge: Cambridge University Press, 1985), p. 135.

9. Fahmy, *Negotiating for Peace*, p. 282.

10. These arguments, with slight variations, are advanced by John Waterbury, *The Egypt of Nasser and Sadat* (Princeton, N.J.: Princeton University Press, 1983), p. 401; Mohammed Sid-Ahmed, "Egypt: The Islamic Issue," *Foreign Policy* (Winter 1987–1988), p. 35; Ali E. Hillal Dessouki, "The Primacy of Economics: The Foreign Policy of Egypt," in Korany and Dessouki, *The Foreign Policies of Arab States*, p.

124; and David Hirst and Irene Beeson, *Sadat* (London: Faber and Faber, 1981), pp. 282–283.

11. Waterbury, *The Egypt of Nasser and Sadat*, p. 402.

12. Paul Jabber, "Egypt's Crisis, America's Dilemma," *Foreign Affairs* (Summer 1986), p. 965.

13. See Norma Salem-Babikian, "The Sacred and the Profane: Sadat's Speech to the Knesset," *Middle East Journal* (Winter 1980), pp. 13–24, and Ali E. Hillal Dessouki, "The Limits of Instrumentalism: Islam in Egypt's Foreign Policy," in *Islam in Foreign Policy*, edited by Adeed Dawisha (Cambridge: Cambridge University Press, 1983), p. 90.

14. Sadat, *In Search of Identity*, pp. 332 and 342.

15. Arab acknowledgment of Sadat's sincerity was not confined to individuals but could even sometimes be discerned in quasi-official statements of the rejectionist governments. For example, an editorial in the March 20, 1978, issue of Damascus's *Tishrin*, a newspaper created by Assad, comments that "Israel has missed an historic chance that may not be offered again."

16. Sadat, *In Search of Identity*, pp. 334–335.

17. Haber, et al., *Year of the Dove*, pp. 63–64.

18. Ezer Weizman, *The Battle for Peace* (New York: Bantam Books, 1981), pp. 59–61.

19. P. J. Vatikiotis, *History of Egypt* (Baltimore, Md.: Johns Hopkins University Press, 1980), p. 412. See also Doreen Kays, *Frogs and Scorpions: Egypt, Sadat, and the Media* (London: Frederick Muller, 1984), p. 17, and Hirst and Beeson, *Sadat*, p. 275.

20. Joseph Montville, "The Psychological Tasks of Arab-Israeli Peace Diplomacy," an unpublished account of discussions with Egyptian and Israeli intellectuals, 1984.

21. The telegram read in part: "We realize the dimensions of the present situation and follow with all confidence your courageous steps for peace based on justice." Quoted in *The New York Times*, November 20, 1977.

22. See, for example, Quandt, *Camp David*, p. 152.

23. Fahmy, *Negotiating for Peace*, p. 261.

24. Joseph Kraft, "Letter from Riyadh," *The New Yorker*, June 26, 1978, p. 72.

25. See Jimmy Carter, *Keeping Faith: Memoirs of a President* (New York: Bantam Books, 1982), p. 298, and Daniel Dishon, "Sadat's Arab Adversaries," *The Jerusalem Quarterly* (Summer 1978), p. 7.

26. See *Newsweek* (December 12, 1977), pp. 54–57, for interviews with Hussein and Sadat. Hussein remarked that "Sadat has broken the mold of conventional thinking and demolished psychological barriers. It took an awful lot of moral courage." Sadat had similarly warm comments about Hussein: "King Hussein has been very understanding. When I was in Jerusalem, he put my speech in the Knesset on Jordanian television. . . . He was true to himself and to his people."

27. *The New York Times*, December 5, 1977.

28. Dishon, "Sadat's Arab Adversaries," p. 3.

29. See Carter, *Keeping Faith*, p. 301: "They expressed their unequivocal support for Sadat. . . , but merely smiled when I urged them to make this known through their public statements."

30. Meeting with Vance in Cairo on December 10, 1977, Sadat was generous in his comments about the Saudi position after his trip to Israel. See Quandt, *Camp David*, p. 153.

31. See *The New York Times*, November 18, 19, and 21, 1977.

32. Described in Hirst and Beeson, *Sadat*, p. 291.

33. Emile Sahliyeh, *In Search of Leadership: West Bank Politics Since 1967* (Washington, D.C.: Brookings Institution, 1988), p. 70.

34. Weizman, *The Battle for Peace*, p. 296.

Chapter 9

1. William Quandt, *Camp David: Peacemaking and Politics* (Washington, D.C.: Brookings Institution, 1986), p. 181.

2. Jimmy Carter, *Keeping Faith: Memoirs of a President* (New York: Bantam Books, 1982), p. 316.

3. See Chapter 7, Note 1, above.

4. For the text of the nine-point proposal of February 3, 1978, outlining U.S. ideas on the nature of a viable transitional arrangement, see Quandt, *Camp David*, p. 171.

5. Eitan Haber, Zeev Schiff, and Ehud Yaari, *The Year of the Dove* (New York: Benniton Books, 1979), p. 171.

6. See Mohamed Ibrahim Kamel, *The Camp David Accords: A Testimony* (London: Routledge and Kegan Paul, 1986), pp. 363–368. The discussion between Sadat and Foreign Minister Kamel, who sought the meeting in order to explain his reasons for resigning, is a lucid and fair summation of the cases for and against the Camp David Accords from the Egyptian standpoint.

7. For an analysis of the determinants of Saudi policy after Camp David, see Adeed Dawisha, "Saudi Arabia and the Arab-Israel Conflict: The Ups and Downs of Pragmatic Moderation," *International Journal* (Autumn 1983), pp. 674–689.

8. Patrick Seale, "The Egypt-Israel Treaty and its Implications," *The World Today* (May 1979), pp. 189–196.

9. Emile Sahliyeh, "Jordan and the Palestinians," in *The Middle East: Ten Years After Camp David*, edited by William B. Quandt (Washington, D.C.: Brookings Institution, 1988), p. 286.

10. For the text of Jordan's questions and the U.S. answers, see Quandt, *Camp David*, pp. 388–396.

11. The radicalization of West Bank politics in the late 1970s is described in Emile Sahliyeh, *In Search of Leadership: West Bank Politics Since 1967* (Washington, D.C.: Brookings Institution, 1988), pp. 71–80.

12. Seale, "The Egypt-Israel Treaty," p. 195. See also P. J. Vatikiotis, *Arab and Regional Politics in the Middle East* (London: Croom Helm, 1984), pp. 117–124, for a discussion of the Arab realignment after Camp David in the historical context of traditional rivalries between the Fertile Crescent and Egypt.

13. In May 1979 Sadat accurately forecast the future of the accommodation between Syria and Iraq: "[Assad] has recently tried to save his neck by forging an alliance with Iraq. But it cannot work, anymore than putting a cat and some mice

in the same box." Joseph Kraft, "Letter from Riyadh," *The New Yorker,* June 26, 1978, p. 98.

14. Habcr ct al. *The Year of the Dove,* p. 28.

15. After having himself been treated to one of Sadat's rundowns on the character defects of the Arab world's principal leaders, Joseph Kraft notes that Prime Minister Mustapha Khalil and Minister of State Boutros Boutros-Ghali "regularly tried to tone down the President's strictures on other Arab leaders." Kraft, "Letter from Riyadh," p. 100.

16. Arthur R. Day, "Hussein's Constraints, Jordan's Dilemma," *SAIS Review* (Winter–Spring 1987), p. 89.

17. May Day speech, 1979; cited in Kraft, "Letter from Riyadh," p. 101.

18. See, for example, Boutros Boutros-Ghali, "The Foreign Policy of Egypt in the Post-Sadat Era," *Foreign Affairs* (Spring 1982), pp. 769–788.

19. Bahgat Korany, "The Cold Peace, the Sixth Arab-Israeli War, and Egypt's Public," *International Journal* (Autumn 1983), p. 660.

20. During the Blair House talks the Israelis observed that "Egypt had some 50 treaties with Arab States which called for hostile action against Israel under certain circumstances." Dayan notes that Israel would have liked Egypt to "disengage herself from these treaties; but that was not possible for political reasons." Moshe Dayan, *Breakthrough: A Personal Account of the Egypt-Israel Peace Negotiations* (New York: Alfred A. Knopf, 1981), p. 212.

21. Quandt, *Camp David,* p. 287.

22. Shimon Shamir, "Israeli Views of Egypt and the Peace Process," in Quandt, *Ten Years After Camp David,* p. 198. Samuel W. Lewis also notes the influence of the Likud extreme right in hardening Israel's position in the autonomy negotiations ("The United States and Israel," in Quandt, *Ten Years After Camp David,* p. 224).

23. Naomi Chazan, "Domestic Developments in Israel," in Quandt, *Ten Years After Camp David,* p. 167.

24. Thomas W. Lippmann, *Egypt after Nasser: Sadat, Peace, and the Mirage of Prosperity* (New York: Paragon House, 1989), p. 219.

25. Mohamed Hasaneyn Heikal, *Autumn of Fury: The Assassination of Sadat* (New York: Random House, 1983), p. 267. Part 6 of this work, Chapters 2–4, describes in detail the circumstances of the assassination and the motives of the assassins.

26. Bernard Lewis, *The Political Language of Islam* (Chicago: University of Chicago Press, 1988), p. 153, Note 14.

Chapter 10

1. Quoted in *The New York Times,* November 10, 1987.

2. See Aaron David Miller, "The PLO and the Peace Process: The Organizational Imperative," *SAIS Review* (Winter–Spring 1987), for an analysis of the divisions within the PLO that brought Arafat to break with consensus decisionmaking and conclude the February 1985 framework agreement with Hussein.

3. See Mohammed Sid-Ahmad, "Egypt: The Islamic Issue," *Foreign Policy* (Winter 1987–1988), p. 24. Sid-Ahmad notes that Mubarak's decision to slow the normalization

process was prompted not only by the Israeli invasion of Lebanon and the Sabra and Shatila massacres, but also by Israel's refusal to return to Egypt the disputed sliver of territory in the Sinai known as Taba. (The Taba dispute was resolved by arbitration in September 1986.)

4. *Al-Ahram*, March 24, 1988.

5. One proponent of this view is Aharon Yariv, former chief of Israeli military intelligence and now director of Tel Aviv University's Jaffee Center for Strategic Studies. Yariv described his position at a seminar on December 10, 1987, sponsored by the Washington Institute for Near East Policy.

6. Abba Eban, interview with *The New York Times*, November 16, 1987.

7. This discussion of recent Egyptian foreign policy is based on conversations between the author and foreign ministry officials and others during a trip to Cairo, Riyadh, Amman, and Damascus in the winter of 1987–1988.

8. Saad Eddin Ibrahim, *The New Arab Social Order: A Study of the Social Impact of Oil Wealth* (Boulder, Colo.: Westview Press, 1982), p. 3. Ibrahim remarks that the extensive network of economic and social bonds notwithstanding, "the quality of this unity is a far cry from what Arab nationalists have dreamt of in this twentieth century."

9. See Abdel Monem Said Aly, *Back to the Fold? Egypt and the Arab World* (Washington, D.C.: Georgetown University Center for Contemporary Arab Studies, 1988), p. 9. Aly argues that the movement Mubarak has encouraged toward political democratization and decentralization has accelerated the "re-Arabization of Egyptian politics" by increasing the assertiveness of social, intellectual, professional, and business associations in Egypt. Some of these groups have close economic ties with the Arabs, while others are traditional bastions of pan-Arab sentiment. Aly provides more detail about Egypt's current economic and cultural connections to the rest of the Arab world.

10. Milton Viorst, "Iraq at War," *Foreign Affairs* (Winter 1986–1987), p. 353.

11. See Frederick W. Axelgard, *A New Iraq? The Gulf War and Its Implications for U.S. Policy* (New York: Praeger, 1988), p. 83.

12. Commenting on the Syrian position at a Brookings "conversation" on September 23, 1987, Egyptian Foreign Minister Ismat Abdel Meguid noted dryly that whereas Syria opposed Egypt's attendance at a Middle East peace conference, Egypt supported the right of Syria to participate.

13. Several months after the Amman summit, Egypt formally restated its position that the Arab collective defense pact remained valid and that the peace treaty between Egypt and Israel would not be given priority over Egypt's Arab commitments. See Ali E. Hillal Dessouki, "Egyptian Foreign Policy Since Camp David," in *The Middle East: Ten Years After Camp David*, edited by William B. Quandt (Washington, D.C.: Brookings Institution, 1988), p. 97.

14. Cairo's *al-Akhbar* of June 2, 1988, carries the official account of the episode.

15. *The New York Times*, June 10, 1988.

Chapter 11

1. Quoted in Raymond W. Baker, *Egypt's Uncertain Revolution Under Nasser and Sadat* (Cambridge, Mass.: Harvard University Press, 1978), p. 47.

2. Nadav Safran, *Egypt in Search of Political Community* (Cambridge, Mass.: Harvard University Press, 1981), p. 95.

3. Ibid., p. 144.

4. Fouad Ajami, "The Arab Road," in *Pan-Arabism and Arab Nationalism*, edited by Tawfic E. Farah (Boulder, Colo.: Westview Press, 1987), p. 118.

5. Fouad Ajami, *The Arab Predicament: Arab Political Thought and Practice Since 1967* (Cambridge: Cambridge University Press, 1981), p. 115.

6. Abdel Monem Said Aly, *Back to the Fold? Egypt and the Arab World* (Washington, D.C.: Georgetown University Center for Contemporary Arab Studies, 1988), p. 6.

7. Some recent surveys in Egypt indicate an upsurge of pan-Arab sentiment. One such survey, conducted by Nader Fergani on the Egyptian work force in 1985, showed that 73.7 percent of the respondents favored some degree of unity with other Arab countries. See Aly, *Back to the Fold?* p. 8.

8. Abdel Monem Said Aly, "Egypt: A Decade after Camp David," in *The Middle East: Ten Years After Camp David*, edited by William B. Quandt (Washington, D.C.: Brookings Institution, 1988), p. 67.

9. Conversation with the author, November 1987.

10. The rivalry between the Egyptian and Syrian wings of the Muslim Brotherhood—and their differing outlooks on the world—was highlighted in the winter of 1980–1981 in an incident concerning the U.S. hostages in Iran. (I ask the reader's forbearance in citing an event in which I was involved while political counselor at the U.S. embassy in Cairo.) During one of a series of meetings with Muslim Brotherhood Supreme Guide Omar Talmasani (for the purpose of understanding and making understood each other's views), Talmasani noted that hostage-taking was contrary to Islam and offered to intervene with the Iranian clerics to try to bring about the release of the U.S. citizens. Within a few days he set off for Geneva to meet with Iranian representatives. His efforts failed—and that seemed to be the end of a magnanimous humanitarian mission. It was not long, however, before the Syrians published an exposé of the affair in an effort to embarrass the Egyptians for being insufficiently militant. The Egyptian press, with an evident shrug of its shoulders, picked up the item and ran a three-inch summary of the facts.

11. Ahmad Yousef Ahmad, "The Dialectics of Domestic Environment and Role Performance: The Foreign Policy of Iraq," in *The Foreign Policies of Arab States*, edited by Bahgat Korany and Ali E. Hillal Dessouki (Boulder, Colo.: Westview Press, 1984), p. 160.

12. Raymond A. Hinnebusch, Jr., "Revisionist Dreams, Realist Strategies: The Foreign Policy of Syria," in Korany and Dessouki, *The Foreign Policies of Arab States*, pp. 300–301.

Chapter 12

1. On this point, see William B. Quandt, "U.S. Policy toward the Arab-Israeli Conflict," in *The Middle East: Ten Years After Camp David*, edited by William B. Quandt (Washington, D.C.: Brookings Institution, 1988), p. 379.

2. On November 20, 1988, Egypt, over the strong objections of Israel, formally recognized the "independent Palestinian state" that the Palestine National Council had declared five days earlier in Algiers.

3. *Al-Ahram*, February 25, 1989.

Bibliography

Abdalla, Ismail-Sabri. *Images of the Arab Future.* New York: St. Martin's Press, 1983.

Ahmad, Ahmad Yousef. "The Dialectics of Domestic Environment and Role Performance: The Foreign Policy of Iraq," in *The Foreign Policies of Arab States,* edited by Bahgat Korany and Ali E. Hillal Dessouki. Boulder, Colo.: Westview Press, 1984.

Ahmed, Jamel Mohammed. *The Intellectual Origins of Egyptian Nationalism.* London: Oxford University Press, 1960.

Ajami, Fouad. "Stress in the Arab Triangle." *Foreign Policy,* Winter 1977–1978.

———. *The Arab Predicament: Arab Political Thought and Practice Since 1967.* Cambridge: Cambridge University Press, 1981.

———. "The Arab Road," in *Pan-Arabism and Arab Nationalism,* edited by Tawfic E. Farah. Boulder, Colo.: Westview Press, 1987.

———. "The End of Pan-Arabism." *Foreign Affairs.* Winter 1978–1979.

———. "The Struggle for Egypt's Soul." *Foreign Policy.* Summer 1979.

Ali, Abdullah Yusuf. *The Holy Qur-an: Text, Translation and Commentary.* Washington, D.C.: The Islamic Center, 1934.

Aly, Abdel Monem Said. *Back to the Fold? Egypt and the Arab World.* Washington, D.C.: Georgetown University Center for Contemporary Arab Studies, 1988.

———. "Egypt: A Decade after Camp David," in *The Middle East: Ten Years After Camp David,* edited by William B. Quandt. Washington, D.C.: Brookings Institution, 1988.

Ammar, Hamed. *Growing Up in an Egyptian Village.* New York: Octagon Books, 1966.

Antonius, George. *The Arab Awakening.* London: Hamish Hamilton, 1938.

Axelgard, Frederick W. *A New Iraq? The Gulf War and Its Implications for U.S. Policy.* New York: Praeger, 1988.

Baker, Raymond W. *Egypt's Uncertain Revolution Under Nasser and Sadat.* Cambridge, Mass.: Harvard University Press, 1978.

Ball, George W. "From Partial Peace to Real Peace in the Mideast." *Worldview,* December 1979.

Ben-Gurion, David. *My Talks with Arab Leaders.* New York: Third Press, 1973.

Berque, Jacques. *Histoire sociale d'un village Egyptien au XXème siècle.* The Hague: Mouton, 1957.

Blackman, Winifred S. *The Fellahin of Upper Egypt.* London: Frank Cass and Co., 1968 (first published in 1927).

Boutros-Ghali, Boutros. "The Foreign Policy of Egypt," in *Foreign Policies in a World of Change,* edited by J. E. Black and K. W. Thompson. New York: Harper and Row, 1963.

———. "The Foreign Policy of Egypt in the Post-Sadat Era." *Foreign Affairs*, Spring 1982.

———. "Monde arabe et Tiers Monde." *Eléments*, No. 89, pp. 33–42, 1971.

Breasted, J. H. *A History of Egypt*. New York: Scribners, 1909.

Brugsch, Heinrich Karl. *A History of Egypt Under the Pharaohs*, Vol. 2. London: J. Murray, 1879.

Brzezinski, Zbigniew. *Power and Principle: Memoirs of the National Security Adviser, 1977–1981*. New York: Farrar, Strauss, Giroux, 1983.

Burrell, R. Michael, and Kelidar, Abbas R. *Egypt: The Dilemmas of a Nation*. Beverly Hills, Calif.: Sage Publications, 1977.

Cantori, Louis J. "Egyptian Policy under Mubarak: The Politics of Change and Continuity," in *The Middle East after the Israeli Invasion of Lebanon*, edited by Robert O. Freedman. Syracuse, N.Y.: Syracuse University Press, 1986.

Carter, Jimmy. *Keeping Faith: Memoirs of a President*. New York: Bantam Books, 1982.

Chazan, Naomi. "Domestic Developments in Israel," in *The Middle East: Ten Years After Camp David*, edited by William B. Quandt. Washington, D.C.: Brookings Institution, 1988.

Colombe, Marcel. "L'Egypte et les origines du nationalisme arabe." *L'Afrique et l'Asie*, No. 14, 1951.

Cooper, Mark N. *The Transformation of Egypt*. Baltimore, Md.: Johns Hopkins University Press, 1982.

Dawisha, Adeed. *Egypt in the Arab World: The Elements of Foreign Policy*. New York: John Wiley and Sons, 1976.

———. "Saudi Arabia and the Arab-Israel Conflict: The Ups and Downs of Pragmatic Moderation." *International Journal*, Autumn 1983.

———. "Syria and the Sadat Initiative." *The World Today*, May 1978.

———. *The Arab Radicals*. New York: Council on Foreign Relations, 1986.

Day, Arthur R. *East Bank/West Bank: Jordan and the Prospects for Peace*. New York: Council on Foreign Relations, 1986.

———. "Hussein's Constraints, Jordan's Dilemma." *SAIS Review*, Winter–Spring 1987.

Dayan, Moshe. *Breakthrough: A Personal Account of the Egypt-Israel Peace Negotiations*. New York: Alfred A. Knopf, 1981.

Deeb, Marius. *Party Politics in Egypt: The Wafd and Its Rivals, 1919–39*. London: Ithaca Press, 1979.

Dekmejian, R. Hrair. *Egypt Under Nasir: A Study in Political Dynamics*. Albany: State University of New York Press, 1971.

Dessouki, Ali E. Hillal. "Egyptian Foreign Policy Since Camp David," in *The Middle East: Ten Years After Camp David*, edited by William B. Quandt. Washington, D.C.: Brookings Institution, 1988.

———. "The Limits of Instrumentalism: Islam in Egypt's Foreign Policy," in *Islam in Foreign Policy*, edited by Adeed Dawisha. Cambridge: Cambridge University Press, 1983.

———. "The Primacy of Economics: The Foreign Policy of Egypt," in *The Foreign Policies of Arab States*, edited by Bahgat Korany and Ali E. Hillal Dessouki. Boulder, Colo.: Westview Press, 1984.

Dishon, Daniel. "Sadat's Arab Adversaries." *The Jerusalem Quarterly*, Summer 1978.

Eban, Abba. *An Autobiography*. New York: Random House, 1977.

Eilts, Hermann F. "Improve the Framework." *Foreign Policy*, Winter 1980–1981.

_____. "The Mideast: Impressive Achievements and Sober Hopes." *Worldview*, December 1979.

Fahmy, Ismail. *Negotiating for Peace in the Middle East*. Baltimore, Md.: Johns Hopkins University Press, 1983.

Faksh, Mahmud A. "Egypt Under Mubarak: The Uncertain Path." *Behind the Headlines*, Vol. 41, No. 3, 1983.

Fernandez-Armesto, Felipe. *Sadat and His Statecraft*. London: Kensal Press, 1982.

Gardiner, Sir Alan. *Egypt of the Pharaohs*. London: Oxford University Press, 1966.

Gershoni, Israel, and Jankowski, James P. *Egypt, Islam, and the Arabs: The Search for Egyptian Nationhood, 1900–1930*. London: Oxford University Press, 1986.

Gibb, H.A.R. *Mohammedanism*. London: Oxford University Press, 1949.

Golan, Matti. *The Secret Conversations of Henry Kissinger*. New York: Quadrangle, 1976.

Haber, Eitan; Schiff, Zeev; and Yaari, Ehud. *The Year of the Dove*. New York: Benniton Books, 1979.

Haim, Sylvia G. *Arab Nationalism: An Anthology*. Berkeley: University of California Press, 1962.

Handel, Michael. *The Diplomacy of Surprise: Hitler, Nixon, Sadat*. Cambridge, Mass.: Harvard University Center for International Affairs, 1981.

Heikal, Mohamed Hasaneyn. *Autumn of Fury: The Assassination of Sadat*. New York: Random House, 1983.

_____. "Egyptian Foreign Policy." *Foreign Affairs*, July 1978.

_____. *Nasser, The Cairo Documents*. London: New English Library, 1972.

_____. *The Road to Ramadan*. New York: Quadrangle, 1975.

_____. *The Sphinx and the Commissar*. New York: Harper and Row, 1978.

Herodotus. *The History of Herodotus*. London: J. M. Dent and Sons, 1912.

Hinnebusch, Raymond A., Jr. *Egyptian Politics Under Sadat*. Cambridge: Cambridge University Press, 1985.

_____. "Revisionist Dreams, Realist Strategies: The Foreign Policy of Syria," in *The Foreign Policies of Arab States*, edited by Bahgat Korany and Ali E. Hillal Dessouki. Boulder, Colo.: Westview Press, 1984.

Hirst, David, and Beeson, Irene. *Sadat*. London: Faber and Faber, 1981.

Hitti, Philip K. *The Arabs*. Princeton, N.J.: Princeton University Press, 1943.

Holt, P. M. *Egypt and the Fertile Crescent, 1516–1922*. Ithaca, N.Y.: Cornell University Press, 1966.

Hopwood, Derek. *Egypt: Politics and Society, 1945–1984*. London: Allen and Unwin, 1985.

Horelick, Arnold L. "Soviet Policy in the Middle East," in *Political Dynamics in the Middle East*, edited by Paul Y. Hammond and Sidney S. Alexander. New York: American Elsevier, 1972.

Hourani, Albert. *Arabic Thought in the Liberal Age, 1798–1939*. London: Oxford University Press, 1962.

Hudson, Michael C. *Arab Politics: The Search for Legitimacy*. New Haven, Conn.: Yale University Press, 1977.

Al-Husri, Sati. "Muslim Unity and Arab Unity," in *Arab Nationalism*, edited by Sylvia Haim. Berkeley: University of California Press, 1962.

Ibrahim, Saad Eddin. "Anatomy of Egypt's Militant Islamic Groups: Methodological Note and Preliminary Findings." *International Journal of Middle East Studies*, December 1980.

———. "Islamic Militancy as a Social Movement: The Case of Two Groups in Egypt," in *Islamic Resurgence in the Arab World*, edited by Ali E. Hillal Dessouki. New York: Praeger, 1982.

———. *The New Arab Social Order: A Study of the Social Impact of Oil Wealth*. Boulder, Colo.: Westview Press, 1982.

Indyk, Martin. *To the Ends of the Earth: Sadat's Jerusalem Initiative*. Cambridge, Mass.: Harvard University Press, 1984.

Insight Team of *The Sunday Times*. *Insight on the Middle East War*. London: Andre Deutsch, 1974.

Issawi, Charles. *The Arab World's Legacy*. Princeton, N.J.: Darwin Press, 1981.

———. "The Bases of Arab Unity." *International Affairs*, January 1955.

Jabber, Paul. "Egypt's Crisis, America's Dilemma." *Foreign Affairs*, Summer 1986.

Jankowski, James P. "Egyptian Responses to the Palestine Problem in the Inter-War Period." *International Journal of Middle East Studies*, August 1980.

Kamel, Mohamed Ibrahim. *The Camp David Accords: A Testimony by Sadat's Foreign Minister*. London: Routledge and Kegan Paul, 1986.

Kays, Doreen. *Frogs and Scorpions: Egypt, Sadat, and the Media*. London: Frederick Muller, 1984.

Kerr, Malcolm H. *Egypt Under Nasser*. New York: Foreign Policy Association (Headline Series, No. 161), 1963.

———. "Egyptian Foreign Policy and the Revolution," in *Egypt Since the Revolution*, edited by P. J. Vatikiotis. New York: Praeger, 1968.

———. "Regional Arab Politics and the Conflict with Israel," in *Political Dynamics in the Middle East*, edited by Paul Y. Hammond and Sidney S. Alexander. New York: American Elsevier, 1972.

———. *The Arab Cold War, 1958–1964*. London: Oxford University Press, 1965.

Kerr, Malcolm H., and Yassin, El Sayed, editors. *Rich and Poor States in the Middle East: Egypt and the New Arab Order*. Boulder, Colo.: Westview Press, 1982.

Kirk, George E. *A Short History of the Middle East*. New York: Praeger, 1955.

Kissinger, Henry A. *White House Years*. Boston: Little, Brown, 1979.

———. *Years of Upheaval*. Boston: Little, Brown, 1982.

Korany, Bahgat. "The Cold Peace, the Sixth Arab-Israeli War, and Egypt's Public." *International Journal*, Autumn 1983.

———. "The Dialectics of Inter-Arab Relations," in *The Arab-Israeli Conflict: Two Decades of Change*, edited by Yehuda Lukacs and Abdalla M. Battah. Boulder, Colo.: Westview Press, 1988.

Korany, Bahgat, and Dessouki, Ali E. Hillal, editors. *The Foreign Policies of Arab States*. Boulder, Colo.: Westview Press, 1984.

Kraft, Joseph. "Letter from Riyadh." *The New Yorker*, June 26, 1978.

Lacouture, Jean. *Nasser: A Biography*. New York: Alfred A. Knopf, 1973.

Lacouture, Jean and Simone. *Egypt in Transition*. New York: Criterion Books, 1958.

Laqueur, Walter Z. *Confrontation: The Middle East War and World Politics.* London: Wildwood House, 1974.

Lesch, Ann Mosely. *Arab Politics in Palestine, 1917–1939.* Ithaca, N.Y.: Cornell University Press, 1979.

Lewis, Bernard. *The Arabs in History.* London: Hutchinson House, 1950.

——. *The Political Language of Islam.* Chicago: University of Chicago Press, 1988.

Lewis, Samuel. "The United States and Israel," in *The Middle East: Ten Years After Camp David,* edited by William B. Quandt. Washington, D.C.: Brookings Institution, 1988.

Lippmann, Thomas W. *Egypt After Nasser: Sadat, Peace and the Mirage of Prosperity.* New York: Paragon House, 1989.

Little, Tom. *Egypt.* New York: Praeger, 1958.

Lukacs, Yehuda, and Battah, Abdallah, editors. *The Arab-Israeli Conflict.* Boulder, Colo.: Westview Press, 1988.

Macdonald, R. W. *The League of Arab States: A Study in the Dynamics of Regional Organization.* Princeton, N.J.: Princeton University Press, 1965.

Mansfield, Peter. *Nasser's Egypt.* Middlesex, England: Penguin Books, 1965.

Marsot, Afaf Lutfi al-Sayyid. *A Short History of Modern Egypt.* Cambridge: Cambridge University Press, 1985.

——. *Protest Movements and Religious Undercurrents in Egypt: Past and Present.* Washington, D.C.: Georgetown University Center for Contemporary Arab Studies, 1984.

McLaurin, R. D. *Foreign Policy Making in the Middle East: Domestic Influences on Policy in Egypt, Iraq, Israel, and Syria.* New York: Praeger, 1977.

Miller, Aaron David. *The Arab States and the Palestine Question.* New York: Praeger, 1986.

——. "The Arab-Israeli Conflict, 1967–1987: A Retrospective." *Middle East Journal,* Summer 1987.

——. "The PLO and the Peace Process: The Organizational Imperative." *SAIS Review,* Winter–Spring 1987.

Mitchell, Richard. *The Society of Muslim Brothers.* London: Oxford University Press, 1969.

Mohieddin, Khaled. "Foreign Policy Since 1952: An Egyptian View," in *Egypt Since the Revolution,* edited by P. J. Vatikiotis. New York: Praeger, 1968.

Montville, Joseph. "The Psychological Tasks of Arab-Israeli Peace Diplomacy." Unpublished account of discussions with Arab and Israeli intellectuals, 1984.

Nasser, Gamal Abdel. *Egypt's Liberation: The Philosophy of the Revolution.* Washington, D.C.: Public Affairs Press, 1956.

——. *The Palestinian Problem (Correspondence Exchanged Between Nasser and John F. Kennedy on the Palestinian Problem).* Cairo: UAR Information Department, 1961.

——. *The Philosophy of the Revolution.* Buffalo, N.Y.: Smith, Keynes and Marshall, 1959.

Neguib, Mohammed. *Egypt's Destiny.* London: Victor Gollancz, 1955.

Noble, Paul. "The Arab System," in *The Foreign Policies of Arab States,* edited by Bahgat Korany and Ali E. Hillal Dessouki. Boulder, Colo.: Westview Press, 1984.

Nuseibeh, Hazem Zaki. *The Ideas of Arab Nationalism*. Ithaca, N.Y.: Cornell University Press, 1956.

Pfeiffer, Robert H. *Introduction to the Old Testament*. New York: Harper and Brothers, 1941.

Quandt, William B. *Camp David: Peacemaking and Politics*. Washington, D.C.: Brookings Institution, 1986.

_____. *Decade of Decisions: American Policy Toward the Arab-Israeli Conflict, 1967–1976*. Berkeley: University of California Press, 1977.

_____. *The Middle East: Ten Years After Camp David*. Washington, D.C.: Brookings Institution, 1988.

_____. "United States Policy in the Middle East: Constraints and Commitments," in *Political Dynamics in the Middle East*, edited by Paul Y. Hammond and Sidney S. Alexander. New York: American Elsevier, 1972.

Rabin, Yitzhak. *The Rabin Memoirs*. Boston: Little, Brown, 1979.

Rawlinson, George. *History of Egypt*. New York: John W. Lovell, 1880.

Rejwan, Nissim. *Nasserist Ideology: Its Exponents and Critics*. New York: John Wiley and Sons, 1974.

Riad, Mahmoud. *The Struggle for Peace in the Middle East*. London: Quartet Books, 1982.

Sachar, H. M. *Egypt and Israel*. New York: Richard Marek Publishers, 1981.

Sadat, Anwar. *Egypt and the New Arab Reality: A Working Paper by Anwar Sadat*. Cairo: Ministry of Information, 1980.

_____. *In Search of Identity: An Autobiography*. London: Collins, 1978.

_____. *Revolt on the Nile*. New York: John Day, 1957.

Safran, Nadav. *Egypt in Search of Political Community*. Cambridge, Mass.: Harvard University Press, 1981.

Sahliyeh, Emile. *In Search of Leadership: West Bank Politics Since 1967*. Washington, D.C.: Brookings Institution, 1988.

_____. "Jordan and the Palestinians," in *The Middle East: Ten Years After Camp David*, edited by William B. Quandt. Washington, D.C.: Brookings Institution, 1988.

Salem-Babikian, Norma. "The Sacred and the Profane: Sadat's Speech to the Knesset." *Middle East Journal*, Winter 1980.

Salame, Ghassan. "Inter-Arab Politics: The Return of Geography," in *The Middle East: Ten Years After Camp David*, edited by William B. Quandt. Washington, D.C.: Brookings Institution, 1988.

Saunders, Harold H. "Reconstituting the Arab-Israeli Peace Process," in *The Middle East: Ten Years After Camp David*, edited by William B. Quandt. Washington, D.C.: Brookings Institution, 1988.

_____. *The Other Walls: The Politics of the Arab-Israeli Peace Process*. Washington, D.C.: American Enterprise Institute, 1985.

Schwantes, Siegfried J. *A Short History of the Ancient Near East*. Grand Rapids, Mich.: Baker Book House, 1965.

Seale, Patrick. "Sadat in Jerusalem." *New Statesman*. November 25, 1977.

_____. "The Egypt-Israel Treaty and its Implications." *The World Today*, May 1979.

_____ . *The Struggle for Syria: A Study in Post War Arab Politics, 1945–1958.* London: Oxford University Press, 1965.

Semple, Ellen Churchill. *The Geography of the Mediterranean Region.* New York: Henry Holt and Co., 1931.

Shamir, Shimon. "Israeli Views of Egypt and the Peace Process," in *The Middle East: Ten Years After Camp David,* edited by William B. Quandt. Washington, D.C.: Brookings Institution, 1988.

_____ . "Egyptian Rule (1832–1840) and the Beginning of the Modern Period in the History of Palestine," in *Egypt and Palestine,* edited by Ammon Cohen and Gabriel Baer. New York: St. Martin's Press, 1984.

Sharabi, Hisham B. *Nationalism and Revolution in the Arab World.* Princeton, N.J.: D. Van Nostrand Company, 1966.

Sharabi, Hisham B., editor. *The Next Arab Decade: Alternative Futures.* Boulder, Colo.: Westview Press, 1988.

Sheehan, Edward R. F. *The Arabs, Israelis and Kissinger.* New York: Reader's Digest Press, 1976.

Shinnie, P. L. "The Legacy to Africa," in *The Legacy of Egypt,* edited by J. R. Harris. Oxford: Clarendon Press, 1971.

Sid-Ahmed, Mohammed. "Egypt: The Islamic Issue." *Foreign Policy,* Winter 1987–1988.

Springborg, Robert. *Family, Power, and Politics in Egypt: Sayed Bey Marei—His Clan, Clients, and Cohorts.* Philadelphia: University of Pennsylvania Press, 1982.

Stephens, Robert. *Nasser: A Political Biography.* London: Allen Lane, Penguin Press, 1971.

Toynbee, Arnold J. *A Study of History.* London: Oxford University Press, 1934.

_____ . *Between Niger and Nile.* London: Oxford University Press, 1965.

Vance, Cyrus. *Hard Choices: Critical Years in America's Foreign Policy.* New York: Simon and Schuster, 1983.

Vatikiotis, P. J. *Arab and Regional Politics in the Middle East.* London: Croom Helm, 1984.

_____ . *Nasser and His Generation.* London: St. Martin's Press, 1978.

_____ . "The Foreign Policy of Egypt," in *Foreign Policy in World Politics,* edited by R. C. Macridis. London: Prentice-Hall, 1962.

_____ . *The History of Egypt.* Baltimore, Md.: Johns Hopkins University Press, 1980.

_____ . "The Politics of the Fertile Crescent," in *Political Dynamics of the Middle East,* edited by Paul Y. Hammond and Sidney S. Alexander. New York: American Elsevier, 1972.

Vaucher, Georges. *Gamal Abdel Nasser et Son Equipe.* Paris: René Juillard, 1960.

Viorst, Milton. "Iraq at War." *Foreign Affairs,* Winter 1986–1987.

Waterbury, John. *Egypt: Burdens of the Past/Options for the Future.* Bloomington, Ind.: American Universities Field Staff, 1978.

_____ . *The Egypt of Nasser and Sadat.* Princeton, N.J.: Princeton University Press, 1983.

Waterfield, Gordon. *Egypt.* New York: Walker and Co., 1967.

Weir, Sir Michael. "Egypt's External Relations," in *Egypt: Internal Challenges and Regional Stability*, edited by Lillian Craig Harris. London: Routledge and Kegan Paul, 1988.

Weizman, Ezer. *The Battle for Peace*, New York: Bantam Books, 1981.

Williams, Ronald J. "Egypt and Israel," in *The Legacy of Egypt*, edited by J. R. Harris. Oxford: Clarendon Press, 1971.

Wynn, Wilton, *Nasser of Egypt: The Search for Dignity*. Cambridge, Mass.: Arlington Books, 1959.

Index

AAC. *See* Arab Cooperation Council
Abdel Meguid, Ismat, 113, 169(n12)
Abduh, Mohammed, 14, 86
Abu Ghazala, Abd al-Halim, 107
al-Afghani, Jamal ed-Din, 14
Alexandria, 22
Algeria, 48, 52, 59, 112-113
Algiers summit, 112-114
Ali, Mohammed, 11-12, 86
Amman summit, 102-103, 107, 108,
    110-112
Anglo-Egyptian treaty, 26
Aoun, Michel, 126
Arab Cooperation Council, 126
Arab-Israeli conflict
    Egyptian influence on, xiii, xiv
    and Egyptian-Israeli peace treaty, 103
    future of, 128-130
    June War, 33-34
    October War, 46-50, 161(n3)
    Palestine War, 23-25, 159(n9)
    See also Middle East negotiations;
        Palestinians
Arab League, 19, 65, 98, 126
Arab Organization for Industrialization,
    111
Arabs
    conquest of Egypt by, 8-9, 118
    interrelations among, 62-66, 102-
        106, 113-114, 119-123, 124-129.
        See also Algiers summit; Amman
        summit; Baghdad summit; Foreign
        relations, with Arab states; Pan-
        Arabism
    See also Arab-Israeli conflict; Middle
        East negotiations

Arafat, Yasser
    and Gulf War, 104
    and October War, 44, 48
    and negotiations, 54, 60, 66, 70, 105,
        113, 125
    See also Palestine Liberation
        Organization
al-As, Amr Ibn, 8
al-Assad, Hafiz, 42, 123, 126
    and 1977 negotiations, 74, 87-88
    October War and aftermath, 44, 46,
        49, 50-53
    and Saudi-Kuwait mediation, 62, 64,
        66
Assam, Abd al-Rahman, 19
Atherton, Alfred L., 92

Ba'ath party, 30-33, 51-52, 72-73, 119,
    122-123
Baghdad Pact, 27-28
Baghdad summit, 97-99
al-Banna, Hassan, 18, 39-40
Begin, Menachem, 68-69, 99, 100, 151,
    153-154
Ben-Gurion, David, 28
Beni Morr, 22-23
Beybars, 10
Blair House talks, 99, 168(n20)
Boutros-Ghali, Boutros, 85, 168(n18)
Byzantium, 8

Camp David Accords. *See* Middle East
    negotiations, Camp David Accords
Carter, Jimmy, 68, 76-77, 92-95, 100,
    151-152, 154, 155, 164(n1). *See
    also* Middle East negotiations,
    Camp David Accords

Ceauşescu, Nicolae, 78, 164(n2)
Constitutional Nationalists, 14–15
Culture
  influence of geography on, 1–3, 117
  influences on Egyptian, 9, 19, 117–
  119
  Saudi versus Egyptian, 62
  village, 38, 160(nn 4, 6)
  See also Identity; Ideology;
    Leadership

Dayan, Moshe, 68–69, 77, 78, 162(n1),
  165(n3), 168(n20)
Defense, 24, 28. See also Military

Eban, Abba, 51, 107, 169(n6)
Economy
  and foreign investment, 57
  and foreign policy, 82–83, 110, 116,
  120–121
  and urban unrest, 57–58, 81
  See also Arab Cooperation Council;
    Foreign aid
Education, 11–12
Egypt. See Culture; Economy; History;
  Politics; Religion
Egyptian-Israeli peace treaty. See
  Middle East negotiations,
  Egyptian-Israeli peace treaty
Egyptian nationalism, xiii, xv, 12, 14–
  16, 18–19, 55–56
  and Jerusalem initiative, 86–87
  See also Identity; Pan-Arabism
Eilts, Hermann F., 92, 164(n30)

Fahd, Crown Prince, 63, 97
Fahmy, Ismael, 66, 79, 80, 163(n1),
  164(n2)
Fawzi, Hussein, 119
Federation of Arab Republics, 43–44,
  59, 66
Feisal, King, 45, 49
Foreign aid
  from Arab states, 57, 61, 73, 83, 90,
  98, 110

and foreign policy, 116. See also
  Foreign policy, and economics
  after June War, 34, 41
  from United States, 82–83, 98
Foreign policy
  and decisionmaking processes, 79–84
  and economics, 57–58, 61–62, 73, 81,
  82–83, 110, 120–121
  and Egyptian ideologies, 26–35, 55–
  56, 86–87, 119–123
  and Egyptian leadership, 21–22, 115–
  117
  Egyptian Middle East, xiii, xiv–xv,
  24, 26, 106–107, 109–110, 169(n13)
  and Gulf War, 104
  Palestinian issue and, 18, 19–20, 28,
  33, 90–91, 100–101, 107–108,
  170(n2)
  See also Foreign relations
Foreign relations
  Ancient Egypt and, 3–7
  with Arab states, 31–33, 40–45, 58–
  66, 71, 87–91, 97–98, 99, 108,
  110–113, 159(n8)
  with Israel, 6–7, 87, 99, 103, 106–
  108, 157(n14)
  with United States, 116–117
  See also Middle East negotiations;
    Palestinians, and Egypt

Gamasy, Mohammed Abdel Ghani, 80,
  165(n5)
Geography, 24
  and cultural development, 1–3, 117
Gulf War, 103–104, 109, 111–112

al-Hakim, Tawfic, 119
Hassan, King, 89, 108
Heikal, Mohamed Hasaneyn, 24, 38–
  39, 159(n9)
History
  of Ancient Egypt, 3–12, 156(n1)
  and Egyptian strategic interests, 24,
  117–119
  foreign dominance, 7–12, 25, 156(nn
  5, 10)

Western colonialism, 13–16, 24, 159(n11)
al-Husri, Sati, 19
Hussein, King
  and Algiers summit, 113
  Camp David and, 93, 96
  and Egypt, 88, 98, 108, 166(n26)
  and negotiations, 53, 66, 70–71, 105, 111, 114
  and October War, 47–48
  See also Jordan
Hussein, Saddam, 112, 113

Ibrahim, Pasha, 11
Identity
  and Egyptian history, xiii–xv, 3, 6, 9–10, 11–12, 117–119
  religious, ethnic, and political, 13–17, 122, 157–158(n2)
  See also Egyptian nationalism; Islam; Pan-Arabism
Ideology
  and foreign policy formulation, xv, 13, 117–123, 159(n18)
  and Nasser, 29
  and Sadat, 38, 41
  See also Egyptian nationalism; Pan-Arabism
Intifadah. See Palestinians, uprising by
Iran, 96, 103–104. *See also* Gulf War
Iraq
  and Arabism, 19–20, 31–33, 72
  and Ba'athism, 122
  Baghdad Pact, 28
  and Egypt, 111–112
  Gulf War, 104, 109
  and negotiations, 60, 112, 125
  October War, 48, 49
  and Syria, 64, 89, 96, 97, 167–168(n13)
Islam
  and Egyptian identity, 9–10, 12, 13–14, 17, 101, 118, 157–158(n2), 160(n4)
  history of, 8–10
  pan-, 14, 119, 121–122

Islambouli, Khaled, 101
Islamic Conference Organization, 108
Islamic Congress, 40, 41
Israel
  Camp David Accords, 93–94, 96
  and military actions, 28, 33, 99
  Nasser on, 24–25
  and peace negotiations, 67, 68–69, 70, 71, 100, 125, 127–128, 168(n22)
  See also Arab-Israeli conflict; Begin, Menachem; Foreign relations, with Israel; Middle East negotiations

Jerusalem initiative. *See* Middle East negotiations, Jerusalem initiative
Jordan
  and Camp David Accords, 93–94, 96
  and Egypt, 89, 98, 108, 109, 111
  June War, 33
  and negotiations, 53, 58, 67, 70–71
  October War, 47–48, 49
  and PLO, 34, 44
  and Saudi Arabia, 73
  See also Hussein, King
June War. *See* Arab-Israeli conflict, June War

Kamel, Mohamed Ibrahim, 94–95, 163(n1), 167(n6)
Kamil, Mustapha, 15–16
Kassem, Abdel Karim, 31–32
al-Kawakebi, Abdel Rahman, 17
Khalil, Mustapha, 85, 168(n15)
Kissinger, Henry, 51, 52–53
Kuwait
  and Egypt, 89, 98
  and mediation, 60, 61, 62–66
  October War, 48

Leadership, 21–22, 25, 26, 115–117. *See also* Mubarak, Hosni; Nasser, Gamal Abdel; Sadat, Anwar
Lebanon, 16, 60–61, 64, 126. *See also* Palestine Liberation Organization, in Lebanon

Leeds Castle Conference, 92
Libya, 42–44, 48, 49, 59–60, 126
Lutfi al-Sayyid, Ahmad, 16, 118

Mahfouz, Nagib, 119
Mansour, Anis, 119
Marei, Sayed, 165(n3)
Marwan, Ashraf, 63
Mena House conference, 88–89
Middle East, xiii, 24, 45, 62, 71, 84.
    See also Arab-Israeli conflict;
    Arabs; Middle East negotiations
Middle East negotiations, 127–130
  Camp David Accords, 93–97, 106,
    107, 144–155
  competing interests and ideologies
    in, 123, 124–128
  disengagement agreements, 50–54,
    161(n6)
  Egyptian-Israeli peace treaty, 99, 103,
    106, 107, 124–125, 168(n20)
  Jerusalem initiative, 77, 78–91, 133–
    143, 166(n15)
  Jordanian-PLO 1985 agreement, 105
  1977 Geneva preparations, 67–77,
    163(nn 10, 15), 164(n27)
  Saudi-Kuwait mediations, 61, 62–66
Military, 159(n9)
  and foreign policy, 28, 80, 86, 109–
    110, 166(n21)
Mit Abul Kom (village), 37
Mohieddin, Khaled, 56, 159(n18)
Morocco, 48, 74, 89, 108
Mubarak, Hosni
  accession of, 103
  foreign policy of, xiv, 106, 108, 109,
    116, 168–169(n3)
  Palestinian issue and, 108, 111
Muslim Brotherhood, 18, 39–40, 56–
    57, 104, 108, 121, 170(n10)

Naguib, Mohammed, 25–26
al-Nahas, Mustapha, 19, 20
Napoleon, Bonaparte, 11–12
Nasser, Gamal Abdel
  early years, 22–25, 159(n11)

foreign policy of, 22, 26, 115
influence of, xiii, 21
and pan-Arabism, 26–35, 42
Nationalism. See Egyptian nationalism;
    Pan-Arabism
National Progressive Unionist
    Grouping (NPUG), 56
Negotiations. See Middle East
    negotiations
New Wafd party, 56
Nile River, 1, 2–3, 117–118
Nixon, Richard, 52
NPUG. See National Progressive
    Unionist Grouping
Numeiry, Ja'afar, 42, 59, 89, 92
Nuri al-Said, 20, 27

October War. See Arab-Israeli conflict,
    October War
Oil, 48–49, 66, 120, 161(n4). See also
    Saudi Arabia
Oman, 89
Ottomans, 10–12

Palestine Liberation Organization
    (PLO)
  and Egypt, 90–91, 105. See also
    Foreign policy, Palestinian issue
    and
  factions within, 60, 105, 127–128,
    162(n8)
  formation of, 34–35
  in Lebanon, 64, 65, 103, 105
  and military operations, 44, 48, 52,
    90
  and negotiations, 54, 60, 66, 67, 69–
    70, 76, 125, 128
  and Palestine National Council of
    1988, 111
  and Palestinian uprising, 113–114
  and Saudi Arabia, 73
  and Syria, 61, 74–75, 105, 164(n23)
  See also Palestinians
Palestine War. See Arab-Israeli conflict,
    Palestine War
Palestinians

and Camp David Accords, 94–95,
96–97, 99
and Egypt, 18, 19–20, 28, 33, 40,
90–91, 100–101, 122. *See also*
Foreign policy, Palestinian issue
and
and Gulf War, 104
representation for, 52, 69–70, 74–75,
76, 113, 125
uprising by, 102, 105–106, 112–114,
127–128, 129
See also Palestine Liberation
Organization
Pan-Arabism
Arab merger attempts, 29–33
contemporary attitudes toward, 119–
121, 169(nn 8, 9), 170(n7)
and Egyptian identity, xiii–xv, 11, 12,
110, 119
and Egyptian-Syrian dispute, 62, 71–
73
and Nasser, 26–27, 34–35, 158(n9)
October War and, 46–50
rise of, 16–20, 24, 29, 160(n24)
See also Arabs, interrelations among;
Foreign relations, with Arab states
Pan-Islam. *See* Islam, pan-
Peres, Shimon, 108
PLO. *See* Palestine Liberation
Organization
Politics
and Egyptian cultural history, 2–3,
21–22, 117
before independence, 17–20
and oil, 48–49
and political parties, 56–57, 58, 120
and Sadat, 36–37, 41, 43, 50
See also Foreign policy; Foreign
relations; Leadership

Qabus, Sultan, 89
Qadhafi, Muammar, 42, 43–44, 59–60,
126

Rabin, Yitzhak, 53
Religion

Christianity and Arabism, 17
and Sadat, 40
See also Islam
Resolution 242. *See* United Nations,
Security Council Resolution 242
Riad, Mahmoud, 65

Sadat, Anwar
and Camp David Accords, 92–95,
99, 152, 153, 154
early years, 37–40, 161(n11)
and Egyptian isolation, 97–98,
168(n15)
foreign policy of, 22, 40–45, 57–58,
59–60, 100–101, 115, 116–117,
164(n30)
influence of, xiii, 36–37, 160–161(n9)
Jerusalem initiative by, 78–91, 133–
143, 164(n1), 164–165(n2), 165(nn
3, 5), 166(n26)
1977 negotiations, 68, 69, 70, 71–73,
76–77
October War and aftermath, 46–54
and political parties, 56–57
and Saudi-Kuwait mediation, 62–66
Saladin, 10
Saudi Arabia
and Camp David Accords, 93–94,
95–96
and Egypt, 28, 42, 44–45, 59, 61–62,
87, 88, 89–90, 97–98, 109, 111,
166(n29)
and Gulf War, 103
mediations by, 60, 62–66, 126
and 1977 negotiations, 67, 73–74
October War, 48
Shamir, Yitzhak, 127
Shi'ism, 103–104
al-Sibai, Yusuf, 90
Sid-Ahmad, Mohammed, 168(n3)
Sinai, 34, 36, 42, 95
Sinai II, 53–54
Sudan, 26, 42, 59, 74, 89
Suez Canal, 29, 34
Syria
Arabism and, 16, 19–20, 72–73

and Arab-Israeli conflict, 126–128
and Arab mergers, 29–31, 42–43
and Ba'athism, 122–123
and Egypt, 28, 32–33, 44–45, 58–59,
   66, 88–89, 112, 169(n12)
Gulf War, 104
and Iraq, 96, 97, 167–168(n13)
and Lebanese War, 60–61, 62–66,
   126–127
and 1977 negotiations, 67, 68, 70,
   71, 72–73, 74–75
October War and aftermath, 46–47,
   50–54
and Palestinians, 74–75, 105, 122,
   125, 164(n23)
and Saudi Arabia, 73

Tahtawi, Rifa'a, 14
Talmasani, Omar, 170(n10)
Tuhamy, Hassan, 68, 77, 78, 95,
   165(n3)
Tunisia, 74, 89

UAR. *See* United Arab Republic
UN. *See* United Nations
Union of Soviet Socialist Republics
   (USSR)
and Middle East aid, 30, 34
and negotiations, 60, 67
and Sadat, 43, 45
United Arab Republic (UAR), 29–32

United Nations (UN)
Security Council Resolution 242,
   111, 112, 125, 131–132
Security Council Resolution 338, 49,
   132
United States (U.S.)
aid to Egypt, 82–83, 98
Camp David Accords, 93–94, 96
Eisenhower Doctrine, 30
and negotiations, 52–54, 59, 67, 70,
   71, 113, 128–130
and October War, 47, 48, 49, 50
and Sadat, 45, 116–117
See also Carter, Jimmy
Unrest, 57–58, 81–82
Urabi, Ahmad Bey, 15, 86
U.S. *See* United States
USSR. *See* Union of Soviet Socialist
   Republics

Vance, Cyrus, 69, 77, 95, 162(n1),
   167(n30)

Wafd party, 18–19, 26
Weizman, Ezer, 85, 163(n1)
West Bank, 52, 68, 93–95, 96–97, 99.
   See also Palestinians
World War II, 39

Yemen, 32, 33, 40–41

Zaghloul, Saad, 18, 86